PREFACE

It is easier to follow a political campaign than to understand it. We read about it in the press, view it on television, and occasionally even see or hear a candidate in person. We observe only what others—the candidates, their advisers, reporters, or a host of other self-interested participants—want us to see, and we are expected to use their views to make a judgment on election day.

There is more, however, to presidential elections than meets the eye. Campaign planners work hard to design a strategy to maximize their vote. They understand the intricacies of the process. They know how the system works, who its beneficiaries are, and where to concentrate their campaign resources. They understand the requirements of finance legislation—how to comply with it, get around it, and take advantage of it. They appreciate the psychological and social motivations of voters and have a feel for which appeals are likely to be most effective most of the time. They are aware of party rules and the ways to build a winning coalition during the nomination period. They can sense the rhythm of conventions and know when events should be scheduled and how various interests can be placated and orchestrated. They know how to organize and plan a general election campaign and how best to present their candidate to the voters. They can usually predict what will happen in the election and interpret the results so as to enhance their political position and governing potential. They do not need to read this book.

On the other hand, people who want to get behind the scenes of presidential campaigns, who want to know the reasons that particular strategies are adopted and certain tactics utilized, should benefit from the information contained in this book.

The Road to the White House: The Politics of Presidential Elections is a straightforward "nuts and bolts" discussion of how the system is designed and works. It is primarily concerned with facts, not opinions; with practice, not theory; with implications, not speculations. It summarizes the state of the art and science of presidential electoral politics.

The third edition has been thoroughly updated. Like the first two, it is organized into four main parts. The first discusses the arena in which the election occurs. Its three chapters examine the electoral system, campaign finance, and the political environment. Chapter 1 provides a historical overview of nominations as well as elections, while chapters 2 and 3 examine recent developments. Highlighted are the political considerations that candidates need to consider as they plan and structure their presidential campaigns.

Parts II and III are organized sequentially. They describe the distinct yet related stages of the presidential campaign: delegate selection, nominating conventions, and the general election. Chapter 4 examines reforms in the selection of convention delegates and their impact on voters, candidates, and the parties. Chapter 5 carries this discussion to the nominating convention, describing its purposes, procedures, policies, and politics. In Chapter 6, the organization, strategy, and tactics of the general election are discussed. Chapter 7 describes the projection and targeting of candidate images. It examines how the media cover the campaign, how the candidates try to affect that coverage, and how all of this affects the electorate on election day. Detailed illustrations from recent elections are used throughout these chapters.

The fourth part looks at the election and beyond by exploring its implications for the government and for the political system. Chapter 8 discusses and evaluates the presidential vote by asking such questions as: Does it provide a mandate? Does it influence the President's ability to govern? Chapter 9 considers problems in the electoral system and possible reforms. It examines some of the major difficulties that have affected the political system and proposals advanced for dealing with them: how the electoral process can be made more equitable; how it can be made more responsive to popular choice; and how that choice can be conveyed more effectively to elected and appointed officials.

These questions are not easy to answer. Students of the American political system have been debating them for some time, and that debate is likely to continue. Without information on how the system works, we cannot intelligently participate in it or improve it. In the case of presidential politics, ignorance is definitely not bliss.

The road to the White House is long and arduous. In fact, it has become more difficult to travel than in the past. Yet, surprisingly, there are more travelers. Evaluating their journey is essential to rendering an intelligent judgment on election day. However, more is at stake than simply choosing the occupants of the presidential and vice presidential offices. The system itself is on trial in every presidential election. That is why it is so important to understand and appreciate the intricacies of the process. Only an informed citizenry can determine whether the nation is being well served by the way we go about choosing our President.

Few books are written alone, and this one is no exception. For the first edition I was fortunate to have had the wise counsel of my colleagues Richard L. Cole and Hugh L. LeBlanc and the comments of outside reviewers Jay S. Goodman (Wheaton College), James Lengle (Georgetown University), Robert T. Nakamura (Dartmouth College), Lester Seligman (University of Illinois), Earl Shaw (University of Minnesota), and William H. Steward (University of Alabama). I also benefited from the advice and experience of two friends, Jeff Fishel of American University and Paul Wilson who were willing to share their extensive knowledge of presidential politics with me.

In the second edition, I was again fortunate to have received close, careful, and extraordinarily helpful readings from Hugh L. LeBlanc and Earl Shaw as well as from James W. Davis (Washington University).

For the third edition, I am greatly indebted to Mark Drozdowski, a former George Washington University undergraduate in political science, for his aid in researching and synthesizing the new literature. My most vivid memory of Mark's industry came during an early summer morning—3:30 a.m. to be exact—when my wife and I were loading the car for a ten-hour drive to Vermont with our two small children. Suddenly, I heard my name, turned around, and saw Mark with his latest draft. Needless to add, I was and remain very impressed by his work.

The third edition has also profited enormously from the criticism of Tony Corrado (Colby College), Hugh L. LeBlanc (The George Washington University), Earl Shaw (University of Minnesota) and Marjorie Randon Hershey (Indiana University). Their detailed comments helped me tighten and strengthen the manuscript as well as improve its scholarship. I would like to extend special thanks to Herbert Alexander (Citizens Research Foundation), Kathleen Frankovic (CBS News), Kevin Coleman (Congressional Research Service), and Timothy Roper (Odell, Roper & Associates) who provided me with specific information in their areas of expertise. Their contributions are noted in the text.

Judith Schneider did her usual herculean job of converting my scribble into computer script. This is the second time she has typed numerous drafts of this book. I am extremely grateful to her once again for another excellent job.

Finally, I wish to extend my thanks to those at St. Martin's Press who have helped me with this and previous editions, to my wife, Cheryl Beil, whose encouragement has been unwavering throughout, and to my sons, Jared and Jeremy, who had to put up with an increasingly grumpy daddy as the deadline for this edition neared.

Stephen J. Wayne

Third Edition

THE ROAD TO
THE WHITE HOUSE

The Politics of Presidential Elections

Third Edition

THE ROAD TO THE WHITE HOUSE

The Politics of Presidential Elections

Stephen J. Wayne

The George Washington University

ST. MARTIN'S PRESS   NEW YORK

Library of Congress Catalog Card Number: 87–060555
© 1988, 1984, 1980 by St. Martin's Press, Inc.
Printed in the United States of America.
21098
fedcba
For information, write St. Martin's Press, Inc.
175 Fifth Ave., New York, NY 10010

Cover design: Darby Downey
Cover photos: Joe Sohm/The Image Works

Cloth ISBN: 0–312–02137–3
Paper ISBN: 0–312–00319–6

To my mother and father,
Mr. and Mrs. Arthur G. Wayne,
and to the memory of my grandmother,
Mrs. Hattie Marks

CONTENTS

II. THE NOMINATION   85

IV. THE ELECTION

8. THE VOTE AND ITS MEANING

9. REFORMING THE ELECTORAL SYSTEM

PART I

THE ELECTORAL ARENA

Chapter 1

PRESIDENTIAL SELECTION: A HISTORICAL OVERVIEW

Introduction

The road to the White House cannot be traversed in a day. It takes months, often years, to travel, and the time is getting longer. Candidates need to have considerable skill and luck to travel it successfully.

The framers of the Constitution worked for several months on the presidential selection system, and their plan has since undergone a number of constitutional, statutory, and precedent-setting changes. Modified by the development of parties, the expansion of suffrage, the growth of the media, and the revolution in modern technology, the system has become more open and participatory but also more contentious, more circuitous, more structured, and more expensive.

This chapter is about that system: why it was created; what needs it was supposed to serve; what compromises were incorporated in the original plan; how it initially operated; what changes have subsequently affected that operation; whom these changes have benefited; and what this suggests about parties, the electorate, and the political system in general.

3

In addressing these questions, I have organized the chapter into four sections. The first discusses the creation of the presidential election process. In doing so, it explores the motives and intentions of the delegates at Philadelphia and describes the procedures for selecting the President within the context of the constitutional and political issues of the day.

The second section examines the development of a nominating system. It explores the three principal methods that have been used—partisan congressional caucuses, brokered national conventions, and state primaries and caucuses—and describes the political forces that helped to shape them and, in the case of the first two modes, destroyed them.

The third part of the chapter discusses presidential elections. It focuses on those decided by the House of Representatives (1800 and 1824), those influenced by Congress (1876), and those that were actually or very nearly unreflective of popular choice (1888, 1960, 1968, and 1976). In doing so, the section highlights the evolution of the Electoral College.

The final part of the chapter examines the current system. It describes its geographic and demographic bases, whom it benefits, and whom it hurts. The section also discusses the system's major-party orientation and its effects on third-party candidacies.

THE CREATION OF THE ELECTORAL COLLEGE

Among the many issues facing the delegates at the Constitutional Convention of 1787 in Philadelphia, the selection of the President was one of the toughest. Seven times during the course of the convention the method for choosing the executive was altered.

The framers' difficulty in designing electoral provisions for the President stemmed from the need to guarantee the institution's independence and, at the same time, create a technically sound, politically effective mechanism that would be consistent with a republican form of government. They were sympathetic with a government based on consent but not with direct democracy. They wanted a system that would choose the most qualified person but not necessarily the most popular. There seemed to be no precise model to follow.

Three methods had been proposed. The Virginia plan, a series of resolutions designed by James Madison and introduced by Governor Edmund Randolph, provided for legislative selection. Eight states chose their governors in this fashion at the time. Having Congress choose the President would be practical and politically expedient. Moreover, members of Congress could have been expected to exercise a considered judg-ment. This was important to the delegates at Philadelphia, since many of them did not consider the average citizen capable of making a reasoned, unemotional choice.

The difficulty with legislative selection was the threat it posed to the institution of the Presidency. How could the executive's independence be preserved if his election hinged on his popularity with Congress and his reelection on the legislature's appraisal of his performance in office? Only if the President were to serve a long term and not be eligible for reelection, it was thought, could his independence be protected so long as Congress was the electoral body. But this also posed problems. Ineligibility provided little incentive for the President to perform well and denied the country the possibility of reelecting a person whose experience and success in office might make him better qualified than anyone else. Reflecting on these concerns, Gouverneur Morris urged the removal of the ineligibility clause on the grounds that "it . . . intended to destroy the great motive to good behavior, the hope of being rewarded by a re-appointment."[1] A majority of the states agreed. Once the ineligibility clause was deleted, however, the terms of office had to be shortened to prevent what the framers feared might become almost indefinite tenure. With a shorter term of office and permanent reeligibility, legislative selection was not nearly as desirable, since it could make the President beholden to the legislature.

Popular election was another alternative, although one that did not generate a great deal of enthusiasm. It was twice rejected in the conven-tion by overwhelming votes. Most of the delegates felt that a direct vote by the people was neither desirable nor feasible.[2] Lacking confidence in the public's ability to choose the best-qualified candidate, many delegates also believed that the size of the country and the poor state of its com-munications and transportation precluded a national campaign and elec-tion. The geographic expanse was simply too large to permit proper supervision and control of the election. Sectional distrust and rivalry also contributed to the problem.

A third alternative was some type of indirect election in which popular sentiment could be expressed but would not dictate the selection. James Wilson first proposed this idea after he failed to generate support for a direct popular vote. Luther Martin, Gouverneur Morris, and Alexan-der Hamilton also suggested indirect popular election through intermedi-aries. However, it was not until the debate over legislative selection divided and eventually deadlocked the delegates that election by electors was seriously considered. The Committee on Unfinished Business proposed the Electoral College compromise on September 4, and it was accepted after a short debate. Viewed as a safe, workable solution to the selection problem, it was deemed consistent with the constitutional and political features of the new government. Popular election was not precluded, but neither was it encouraged by the compromise.

According to the proposal, presidential electors were to be chosen by the states in a manner designated by their legislatures. In order to ensure their independence, the electors could not simultaneously hold a federal government position. The number of electors was to equal the number of senators and representatives from each state. At a designated time the electors would vote and send the results to Congress, where they would be announced to a joint session by the President of the Senate, the Vice President. The only limitation on the voting was that the electors could not cast *both* their ballots for inhabitants of their own states.[3]

Under the original plan, the person who received a majority of votes cast by the Electoral College would be elected President, and the one with the second highest total would be Vice President. There was no separate ballot for each office. In the event that no one received a majority, the House of Representatives would choose from among the five candidates with the most electoral votes, with each state delegation casting one vote. If two or more individuals were tied for second, then the Senate would select the Vice President from among them. Both of these provisions were subsequently modified by the Twelfth Amendment to the Constitution.

The electoral system was a dual compromise. Allowing state legislatures to establish the procedures for choosing electors was a concession to the proponents of a federal system; having the House of Representatives decide, if there was no Electoral College majority, was designed to please those who favored a stronger national government. Designating the number of electors to be equal to a state's congressional delegation gave the larger states an advantage in the initial voting for President; balloting by states in the House if the Electoral College was not decisive benefited the smaller states.

The large-small state compromise was critical to the acceptance of the Electoral College plan. It was argued during the convention debates that in practice the large states would nominate the candidates for President and the small states would exercise the final choice.[4] So great were sectional rivalry and distrust at the time, the prospect of a majority of the college's agreeing on anyone other than George Washington seemed remote.

THE DEVELOPMENT OF NOMINATING SYSTEMS

While the Constitution prescribed a system for electing a President, it made no reference to the nomination of candidates. Political parties had not emerged prior to the Constitutional Convention. Factions existed, and the framers of the Constitution were concerned about them, but the development of a party system was not anticipated. Rather, it was assumed that electors whose interests were not tied to the national government would make an independent judgment in choosing the best possible person as President.

In the first two elections the system worked as intended. George Washington was the unanimous choice of the electors. There was, however, no consensus on who the Vice President should be. The eventual winner, John Adams, benefited from some discussion and informal lobbying by prominent individuals prior to the vote.[5]

A more organized effort to agree on candidates was undertaken four years later. Partisan alliances were beginning to develop in Congress. Members of the two principal groups, the Federalists and the Anti-Federalists, met separately to recommend individuals. The Federalists chose Vice President Adams; the Anti-Federalists picked Governor George Clinton of New York.

With political parties evolving during the 1790s, the selection of the electors quickly became a partisan contest. In 1792 and 1796 a majority of the state legislatures chose them directly. Thus, the political group that controlled the legislature also controlled the selection. Appointed for their political views, electors were expected to exercise a partisan judgment. When in 1796 a Pennsylvania elector did not, he was accused of faithless behavior. Wrote one critic in a Philadelphia newspaper: "What, do I chuse Samuel Miles to determine for me whether John Adams or Thomas Jefferson shall be President? No! I chuse him to act, not to think."[6]

Washington's decision not to serve a third term forced Federalist and Anti-Federalist members of Congress to recommend the candidates in 1796. Meeting separately, party leaders agreed among themselves on the tickets. The Federalists urged their electors to vote for John Adams and Thomas Pinckney, while the Anti-Federalists (or Republicans, as they began to be called) suggested Thomas Jefferson and Aaron Burr.

Since it was not possible to indicate the presidential and vice presidential choices on the ballot, Federalist electors, primarily from New England, decided to withhold votes from Pinckney (of South Carolina) to make certain that he did not receive the same number as Adams (of

Massachusetts). This enabled Jefferson to finish ahead of Pinckney with 68 votes compared with the latter's 59, but behind Adams, who had 71. Four years of partisan differences followed between a President who, though he disclaimed a political affiliation, clearly favored the Federalists in appointments, ideology, and policy, and a Vice President who was the acknowledged leader of the opposition party.

Beginning in 1800, partisan caucuses composed of members of Congress met for the purpose of recommending the party's nominees. The Republicans continued to choose candidates in this manner until 1824; the Federalists did so only until 1808. In the final two presidential elections in which the Federalists ran candidates, 1812 and 1816, top party leaders, meeting in secret, decided on the nominees.[7]

"King caucus" violated the spirit of the Constitution. It effectively provided for Congress to pick the nominees. After the decline of the Federalists, the nominees were, in fact, assured of victory—a product of the dominance of the Jeffersonian Republican party as well as the success of the caucus in obtaining support for its candidates.

There was opposition within the caucuses. In 1808, Madison prevailed over James Monroe and George Clinton. In 1816, Monroe overcame a strong challenge from William Crawford. In both cases, however, the electors united behind the successful nominee. In 1820, they did not. Disparate elements within the party selected their own candidates.

Although the caucus was the principal mode of candidate selection during the first part of the nineteenth century, it was never formally institutionalized as a nominating body. How meetings were called, by whom, and when varied from election to election. So did attendance. A sizable number of representatives chose not to participate at all. Some stayed away on principle; others did so because of the choices they would have to make. In 1816 less than half of the Republican members of Congress were at their party's caucus. In 1820 only 20 percent attended, and the caucus had to adjourn without formally supporting President Monroe and Vice President Tompkins for reelection. In 1824 almost three-fourths of the members boycotted the session.

The 1824 caucus did nominate candidates. But with representatives from only four states constituting two-thirds of those attending, the nominee, William Crawford, failed to receive unified party support. Other candidates were nominated by state legislatures and conventions, and the electoral vote was divided. With no candidate obtaining a majority, the House of Representatives had to make the final decision. John Quincy Adams was selected on the first ballot. He received the votes of 13 of the 24 state delegations.

The caucus was never resumed. In the end it fell victim to the decline of one of the major parties, the decentralization of political power, and Andrew Jackson's stern opposition. The Federalists had collapsed as a viable political force. As the Republican party grew from being the majority party to the only one, factions developed within it, the two principal ones being the National Republicans and the Democratic-Republicans. In the absence of a strong opposition there was little to hold these factions together. By 1830 they had split into two separate groups, one supporting and one opposing President Jackson.

Political leadership was changing as well. A relatively small group of individuals had dominated national politics for the first three decades after the 1787 Constitution. Their common experience in the war, the Constitutional Convention, and the early government produced personal contacts, political influence, and public respect that contributed to their ability to agree on candidates and to generate public support for them.[8]

Their successors had neither the tradition nor the national orientation in which to cast their presidential votes. Most owed their prominence and political clout to state and regional areas. Their loyalties reflected these bases of support.

The growth of party organizations at the state and local level affected the nomination system. In 1820 and 1824 it produced a decentralized mode of selection. State legislatures, caucuses, and conventions nominated their own candidates. Support was also mobilized on regional levels.

Whereas the congressional caucus had become unrepresentative, state-based nominations suffered from precisely the opposite problem. They were too representative of sectional interests and produced too many candidates. Unifying diverse elements behind a national ticket proved extremely difficult, although Jackson was successful in 1824 and again in 1828. Nonetheless, a system that was more broadly based than the old caucus and that could provide a decisive and mobilizing mechanism was needed. National nominating conventions filled the void.

The first such convention was held in 1831 by the Anti-Masons. A small but relatively active third party, it had virtually no congressional representation. Unable to utilize a caucus, the party turned instead to a general meeting, which was held in a saloon in Baltimore, with 116 delegates from thirteen states attending. They decided on the nominees as well as on an address to the people that contained the party's position on the dominant issues of the day.

Three months later a second convention was held in the same saloon by opponents of President Jackson. The National Republicans (or Whigs, as they later became known) also nominated candidates and agreed on an address critical of the administration.

The Democratic-Republicans (or Democrats, as they were later called) met in Baltimore one year later. The impetus for their convention was Jackson's desire to demonstrate popular support for his Presidency as well as to ensure the selection of Martin Van Buren as his running mate. In 1836, Jackson resorted to another convention—this time to handpick Van Buren as his successor.

The Whigs did not hold a convention in 1836. Believing that they would have more success in the House of Representatives than in the nation as a whole, they ran three regional candidates, nominated by the states, who competed against Van Buren in areas of their strength. The plan, however, failed to deny Van Buren an electoral majority. He ended up with 170 votes compared with a total of 124 for his three opponents.

Thereafter, the Democrats and their opponents, first the Whigs and then their Republican successors, held nominating conventions to select their candidates. The early conventions were informal and rowdy by contemporary standards, but they also set the precedents for later meetings.

The delegates decided on the procedures for conducting the convention, policy statements (addresses to the people), and the nominees. Rules for apportioning the delegates were established before the meetings were held. Generally speaking, states were accorded as many delegates as their congressional representation merited, regardless of the number of actual participants. The way in which the delegates were chosen, however, was left up to the states. Local and state conventions, caucuses, or even committees chose the delegates.

Public participation was minimal. Even the party's rank and file had a small role. It was the party leaders who designated the delegates and made the deals. In time it became clear that successful candidates owed their selection to the heads of the powerful state organizations and not to their own political prominence and organizational support. The price they had to pay, however, when calculated in terms of patronage and other types of political payoffs, was often quite high.

Nineteenth-century conventions served a number of purposes. They provided a forum for party leaders, particularly at the state level. They constituted a mechanism by which agreements could be negotiated and support mobilized. By brokering interests, conventions helped unite the disparate elements within the party, thereby converting an organization of state parties into a national coalition for the purpose of conducting a presidential campaign.

Much of the bartering was conducted behind closed doors. Actions on the convention floor often had little to do with the wheeling and dealing that occurred in the smoke-filled smaller rooms. Since there was little public preconvention activity, many ballots were often necessary before the required number, usually two-thirds of the delegates, was reached.

The nominating system buttressed the position of individual state party leaders, but it did so at the expense of rank-and-file participation. The influence of the state leaders depended on their ability to deliver votes. This, in turn, required that the delegates not exercise an independent judgment. To guarantee their loyalty, the bosses controlled their selection.

Demands for reform began to be heard at the beginning of the twentieth century. The Progressive movement, led by Robert La Follette of Wisconsin and Hiram Johnson of California, desired to break the power of state bosses and their machines through the direct election of convention delegates, or alternatively through the expression of a popular choice by the electorate.

Florida became the first state to provide its political parties with such an option. In 1904 the Democrats took advantage of it and held a state-wide vote for convention delegates. One year later, Wisconsin enacted a law for the direct election of delegates to nominating conventions. Others followed suit. By 1912, fifteen states provided for some type of primary election. Oregon was the first to permit a preference vote for the candidates themselves.

The year 1912 was also the first in which a candidate sought to use primaries as a way to obtain the nomination. With almost 42 percent of the Republican delegates selected in primaries, former President Theodore Roosevelt challenged incumbent William Howard Taft. Roosevelt won nine primaries to Taft's one, yet lost the nomination. (See Table 1–1.) Taft's support among regular party leaders who delivered their delegations and controlled the convention was sufficient to retain the nomination. He received one-third of his support from southern delegations, although the Republican party had won only 7 percent of the southern vote in the previous election.

Partially in reaction to the unrepresentative, "boss-dominated" convention of 1912, additional states adopted primaries. By 1916, more than half of them held a Republican or Democratic contest. Although a majority of the delegates in that year were chosen by some type of primary, many of them were not bound to specific candidates. As a consequence, the primary vote did not control the outcome of the conventions.

Table 1-1   NUMBER OF PRESIDENTIAL PRIMARIES AND PERCENTAGE OF CONVENTION DELEGATES FROM PRIMARY STATES, BY PARTY, SINCE 1912*

	Democratic		Republican	
Year	Number of Primaries	Percentage of Delegates	Number of Primaries	Percentage of Delegates
1912	12	32.9 %	13	41.7 %
1916	20	53.5	20	58.9
1920	16	44.6	20	57.8
1924	14	35.5	17	45.3
1928	17	42.2	16	44.9
1932	16	40.0	14	37.7
1936	14	36.5	12	37.5
1940	13	35.8	13	38.8
1944	14	36.7	13	38.7
1948	14	36.3	12	36.0
1952	15	38.7	13	39.0
1956	19	42.7	19	44.8
1960	16	38.3	15	38.6
1964	17	45.7	17	45.6
1968	17	37.5	16	34.3
1972	23	60.5	22	52.7
1976	30	72.6	28	67.9
1980	31	71.4	34	76.0
1984	25	54.0	30†	66.0
1988	29	73.3	31	72.8

Sources: 1912–1964, F. Christopher Arterton, "Campaign Organizations Confused the Media Political Environment," in *Race for the Presidency,* ed. James David Barber (Englewood Cliffs, N.J.: Prentice-Hall, 1978), p. 7; 1968–1980, David E. Price, *Bringing Back the Parties* (Washington, D.C.: The Congressional Quarterly, 1984), p. 209; 1984, *Congressional Quarterly Weekly Report,* June 16, 1984, 1443. 1988 figures compiled by Kevin J. Coleman of the Congressional Research Service of the Library of Congress on the basis of information available to him in March 1987.

*Includes states holding nonbinding presidential preference primaries except for 1988.

†Five of the Republican primaries scheduled for 1984 were actually not held.

The movement toward popular participation was short-lived, however. Following World War I the number of primaries declined. State party leaders, who saw these elections as a threat to their own influence, argued against them on three grounds: they were expensive; they did not attract many voters; and, major candidates tended to avoid them. Moreover, primaries frequently encouraged factionalism, thereby weakening the party's organizational structure.

In response to this criticism the reformers, who supported primaries, could not claim that their principal goal—rank-and-file control over the party's nominees—had been achieved. Public involvement was disappointing. Primaries rarely attracted more than 50 percent of those who voted in the general election, and usually much less. The minority party, in particular, suffered from low turnout. In some states rank-and-file influence was further diluted by the participation of independents.

As a consequence of these factors, some states that had enacted new primary laws reverted to their former method of selection. Others made the primaries advisory rather than mandatory. Fewer delegates were selected in them. By 1936 only fourteen states held Democratic primaries and twelve held Republican ones. Less than 40 percent of the delegates to each convention that year were chosen in this manner. For the next twenty years the number of primaries and the percentage of delegates hovered around this level.

Roosevelt's failure in 1912 and the decline in primaries thereafter made them at best an auxiliary route to the nomination. While some presidential aspirants became embroiled in them, none who depended on them won. In 1920 a spirited contest between three Republicans (General Leonard Wood, Governor Frank Lowden, and Senator Hiram Johnson) failed to produce a convention majority and resulted in party leaders choosing Warren Harding as the standard-bearer. Similarly, in 1952, Senator Estes Kefauver entered thirteen of seventeen presidential primaries, won twelve of them, became the most popular Democratic contender, but failed to win his party's nomination. The reason Kefauver could not parlay his primary victories into a convention victory was that a majority of the delegates were not selected in this manner. Of those who were, many were chosen separately from the presidential preference vote. Kefauver did not contest these separate delegate elections. As a consequence, he obtained only 50 percent of the delegates in states where he actually won the presidential preference vote. Moreover, the fact that most of his wins occurred against little or no opposition undercut Kefauver's claim to being the strongest, most electable Democrat. He had avoided primaries in four states where he feared that he might either lose or do poorly.

Not only were primaries not considered to be an essential road to the nomination, but running in too many of them was interpreted as a sign of weakness, not strength. It indicated a lack of national recognition and/or a failure to obtain the support of party leaders. As a consequence, leading candidates tended to choose their primaries carefully, and the primaries, in turn, tended to reinforce the position of the leading candidates.

Those who did enter primaries did so mainly to test their popularity rather than to win convention votes. Dwight D. Eisenhower in 1952, John

F. Kennedy in 1960, and Richard M. Nixon in 1968 had to demonstrate that being a general, a Catholic, or a once-defeated presidential candidate would not be fatal to their chances. In other words, they needed to prove they could win the general election.

With the possible exception of John Kennedy's victories in West Virginia and Wisconsin, primaries were neither crucial nor decisive for winning the nomination until the 1970s. When there was a provisional consensus within the party, primaries helped confirm it; when there was not, primaries were not able to produce it.[9] In short, they had little to do with whether the party was unified or divided at the time of the convention.

Primary results tended to be self-fulfilling in the sense that they confirmed the front-runner's status. Between 1936 and 1968, the preconvention leader, the candidate who was ahead in the Gallup Poll before the first primary, won the nomination seventeen out of nineteen times. The only exceptions were Thomas E. Dewey in 1940, who was defeated by Wendell Willkie, and Kefauver in 1952, who lost to Adlai Stevenson. Willkie, however, had become the leader in public opinion by the time the Republican convention met. Even when leading candidates lost a primary, they had time to recoup. Dewey and Stevenson, defeated in early primaries in 1948 and 1956, respectively, went on to reestablish their credibility as front-runners by winning later primaries.

This situation changed dramatically after 1968. Largely as a consequence of the tumultuous Democratic convention of that year, whose nominee and platform were allegedly dictated by party "bosses," demands for a larger voice for the party's rank and file increased. In reaction to these demands, the Democratic party began to look into the matter of delegate selection. It enacted a series of reforms designed to ensure broader representation at the convention. To avoid challenges to their delegations, a number of states that had used caucus and convention systems changed to primaries. By 1980, thirty-five states, the District of Columbia, and Puerto Rico were holding delegate elections of one type or another. Approximately three-fourths of the delegates to each convention were chosen in these primary elections.

New finance laws, which provided for government subsidies of preconvention campaigning, and increased media coverage, particularly by television, also added to the incentive to enter primaries. By 1972 both became important. In that year, Senator Edmund Muskie, the leading Democratic contender at the beginning of the process, was forced to withdraw after doing poorly in the early contests, while in 1976, President

Gerald Ford came close to being the first incumbent President since Chester A. Arthur in 1884 to be denied his party's nomination.

In 1972 and thereafter, primaries were used to build popularity rather than simply reflect it. The ability of lesser-known candidates, such as George McGovern and Jimmy Carter, to use the prenomination process to gain public recognition, win delegate support, and become the leading candidates testifies to this new importance of primaries in contemporary politics. Today, they are the road to the nomination. Aspirants can no longer hope to succeed without entering them; incumbents can no longer ignore them.

The impact of primaries has been significant. They have affected the strategies and tactics of the candidates. They have influenced the composition and behavior of the delegates. They have changed the decision-making character of the national conventions. They have shifted power within the party. They have enlarged the selection zone of potential nominees. They have made governing more difficult. Each of these changes will be discussed in the chapters that follow.

THE EVOLUTION OF THE GENERAL ELECTION

The general election has changed as well. The Electoral College no longer operates as it was designed. It now has a partisan coloration. There is greater public participation, although it is still not direct. The system bears a resemblance to its past. While it has become more democratic, it is still not without its biases.

The Electoral College system was one of the few innovative features of the Constitution. It had no immediate precedent, although it bore some relationship to the way the state of Maryland selected its senators. In essence, it was invented by the framers, not synthesized from British and American experience. And it is one aspect of the system that has rarely worked as intended.

Initially, the method by which the states chose their electors varied. Some provided for direct election in a statewide vote. Others had the legislatures do the choosing. Two states used a combination of popular and legislative selection.

As political parties emerged around the turn of the nineteenth century, state legislatures maneuvered the selection process to benefit the party in power. This resulted in the election of more cohesive groups of electors who shared similar partisan views. Gradually, the trend evolved into a winner-take-all system with electors chosen on a statewide basis by popular vote. South Carolina was the last state to move to popular selection. It did so in 1864.

The development of the party system changed the character of the Electoral College. Only in the first two elections, when Washington was the unanimous choice, did the electors exercise a nonpartisan and presumably independent judgment. Within ten years from the time the federal government began to operate, they quickly became the captives of their party and were expected to vote for its candidates. The outcome of the election of 1800 vividly illustrates this new pattern of partisan voting.

The Federalist party supported President John Adams of Massachusetts and Charles C. Pinckney of South Carolina. The Republicans, who had emerged to oppose the Federalists' policies, backed Thomas Jefferson of Virginia and Aaron Burr of New York. The Republican candidates won, but, unexpectedly, Jefferson and Burr received the same number of votes. All electors who had cast ballots for Jefferson also cast them for Burr. Since it was not possible to differentiate the candidates for the Presidency and Vice Presidency on the ballot, the results had to be considered a tie, though Jefferson was clearly his party's choice for President. Under the terms of the Constitution, the House of Representatives, voting by state, had to choose the winner.

On February 11, 1801, after the results of the Electoral College vote were announced by the Vice President—who happened to be Jefferson—the House convened to resolve the dilemma. It was a Federalist-controlled House. Since the winners of the 1800 election were not to take office until March 4, 1801, a "lame duck" Congress would have to choose the next President.[10] A majority of Federalists supported Burr, whom they regarded as the more pragmatic politician. Jefferson, on the other hand, was perceived as a dangerous, uncompromising radical by many Federalists. Alexander Hamilton, however, was outspoken in his opposition to Burr, regarding him as "the most unfit man in the United States for the office of President."[11]

On the first ballot taken on February 11, Burr received a majority of the total votes, but Jefferson received the support of more state delegations.[12] Eight states voted for Jefferson, six backed Burr, and two were evenly divided. This left Jefferson one short of the needed majority. The House took nineteen ballots on its first day of deliberations, and a total of thirty-six, before it finally elected Jefferson. Had Burr promised to be a Federalist President, it is conceivable that he would have won.

The first amendment to reform voting procedures in the Electoral

College was enacted by the new Congress, controlled by Jefferson's party, in 1803. It was accepted by three-fourths of the states in 1804. This amendment to the Constitution—the twelfth—provided for separate voting for President and Vice President. It also refined the selection procedures in the event that the President and/or Vice President did not receive a majority of the electoral vote. The House of Representatives, still voting by states, was to choose from among the three presidential candidates with the most electoral votes, and the Senate, voting by individuals, was to choose from the top two vice presidential candidates. If the House could not make a decision by March 4, the amendment provided for the new Vice President to assume the Presidency until such time as the House could render a decision.

The next nondecisive presidential vote did not occur until 1824. That year, four people received electoral votes for President: Andrew Jackson (99 votes), John Quincy Adams (84), William Crawford (41), and Henry Clay (37). According to the Twelfth Amendment, the House of Representatives had to decide from among the top three, since none had a majority. Eliminated from the contest was Henry Clay, who happened to be Speaker of the House. Clay threw his support to Adams, who won. It was alleged that he did so in exchange for appointment as secretary of state, a charge that Clay vigorously denied. After Adams became President, however, he did appoint Clay to that position.

Jackson was the winner of the popular vote. In the eighteen states that chose electors by popular vote that year (there were twenty-four states in the Union at the time), he received 192,933 votes compared with 115,696 for Adams, 47,136 for Clay, and 46,979 for Crawford. Adams, however, had the backing of more state delegations. He enjoyed the support of the six New England states (he was from Massachusetts), and with Clay's help the representatives of six other states backed his candidacy. The votes of thirteen states, however, were needed for a majority. New York seemed to be the pivotal state and Stephen Van Rensselaer, a Revolutionary War general, the swing representative. On the morning of the vote, Speaker Clay and Representative Daniel Webster tried to persuade Van Rensselaer to vote for Adams. It was said that they were unsuccessful.[13] When the voting began, Van Rensselaer bowed his head as if in prayer. On the floor he saw a piece of paper with "Adams" written on it. Interpreting this as a sign from the Almighty, he dropped the paper in the box. New York went for Adams by one vote, providing him with a bare majority of states.[14]

Jackson, outraged at the turn of events, urged the abolition of the

Electoral College. His claim of a popular mandate, however, is open to question. The most populous state at the time, New York, did not permit its electorate to participate in the selection of electors. Rather, the state legislature made the decision. Moreover, in three of the states in which Jackson won the electoral vote but lost in the House of Representatives, he had fewer popular votes than Adams. He captured the majority of electoral votes in two of these states because the electors were chosen on a district rather than statewide basis.[15]

Opposition to the system mounted, however, and a gradual democratization of the process occurred. More states began to elect their electors directly by popular vote. In 1800, ten of the fifteen had had legislative selection. By 1832, only South Carolina retained this practice.[16]

There was also a trend toward statewide election of an *entire* slate of electors. Those states that had chosen their electors within districts converted to a winner-take-all system in order to maximize their voting power in the Electoral College. This, in turn, created the possibility that there could be a disparity between the popular and electoral vote. A candidate could be elected by winning the popular vote in the big states by small margins and losing the smaller states by large margins.

The next disputed election occurred in 1876. Democrat Samuel J. Tilden received the most votes. He had 250,000 more popular votes and 19 more electoral votes than his Republican rival, Rutherford B. Hayes. Nonetheless, Tilden was one vote short of a majority in the Electoral College. Twenty electoral votes were in dispute. Dual election returns were received from Florida (4), Louisiana (8), and South Carolina (7). Charges of fraud and voting irregularities were made by both parties. The Republicans, who controlled the three state legislatures, contended that Democrats had forcibly prevented newly freed blacks from voting. The Democrats, on the other hand, alleged that many nonresidents and non-registered people had participated. The other disputed electoral vote occurred in the state of Oregon. One Republican elector was challenged on the grounds that he held another federal position at the time and thus was ineligible to be an elector.

Three days before the Electoral College vote was to be officially counted, Congress established a commission to examine and try to resolve the dispute. The electoral commission was to consist of fifteen members: ten from Congress (five Republicans and five Democrats) and five from the Supreme Court. Four of the Supreme Court justices were designated by the act (two Republicans and two Democrats), and they were to choose a fifth justice. David Davis, a political independent, was expected to be selected, but on the day the commission was created, Davis was appointed by the Illinois legislature to the United States Senate. The Supreme Court justices then chose Joseph Bradley, an independent Republican. Bradley sided with his party on every issue. By a strictly partisan vote, the commission validated all the Republican electors, thereby giving Hayes a one-vote margin of victory.[17]

The only other election in which the winner of the popular vote was beaten in the Electoral College occurred in 1888. Democrat Grover Cleveland had a plurality of 95,096 popular votes but only 168 electoral votes compared with 233 for the Republican, Benjamin Harrison. Cleveland's loss of Indiana by about 3,000 votes and New York by about 15,000 led to his defeat.

While all other leaders in the popular vote have won a majority of electoral votes, shifts of just a few thousand popular votes in a few states could have altered the results. In 1860, a shift of 25,000 in New York from Abraham Lincoln to Stephen A. Douglas would have denied Lincoln a majority in the Electoral College. A change of less than 30,000 in three states in 1892 would have given Harrison another victory over Cleveland. In 1916, Charles Evans Hughes needed only 3,807 more votes in California to have beaten Woodrow Wilson. Similarly, Thomas E. Dewey could have denied Harry S. Truman a majority in the Electoral College with 12,487 more California votes in 1948. In 1960, a change of less than 9,000 in Illinois and Missouri would have meant that John F. Kennedy lacked an Electoral College majority. In 1968, a shift of only 55,000 votes from Richard M. Nixon to Hubert H. Humphrey in three states (New Jersey, Missouri, and New Hampshire) would have thrown the election into the House—a House controlled by the Democrats. In 1976, a shift of only 3,687 in Hawaii and 5,559 in Ohio would have cost Jimmy Carter the election.[18]

Not only could the results of these elections have been affected by very small voter shifts in a few states, but in 1948, 1960, and 1968 there was the further possibility that the Electoral College itself would not be able to choose a winner. In each of these elections, third-party candidates or independent electoral slates threatened to secure enough votes to prevent either of the major candidates from obtaining a majority. In 1948, Henry Wallace (Progressive party) and Strom Thurmond (States' Rights party) received almost 5 percent of the total popular vote, and Thurmond won 39 electoral votes. In 1960, fourteen unpledged electors were chosen in Alabama and Mississippi.[19] In 1968, Governor George Wallace of Alabama, running on the American Independent party ticket, received almost 10 million popular votes (13.5 percent of the total) and 46 electoral votes. It was clear that close competition between the major parties, combined with a strong third-party movement, provided the Electoral College with its most difficult test.

THE POLITICS OF ELECTORAL COLLEGE VOTING

The Electoral College is not neutral. No system of election can be. The way votes are aggregated does make a difference. It benefits some of the electorate and adversely affects others.

A direct popular election always works to the advantage of the majority; the Electoral College usually does. Most often, it exaggerates the margin of the popular vote leader. Richard Nixon's 301 electoral votes in 1968 provided him with 56 percent of the college; his popular vote percentage was only 43.4 percent. Jimmy Carter's election in 1976 resulted in a smaller disparity. He won 50.1 percent of the popular vote and 55 percent of the electoral vote. In 1980, Ronald Reagan received 51 percent of the popular vote but a whopping 91 percent of the electoral vote.

It must be recalled, however, that while the Electoral College usually expands the margin of the popular vote winner, it has also from time to time led to the defeat of the candidate with the most popular votes. On three occasions, 1824, 1876, and 1888, the plurality winner was a loser in the Electoral College. Although such an electoral loss would be less likely today because the parties are competitive in more states, it is still possible.

The Electoral College contains a number of built-in biases. The most significant of these is the winner-take-all voting that has developed. The presidential and vice presidential candidates who receive a plurality of the popular vote within the state get in almost every instance all its electoral votes. Naturally this benefits the largest states not only because of the number of electoral votes they cast but because the votes are almost always cast in a bloc. Moreover, the advantage that the citizens of the largest states receive increases in direct proportion to their population.[20] (See Figure 1–1 for the relative advantage large populations confer upon the states.) This is why a greater share of campaign time and money is spent in these states.

By giving an edge to the larger and more competitive states, the Electoral College also benefits groups that are geographically concentrated within those states and have cohesive voting patterns. Those who

Figure 1–1   STATE SIZE ACCORDING TO POPULATION: THE
1984 ELECTORAL VOTE

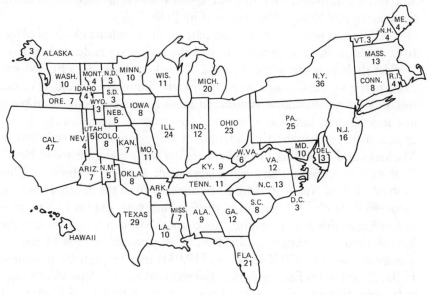

live in the central cities and suburbs have a particular advantage. Jews, Hispanics, and urban blacks fall into this category. However, the black population in general does not because many blacks live in rural and smaller states, particularly in the South. Blue-collar workers and rural dwellers are also disadvantaged.[21]

There is a slight offsetting gain for the very smallest states. That each receives a minimum of three electoral votes regardless of size increases the voting power of sparsely populated states. For example, if Alaska's population of approximately 400,500 were divided by its three electoral votes, there would be one elector for every 133,500 people. Dividing California's population of 23,670,000 by its 47 electoral votes yields one elector for every 567,500 people.[22]

If the voting power of individual states is calculated by region, a bias also occurs. According to Lawrence D. Longley and James D. Dana, Jr., states in the Far West and East are aided, but those in the South, Midwest, and Rocky Mountain areas are hurt.[23]

Additionally, the Electoral College works to the benefit of the two major parties and to the detriment of the minor parties. The winner-take-all system within states, when combined with the need for a majority within the college, makes it difficult for third parties to accumulate enough votes to win an election. To have any effect, third-party support must be geographically concentrated, as George Wallace's was in 1968 and Strom Thurmond's was in 1948, rather than evenly distributed across the country, as Henry Wallace's was in 1948.

Given the limitations on third parties, their realistic electoral objectives would seem to be to defeat one of the major contenders rather than to elect their own candidate. In 1912, Theodore Roosevelt's Bull Moose campaign split the Republican party, thereby aiding the candidate of the minority party, Woodrow Wilson. In more recent elections, third-party and independent candidates have cost the major parties votes but do not appear to have changed the outcome of the election. Truman's loss of Michigan and New York in 1948 apparently was a consequence of Henry Wallace's Progressive party candidacy, while George Wallace in 1968 probably denied Nixon 46 more electoral votes from the South. However, George Wallace's 11.4 percent of the Missouri vote and his 11.8 percent in Ohio probably hurt Humphrey more than Nixon and may explain the loss of these two states by the Democratic candidate. Ford's narrow victory in Iowa in 1976 (632,863 to 619,931) may be partially attributed to the 20,051 votes Eugene McCarthy received as an independent candidate, votes that very likely would have gone to Carter had McCarthy not run.

The impact on third parties is more than simply a question of numbers. It affects the psychology of voting for a candidate who has little chance of winning a majority of the electoral vote. In 1980, the Carter campaign appealed to disaffected Democrats and independents, sympathetic to John Anderson, on precisely these grounds. The "wasted vote" appeal undercut Anderson's ability to raise money and garner political support.[24]

SUMMARY

The quest for the Presidency has been and continues to be influenced by the system designed in Philadelphia in 1787. The objectives of that system were to protect the independence of the institution, to ensure the selection of a well-qualified candidate, and to do so in a way that was politically expedient. It was intended to be consistent with the tenets of a republican form of government.

While many of the objectives are still the same, the system has changed significantly over the years. Of all the factors that have influenced these changes, none has been more important than the advent of political parties. This development created an additional first step in the process—the nomination, which has influenced the selection and behavior of the electors and has affected the operation and the beneficiaries of the Electoral College itself.

The nomination process is necessary to the parties, whose principal interest is to get their leaders elected. At first, members of Congress, meeting in partisan caucuses, decided on the nominees. On the basis of common friendships and shared perspectives they reached a consensus and then used their influence to mobilize support for it. In effect, the system provided for legislative selection of the President in violation of the letter and spirit of the Constitution.

The caucus method broke down with the weakening of the parties, the demise of the Federalists, and the factionalization of the Republicans. It was never restored. In its place developed a more decentralized mode of selection reflective of the increasing sectional composition of the parties.

The new nomination process, controlled by state leaders, operated within the framework of a brokered national convention. There was little rank-and-file participation. The wheeling and dealing was done for the party's electorate, not by them. Demands for greater public involvement eventually opened the system, thereby reducing the influence of state leaders and decreasing the dependence of candidates on them. Power eventually shifted from the political leaders to the candidates themselves, with the people making the final judgment.

Similar trends, rooted in the development of parties and the expansion of suffrage, affected the way in which the electors were selected and voted. Instead of being chosen on the basis of their qualifications, electors were selected on the basis of their politics; instead of being elected as individuals, entire slates of electors were chosen; instead of exercising independent judgment, the electors became partisan agents who were morally and politically obligated to support their party's choice. The predictable soon happened: block voting by electors in states.

The desire of the populace for greater participation also had an effect. It accelerated the movement to choose the electors directly by the people, which resulted in an increased likelihood of the electoral vote's reflecting, even exaggerating, the popular vote. Only three times in American history was the plurality winner not elected. However, the shift of a very small number of votes in a few states could have altered the results of other elections, most recently in 1960, 1968, and 1976. This raises doubts about the adequacy of the system.

The equity of the Electoral College itself has come into question. The way it works benefits the larger, more competitive states with the most electoral votes. Within those states, the groups that are better organized and more geographically concentrated seem to enjoy the greatest advantage. Their vote is maximized by the winner's taking all the state's electoral votes and the state's having a larger share of the total Electoral College. Candidates keep this in mind when planning and conducting their campaigns.

In summary, the electoral system has been decisive and efficient, but questions about its equity remain. It does not jeopardize the President's independence. In fact, it may do just the opposite; it may isolate the selection of President and Vice President too much from that of other officials for national office. It permits a partisan choice but recently has not contributed to the strength of the party inside or outside the government. It facilitates participation in the nomination process but has not substantially raised the level of public involvement in the general election. The winning candidate often obtains only a bare majority or even plurality of the voters, who, in turn, constitute only somewhere between 50 to 60 percent of the voting-age population—hardly the mandate we might expect in a vibrant democratic society.

NOTES

1. Gouverneur Morris, *Records of the Federal Convention*, ed. Max Farrand (New Haven: Yale University Press, 1921), Vol. II, p. 33.

2. The first proposal for direct election was introduced in a very timid fashion by James Wilson, delegate from Pennsylvania. James Madison's *Journal* describes Wilson's presentation as follows: "Mr. Wilson said he was almost unwilling to declare the mode which he wished to take place, being apprehensive that it might appear chimerical. He would say however at least that in theory he was for an election by the people; Experience, particularly in N. York & Massts, shewed that an election of the first magistrate by the people at large, was both convenient & successful mode." Ibid., Vol. I, p. 68.

3. So great was the sectional rivalry, so parochial the country, so limited the number of people with national reputations, that it was feared that electors would tend to vote primarily for those from their own states. To prevent the same states, particularly the largest ones, from exercising undue influence in the selection of both the President and Vice President, this provision was included. It remains in effect today.

4. George Mason declared, "Nineteen times out of twenty, the President would be chosen by the Senate." Ibid., Vol. II, p. 500. The original proposal of the Committee on Unfinished Business was that the Senate should select the President. The delegates substituted the House of Representatives, fearing that the Senate was too powerful with its appointment and treaty-making powers. The principle of equal state representation was retained. Choosing the President is the only occasion on which the House votes by states.

5. Thomas R. Marshall, *Presidential Nominations in a Reform Age* (New York: Praeger, 1981), p. 19.

6. Neal R. Peirce and Lawrence D. Longley, *The People's President* (New Haven: Yale University Press, 1981), p. 36.

7. Marshall, *Presidential Nominations*, p. 20.

8. Ibid., p. 21.

9. Louis Maisel and Gerald J. Lieberman, "The Impact of Electoral Rules on Primary Elections: The Democratic Presidential Primaries in 1976," in Louis Maisel and Joseph Cooper (eds.), *The Impact of the Electoral Process* (Beverly Hills, Calif.: Sage Publications, 1977), p. 68.

10. Until the passage of the Twentieth Amendment, which made January 3 the date when members of Congress took their oath of office and convened, every second session of Congress was a lame duck session.

11. Lucius Wilmerding, *The Electoral College* (New Brunswick, N.J.: Rutgers University Press, 1953), p. 32.

12. There were 106 members of the House (58 Federalists and 48 Republicans). On the first ballot, the vote of those present was 53 to 51 for Burr.

13. Peirce and Longley, *The People's President*, p. 51.

14. Marquis James, *The Life of Andrew Jackson* (Indianapolis: Bobbs-Merrill, 1938), p. 439.

15. William R. Keech, "Background Paper" in *Winner Take All: Report of the Twentieth Century Fund Task Force on Reform of the Presidential Election Process* (New York: Holmes and Meier, 1978), p. 50.

16. South Carolina clung to this system until 1860. After the Civil War, it too instituted popular selection.

17. The act that created the commission specified that its decision would be final unless overturned by both houses of Congress. The House of Representatives, controlled by the Democrats, opposed every one of the commission's findings. The Republican Senate, however, concurred. A Democratic filibuster in the Senate was averted by Hayes's promise of concessions to the South, including the withdrawal of federal troops. Tilden could have challenged the findings in court but chose not to do so.

18. Richard M. Scammon and Alice V. McGillivray, *America votes 12* (Washington, D.C.: Congressional Quarterly, 1977), p. 15.

19. In Alabama, slates of electors ran against each other without the names of the presidential candidates appearing on the ballot. The Democratic slate included six unpledged electors and five loyalists. All were elected. The unpledged electors voted for Senator Harry Byrd of Virginia, while the loyalists stayed with the Kennedy-Johnson ticket. In Mississippi, all eight Democratic electors voted for Byrd.

20. Lawrence D. Longley and James D. Dana, Jr., "New Empirical Estimates of the Biases of the Electoral College for the 1980s," *Western Political Quarterly* 37 (Mar. 84), 165.

21. Ibid., 168–170.

22. There are two other, less obvious, biases in the Electoral College. The distribution of electoral votes is calculated on the basis of the census, which occurs every ten years. Thus, the College does not mirror population shifts within this period. Nor does it take into account the number of people who actually cast ballots. It is a state's population, not its turnout, that determines the number of electoral votes it receives, over and above the automatic three.

23. Longley and Dana, "New Empirical Estimates," 169.

24. Independent and third-party candidates have also been hurt by early filing deadlines in certain states. In 1980, Anderson was forced to devote several months and a million dollars to overcoming such legal obstacles. In 1983 the Supreme Court vindicated

his efforts. It held that early deadlines, which limited participation by independent and third-party candidates, violated their first amendment guarantees of freedom of association. A majority of the Court declared that minority-party candidates should be able to get on state ballots after the two major parties have chosen their nominees (*Anderson v. Celebrezze*, 460 U.S. 780, 1982.)

Selected Readings

Best, Judith. *The Case Against Direct Election of the President: A Defense of the Electoral College.* Ithaca, N.Y.: Cornell University Press, 1975.

Bickel, Alexander M. *Reform and Continuity: The Electoral College, the Convention, and the Party System.* New York: Harper & Row, 1971.

Chase, James S. *Emergence of the Presidential Nominating Convention, 1789–1832.* Urbana: University of Illinois Press, 1973.

Congressional Quarterly. *Presidential Elections Since 1789.* Washington, D.C.: Congressional Quarterly, 1983.

Longley, Lawrence D., and Alan G. Braun. *The Politics of Electoral College Reform.* New Haven: Yale University Press, 1975.

Longley, Lawrence D., and James D. Dana, Jr. "New Empirical Estimates of the Biases of the Electoral College for the 1980s." *Western Political Quarterly* 37 (1984), 157–173.

Marshall, Thomas R. *Presidential Nominations in a Reform Age.* New York: Praeger, 1981.

Peirce, Neal R., and Lawrence D. Longley. *The People's President.* New Haven: Yale University Press, 1981.

Roseboom, Eugene H. *A History of Presidential Elections.* New York: Macmillan, 1957.

Sayre, Wallace S., and Judith H. Parris. *Voting for President.* Washington, D.C.: Brookings Institution, 1970.

Sterling, Carleton W. "The Electoral College Biases Revealed, the Conventional Wisdom and Game Theory Models Notwithstanding." *Western Political Quarterly*, 31 (1978), 159–177.

U.S. Congress. House. Committee on the Judiciary. *Electoral College Reform.* Hearings. 91st Cong., 1st sess. Washington, D.C.: Government Printing Office, 1969.

———. Senate. Committee on the Judiciary. *Electing the President.* Hearings. 91st Cong., 1st sess. Washington, D.C.: Government Printing Office, 1969.

———. Senate. Committee on the Judiciary. *The Electoral College and Direct Election.* Hearings. 95th Cong., 1st sess. Washington, D.C.: Government Printing Office, 1977.

———. Senate. Committee on the Judiciary. *Hearings on Direct Popular Election of the President and Vice President of the United States.* 96th Cong., 1st sess. Washington, D.C.: Government Printing Office, 1979.

Chapter 2

CAMPAIGN FINANCE

Introduction

Running for President is very expensive. In 1984 a whopping $137 million was spent by major-party candidates in their quest for the nomination. Another $81 million was expended by the principal candidates in the general election. National, state, and local party committees, political action committees (PACs), and individuals also spent considerable sums on behalf of the Republican and Democratic nominees. According to Herbert E. Alexander, expenditures totaled $325 million for the 1984 presidential election, $50 million more than in the previous election.[1]

The magnitude of these expenditures poses serious problems for presidential candidates, who must raise considerable sums during the preconvention struggle and monitor their expenses closely, make important allocation decisions, and conform to the intricacies of finance laws during both the nomination and general election campaigns. Moreover, such expenditures raise important issues for a democratic selection process. This chapter will explore some of those problems and issues.

The chapter is organized into five sections. The first details the costs of presidential campaigns, paying particular attention to the increase in media expenditures since 1960. The next section looks briefly at the relationship between spending and electoral success. Can money buy elections? Have the big spenders been the big winners? The third section focuses on the contributors, the size of their gifts, and the implications

27

of large donations for a democratic selection process. What happens when the individual's right to give conflicts with government's desire to set limits? Who prevails? Attempts to control spending and subsidize elections are discussed in the fourth section. The final section examines the impact of the new election laws on presidential campaigning and the party system.

THE COSTS OF CAMPAIGNING

Candidates have always spent money in their quest for the Presidency, but it was not until they personally began to campaign across the country that these costs rose sharply. In 1860, Abraham Lincoln spent an estimated $100,000. One hundred years later, John Kennedy and Richard Nixon were each spending one hundred times that amount. In the twelve years following the 1960 general election, expenditures quadrupled. Table 2–1 lists the costs of the major party candidates in presidential elections from 1860 to 1972, the last election in which campaign spending by major party candidates was not restricted to funds provided by the federal government.

Prenomination costs have risen even more rapidly than those in the general election. Until the 1960s, large expenditures were the exception, not the rule. General Leonard Wood spent an estimated $2 million in an unsuccessful quest for the Republican nomination in 1920. The contest between General Dwight D. Eisenhower and Senator Robert A. Taft in 1952 cost about $5 million, a total that was not exceeded until 1964, when Nelson Rockefeller and Barry Goldwater together spent approximately twice that amount.

In recent years prenomination expenditures have skyrocketed. The increasing number of primaries, participatory caucuses, and candidates has been largely responsible for the rise. In the 1950s these preconvention contests were optional; in the 1970s and 1980s they have been mandatory. Even incumbent Presidents have to enter. And they spend money even when they are not challenged. In 1984 the Reagan campaign committee spent almost $28 million during the nomination period, much of it on voter registration drives for the general election.

To campaign effectively in several states simultaneously requires considerable money to pay for professional services, large organizations, and direct and indirect voter contact. Identifying potential supporters, contacting them, and getting them to the polls is expensive. The need for television advertising and the costs of it have increased significantly. As

Table 2-1   COSTS OF PRESIDENTIAL GENERAL ELECTIONS, 1860–1972,
MAJOR PARTY CANDIDATES

Year	Republican		Democratic	
1860	$100,000	Lincoln*	$50,000	Douglas
1864	125,000	Lincoln*	50,000	McClellan
1868	150,000	Grant*	75,000	Seymour
1872	250,000	Grant*	50,000	Greeley
1876	950,000	Hayes*	900,000	Tilden
1880	1,100,000	Garfield*	335,000	Hancock
1884	1,300,000	Blaine	1,400,000	Cleveland*
1888	1,350,000	Harrison*	855,000	Cleveland
1892	1,700,000	Harrison	2,350,000	Cleveland*
1896	3,350,000	McKinley*	675,000	Bryan
1900	3,000,000	McKinley*	425,000	Bryan
1904	2,096,000	T. Roosevelt*	700,000	Parker
1908	1,655,518	Taft*	629,341	Bryan
1912	1,071,549	Taft	1,134,848	Wilson*
1916	2,441,565	Hughes	2,284,590	Wilson*
1920	5,417,501	Harding*	1,470,371	Cox
1924	4,020,478	Coolidge*	1,108,836	Davis
1928	6,256,111	Hoover*	5,342,350	Smith
1932	2,900,052	Hoover	2,245,975	F. Roosevelt*
1936	8,892,972	Landon	5,194,741	F. Roosevelt*
1940	3,451,310	Willkie	2,783,654	F. Roosevelt*
1944	2,828,652	Dewey	2,169,077	F. Roosevelt*
1948	2,127,296	Dewey	2,736,334	Truman*
1952	6,608,623	Eisenhower*	5,032,926	Stevenson
1956	7,778,702	Eisenhower*	5,106,651	Stevenson
1960	10,128,000	Nixon	9,797,000	Kennedy*
1964	16,026,000	Goldwater	8,757,000	Johnson*
1968†	25,402,000	Nixon*	11,594,000	Humphrey
1972	61,400,000	Nixon*	30,000,000	McGovern

Source: Herbert E. Alexander, *Financing Politics* (Washington, D.C.: Congressional Quarterly, 1980), p. 5. Copyrighted material reprinted with permission of Congressional Quarterly Inc.
*Indicates winner.
†George Wallace spent an estimated $7 million as the candidate of the American Independent party in 1968.

a consequence, preconvention expenditures since 1968 have actually exceeded those in the general elections. Table 2–2 lists the totals spent in the last six prenomination campaigns. These costs are likely to increase in 1988.

The media, particularly television, account for much of the spending. This was not always so. When campaigns were conducted in the press, expenses were relatively low. Electioneering, as carried on by a highly partisan press before the Civil War, had few costs other than for

Table 2–2   COSTS OF PRESIDENTIAL NOMINATION CAMPAIGNS, 1964–1984 (IN MILLIONS OF DOLLARS)

Year	Republican	Democratic
1964	$10	(uncontested)
1968	20	$ 25
1972	(virtually uncontested)*	33.1
1976	26.1	40.7
1980	86.1	41.7
1984	28.0	107.7

Sources: 1964–1972, Herbert E. Alexander, *Financing Politics* (Washington, D.C.: Congressional Quarterly, 1976), pp. 45–47; 1976–1984, Federal Election Commission, Final Reports.
   *Representative John M. Ashbrook spent $740,000 and Representative Paul N. McCloskey spent $550,000 in challenging President Richard M. Nixon for the nomination. Alexander, *Financing Politics*, p. 46.

the occasional biography and campaign pamphlet printed by the party and sold to the public at less than cost.

With the advent of more active public campaigning toward the middle of the nineteenth century, candidate organizations turned to buttons, billboards, banners, and pictures to symbolize and illustrate their campaigns. By the beginning of the twentieth century, the cost of this type of advertising in each election exceeded $150,000—a lot then, but a minuscule amount by contemporary standards.[2]

In 1924, radio was employed for the first time in presidential campaigns. The Republicans spent approximately $120,000 that year, while the Democrats spent only $40,000.[3] Four years later, however, the two parties together spent over $1,000,000. Radio expenses continued to equal or exceed a million dollars per election for the next twenty years.[4]

Television emerged as a vehicle for presidential campaigning in 1952. Both national party conventions were broadcast live by television as well as radio. While there were only 19 million television sets in the United States, almost one-third of the population were regular television viewers. The number of households with television sets rose dramatically over the next four years. By 1956 an estimated 71 percent had television, and by 1968 the figure was close to 95 percent.

The first spot commercials for presidential candidates appeared in 1952. They became regular fare thereafter, contributing substantially to campaign costs. Film biographies, interview shows, political rallies, and election-eve telethons were all seen with increasing frequency.

Table 2–3   RADIO AND TELEVISION EXPENDITURES FOR PRESIDENTIAL
GENERAL ELECTION CAMPAIGNS, BY PARTY, 1952–1984

Year	Republican	Democratic
1952	$2,046,000	$1,500,000
1956	2,886,000	1,763,000
1960	1,865,000	1,142,000
1964	6,370,000	4,674,000
1968	12,598,000	6,143,000
1972	4,300,000	6,200,000
1976	7,875,000	9,081,321
1980	12,324,000	18,400,000
1984	22,900,000*	18,200,000

Source: Herbert E. Alexander, *Financing Politics* (Washington, D.C.: Congressional Quarterly, 1984),
p. 13. Copyrighted material reprinted with permission of Congressional Quarterly Inc. Figures for 1984
provided to the author by Professor Alexander.
*Includes $2.5 million spent during the prenomination period.

In 1948 no money was spent on television by either party. Twenty
years later, expenses exceeded $18 million for radio and television com-
bined, approximately one-third of the total cost of the campaign. In
recent campaigns that figure has been in the $25-million range, with more
than half the campaign budget of each of the major party candidates
devoted to media activities. This amount, however, while significant, pales
by comparison with the $872 million that Procter and Gamble spent
promoting its products in 1984.[5]

The use of other modern technology has also increased expenditures.
In 1968, Democrats Hubert Humphrey and George McGovern spent
between them $650,000 on polling, while in 1972 the Nixon campaign
alone spent over $1.6 million.[6] If anything, these expenses have increased.
In 1984 the Reagan campaign spent approximately $2 million on polling
for the general election.

Finally, the costs of fund-raising have increased. In the past, candidates depended on a relatively small number of large contributors and
could personally solicit funds. Today, they depend on a relatively large
number of small contributors; mass appeals must be made.

Dwight Eisenhower was the first presidential candidate to make use
of the direct-mail technique to raise money. His letter to *Reader's Digest*
subscribers promising to go to Korea to end the war generated a substan-

tial legacy for his campaign. Barry Goldwater in 1964 and George McGovern in 1972, unable to obtain support from their parties' regular contributors, targeted appeals to partisans and other sympathizers. Their success, even though they had been well behind in the preelection polls, combined with changes in the law that prohibit large gifts yet ultimately require more spending, has made direct-mail solicitation the order of the day for parties and candidates alike. In 1984 the Reagan-Bush Committee raised $11 million out of a total of $16 million in private contributions in this manner.

The costs of these mailings can be considerable. When the price of obtaining the lists is added to the expense of designing, producing, addressing, and sending the letters, the total spent can exceed the amount raised. Philip Crane, the first declared candidate for the 1980 Republican nomination, spent $2 million to raise $1.7 million from 70,000 contributors. Today that cost would be even higher.

Three major issues arise from the problems of large expenditures. One concerns the impact of spending. To what extent does it improve a candidate's chances for success? Another problem pertains to the donors. Who pays, how much can they give, and what do they get for their money? A third relates to the costs. Can expenditures be controlled without impinging on First Amendment freedoms? The next section turns to the first of these questions, the relation of expenditures to winning and losing. Subsequent parts examine the sources of contributions, attempts to regulate contributions and costs, and the impact of the finance laws on presidential elections.

THE CONSEQUENCES OF SPENDING

Is spending related to electoral success? Have candidates with the largest bankrolls generally been victorious? In the general elections at the presidential level, the answers seem to be yes, but it is difficult to determine precisely the extent to which money contributed to victory or simply flowed to the likely winner.

Between 1860 and 1972, the winner outspent the loser twenty-one out of twenty-nine times. (See Table 2–1.) Republican candidates have spent more than their Democratic opponents in twenty-five out of the twenty-nine elections. The four times they did not, the Democrats won. The trend has continued. Although since 1976 expenditures of the major party candidates' organizations cannot exceed a ceiling established by law, money can be spent independently on their behalf. In 1980 and 1984 considerably more was spent in this way for Ronald Reagan than for his Democratic opponents.

What does this all suggest? The pattern of greater spending and electoral victories indicates that the *money contributes to success, but potential success also attracts money.*

Having more funds is an advantage, but it does not guarantee victory. The fact that heavily favored incumbent Richard Nixon outspent rival George McGovern more than two to one in 1972 does not explain McGovern's huge defeat, although it probably portended it. On the other hand, Hubert Humphrey's much narrower defeat by Nixon four years earlier was probably influenced by Humphrey's having spent less than $12 million, compared with over $25 million spent by Nixon. The closer the election, the more the disparity in funds can be a factor.

Theoretically, campaign spending should have a greater impact on the nomination process than on the general election. The need of most candidates to gain visibility, mobilize support, and develop an effective organization normally requires a large outlay of funds. Some of the biggest spenders, however, have been losers. In 1964, Nelson Rockefeller spent approximately $5 million, much of it his own money, in losing the Republican nomination to Barry Goldwater. Four years later, an unsuccessful Rockefeller spent $8 million without entering a single primary. And in 1980 John Connally spent $13.7 million, yet had only one delegate pledged to him at the time of his withdrawal—the most expensive delegate in history!

There are, of course, examples of successful candidates for their party's nomination who spent more. John Kennedy's financial resources in 1960 not only aided his campaign in critical primaries, such as the West Virginia contest with Humphrey, but also discouraged challengers in several others, such as California and Ohio. In 1972, McGovern was able to spend $4 million, one-third of all his prenomination expenses, on the crucial California primary. In 1980 both winning nominees, Ronald Reagan and Jimmy Carter, outspent their opponents, as did Walter Mondale in 1984. Table 2–4 lists the spending by primary candidates in 1984.

Looking at these aggregate amounts, however, may be misleading. In 1984, the loser outspent the winner in half the Democratic primaries and caucuses. Mondale won six contests in which he outspent Gary Hart but also won seventeen where Hart outspent him. Hart, in turn, won nineteen where he outspent Mondale but also won seven where Mondale spent more. Jesse Jackson won one primary, in the District of Columbia,

Table 2–4   PRENOMINATION EXPENDITURES FOR DEMOCRATIC AND
REPUBLICAN CANDIDATES, 1984*

Democrats		Republicans	
Candidate	Expenditures	Candidate	Expenditures
Askew, Reubin O'D	$3,353,234	Reagan, Ronald	$27,955,189
Cranston, Alan	8,176,227		
Glenn, John	14,411,429		
Hart, Gary W.	24,260,585		
Hollings, Ernest F.	2,778,931		
Jackson, Jesse L.	10,090,305		
Larouche, Lyndon Hermyle, Jr.	4,923,407		
McGovern, George Stanley	1,857,182		
Mondale, Walter F.	37,315,417		
Others	504,949		
Total	$107,671,666		$27,955,189

Source: Federal Election Commission, "Presidential Pre-Nomination Campaigns," Final Report (April, 1986), p. 9.
*Some campaigns began as early as 1981. Figures in this table cover net expenditures from the beginning of the campaigns through December 31, 1985.

where he outspent the others, but also won two where the others outspent him. Four years earlier, George Bush tended to do better against Reagan where he spent less and worse where he spent more.[7]

If just caucuses are examined, however, spending seems to have a greater impact, because it contributes more directly than in primaries to the ability of a candidates's organization to mobilize its supporters. Hart's spending in particular was more important than any other factor in explaining the size of his caucuses vote in 1984.[8]

Money is obviously important. Without it, it would be difficult to wage a successful campaign. But the spending of vast sums, particularly by a candidate who is trailing, may be a sign of weakness, not strength. It may indicate that the big spender lacks grass roots support and thus must wage an expensive media campaign to convey his message. This is precisely what Gary Hart did in 1984. He outspent Walter Mondale by substantial amounts in the last seven large primaries, yet he received a plurality of the vote in only two of them.

To summarize, money is essential in getting started. It generates credibility in the eyes of donors, politicians, and the media. It can provide a critical edge in a close contest. It enables candidates to maximize their resources, particularly organizational support, polling, and media, which are vital to the conduct of modern campaigns. These reasons explain why candidates and their organizations devote so much time and effort to raising funds and why the absence of sufficient money can be fatal to a political campaign.

THE SOURCES OF SUPPORT

In addition to the high costs of campaigning and the effect that unequal spending can have on electoral results, another critical issue is the sources of funds and the strings, if any, that are attached to giving. Throughout most of America's electoral history, parties and candidates have depended on large contributors.

At the end of the nineteenth century, in the midst of the industrial boom, the Republicans were able to count on the support of the Astors, Harrimans, and Vanderbilts, while the Democrats looked to financier August Belmont and inventor-industrialist Cyrus McCormick. Corporations, banks, and life insurance companies soon became prime targets of party fund-raisers. The most notorious and probably the most adroit fund-raiser of this period was Mark Hanna. A leading official of the Republican party, Hanna owed most of his influence to his ability to obtain substantial political contributions. He set quotas, personally assessing the amount that businesses and corporations should give. In 1896, and again in 1900, he was able to obtain contributions of $250,000 from Standard Oil. Theodore Roosevelt personally ordered the return of some of the Standard Oil money in 1904 but accepted large gifts from magnates E. H. Harriman and Henry C. Frick.[9] Roosevelt's trust-busting activities during his Presidency led Frick to remark, "We bought the son of a bitch and then he did not stay bought."[10]

Sizable private gifts remained the principal source of party and candidate support until the mid-1970s. The Republicans benefited more than the Democrats from the wealthy contributors known in the campaign vernacular as "fat cats." Only in 1964 was a Democrat—incumbent Lyndon B. Johnson, who enjoyed a large lead in the preelection polls—able to raise more money from large donors than his Republican opponent—Barry Goldwater.

The reluctance of regular Republican contributors to support the Goldwater candidacy forced his organization to appeal to thousands of potential supporters through a direct mailing. The success of this effort in raising $5.8 million from approximately 651,000 people showed the potential of the mails as a fund-raising technique and shattered an unwritten rule of politics: that money could not be raised by mail. In 1968 Alabama Governor George Wallace, running as a third-party candidate, solicited the bulk of his funds in this fashion.

Despite the use of mass mailings and also party telethons to broaden the base of political contributors in the 1960s, dependence on large donors continued to grow. In 1964 over $2 million was raised in contributions of $10,000 or more. Eight years later approximately $51 million was collected in gifts of this size or larger. Some gifts were in the million-dollar range.

The magnitude of these contributions, combined with the heavy-handed tactics of the Nixon fund-raisers in 1971 and 1972, brought into sharp focus the difficulty of maintaining a democratic selection process that was dependent on private funding.[11] Reliance on large contributors, who often did not wish their gifts to be made public, the inequality of funding between parties and candidates, and the high costs of campaigning, especially in the media, all raised serious questions. Were there assumptions implicit in giving and receiving? Could elected officials be responsive to individual benefactors and to the general public at the same time? Put another way, did the need to obtain and keep large contributors affect decision making in a manner that was inconsistent with the tenets of a democratic society? Did the high cost of campaigning, in and of itself, eliminate otherwise qualified candidates from running? Were certain political parties, interest groups, or individuals consistently advantaged or disadvantaged by the distribution of funding? Had the Presidency become an office that only the wealthy could afford—or, worse still, that only those with wealthy support could seek?

FINANCE LEGISLATION OF THE 1970S

Reacting to these issues, Congress in the 1970s enacted far-reaching legislation designed to reduce dependence on large donors, discourage illegal contributions, broaden the base of public support, and control escalating costs at the presidential level. Additionally, the Democratic Congress that passed these laws wanted to equalize the funds available to the Republican and Democratic nominees. Finally, the legislation was designed to buttress the two-party system, making it more difficult for minority candidates and parties to successfully challenge major party nominees for elective office.

One law, the Federal Election Campaign Act of 1971, set ceilings on the amount of money presidential and vice presidential candidates and their families could contribute to their own campaigns and the amount that could be spent on media advertising; it also established procedures for the public disclosure of all contributions over a certain amount.

A second act, the Revenue Act of 1971, created tax credits and deductions to encourage private contributions. It also provided, for the first time, federal subsidies for the general election. Financed by an income-tax checkoff provision, the fund allowed a taxpayer to designate $1 to a special presidential election account. Since the checkoff has been placed in a prominent place on the income-tax form, approximately 25 percent of taxpayers have been approving the use of $1 of their taxes for the fund. Figure 2–1 indicates designations to and disbursements from this fund.

Despite the passage of the funding provision in 1971, it did not go into effect until the 1976 presidential election. Most Republicans had opposed the legislation. In addition to conflicting with their general ideological position that the national government's role be limited, it offset the party's traditional fund-raising advantage. President Nixon was persuaded to sign the bill only after the Democratic leadership agreed to postpone the effective date of the law until after 1972, the year Nixon ran for reelection.

There was also a short but critical delay in the effective date for the disclosure provision of the other 1971 campaign finance act. Signed by the President on February 14, 1972, it was scheduled to take effect in sixty days. This delay precipitated a frantic attempt by both parties to tap large donors who wished to remain anonymous. It is estimated that the Repub-

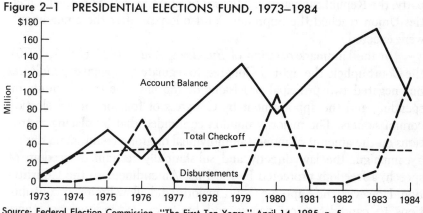

Figure 2–1   PRESIDENTIAL ELECTIONS FUND, 1973–1984

Source: Federal Election Commission, "The First Ten Years," April 14, 1985, p. 5.

licans collected a staggering $20 million, much of it pledged beforehand, during this period. Of this money, approximately $1.5 million came in forms that could not be easily traced.

Even after the disclosure provision went into effect, violations were numerous. Moreover, pressure on corporations, particularly by Nixon campaign officials, resulted in a long list of illegal contributions. The spending of funds on "dirty tricks" and other unethical and illegal activities, such as the burglary of the Democratic National Committee's Watergate headquarters, further aroused public ire and eventually resulted in new and more stringent legislation.

Congress responded by amending the Federal Election Campaign Act of 1971. The new provisions, passed in 1974, included public disclosure provisions, contribution ceilings, campaign-spending limits, and federal subsidies for the nomination process. A six-person commission was established to enforce the law. Two members of the Federal Election Commission (FEC) were to be appointed by the President and four by the Congress.

The amendments were highly controversial. Critics immediately charged a federal giveaway, a robbery of the Treasury. Opponents of the legislation also argued that the limits on contributions and spending violated the constitutionally guaranteed right to freedom of speech, that the funding provisions unfairly discriminated against third-party and independent candidates, and that appointment of four of the commissioners by Congress violated the principle of separation of powers. A suit brought by such diverse individuals and groups as conservative New York Republican Senator James L. Buckley, presidential aspirant and former liberal Democratic senator from Minnesota Eugene McCarthy, the Libertarian party, the Republican party of Mississippi, and the New York Civil Liberties Union reached the Supreme Court one year after the amendments were enacted.

In the landmark decision of *Buckley v. Valeo* (424 U.S. 1, 1976), the Court upheld the right of Congress to regulate campaign expenditures but negated two principal provisions of the law, the overall limits on spending and the appointment by Congress of four of the six election commissioners. The majority opinion contended that by placing restrictions on the amount of money an individual or group could spend during a campaign, the law directly and substantially restrained freedom of speech, a freedom protected by the First Amendment to the Constitution. However, the Supreme Court majority did allow limits on contributions to candidates' campaigns and limits on expenditures of those

KEY PROVISIONS OF CAMPAIGN FINANCE LEGISLATION

Public Disclosure: All contributions of $200 or more must be identified. All expenditures of $200 or more must be reported. Campaign committees are also required to file periodic reports before the election and a final report after it.

Contribution Limits: In any election, including a primary, contributions from an individual cannot exceed $1,000 to a single candidate, $20,-000 to a national political party committee, and $5,000 to other political committees, with the total not to exceed $25,000 in any one year.

Personal contributions from candidates or their immediate families are limited to $50,000 at the prenomination stage and to $50,000 in the general election if a candidate accepts federal funds. Candidates who do not accept federal funds are not limited in what they can contribute to their own campaign. Individuals and political action committees can spend an unlimited amount on their own for candidates of their choice, provided they do not consult or communicate in any way with the candidate's campaign organization.

Campaign Expenses: Candidates who accept public funding cannot spend more than $10 million in their quest for the nomination and $20 million in the general election plus a cost-of-living increment calculated from the base year of 1974. In 1984 these limits were $20.2 million in prenomination expenditures and $40.4 million in the general election. In 1988 they will be approximately $22.3 million in the primaries and caucuses plus an additional 20 percent for fund-raising (a total of about $27 million) and almost $45 million in the general election.

There are also specific spending limits in the states for nomination expenditures. These limits are based on the size of the voting-age population in the state. In 1988 they will range from $444,600 in the smallest states to $7.1 million in the largest state, California. Fund-raising expenses up to 20 percent of all expenditures and accounting and legal fees are exempt from these spending limits. Candidates who do not accept federal funds have no limit on their expenditures. Additionally, the national parties can spend two cents per citizen of voting age in support of their presidential and vice presidential candidates. However, state and local parties can spend unlimited amounts on voluntary efforts to get out the vote.

Matching Funds: Major-party contenders who raise $5,000 in twenty states in contributions of $250 or less, a total of $100,000, are eligible to receive matching grants during the prenomination period, which begins

January 1 of the year in which the election occurs. Only the first $250 of each contribution will be matched.

Communication Notices: All authorized advertisements by candidates' organizations must state the name of the candidate or agent who authorized them. All nonauthorized advertisements must identify the person who made or financed the ad and his or her organizational affiliation, if any.

Compliance Procedures: The Federal Election Commission has authority to investigate possible violations, hold hearings, and assess certain civil penalties. Its decision may be appealed to U.S. District Courts. The Justice Department retains the authority for criminal investigation and prosecution.

candidates who accepted public funds. In doing so, the Court acknowledged that large, often secret, contributions and rapidly increasing expenditures did pose problems for a democratic society, problems on which Congress had power to legislate.

The Court's decision required that the election law be amended once again. It took Congress several months to do so. In the spring of 1976, during the presidential primaries, amendments were enacted that continued public funding of the presidential election and subsidizing of the delegate selection process but did so on a voluntary basis. Candidates did not have to accept government funds, but if they did, as in the past, they were limited in how much they could spend. The amount that could be contributed to a candidate was also limited. The Federal Election Commission was reconstituted, with all six members to be nominated by the President and appointed subject to the advice and consent of the Senate.

In 1979, additional amendments to the Federal Election Campaign Act were passed. Designed to reduce the reporting requirements of the law, they raised the minimum contribution and expenditure that had to be reported and decreased the number of reports that had to be filed. To encourage voluntary activities and higher turnout, the amendments also permitted state and local party committees to purchase an unlimited amount of campaign paraphernalia for candidates for national office and to spend an unlimited amount on registration and get-out-the-vote activities. Known as the "soft money" provision, this amendment has generated considerable controversy because it permits a party to raise and spend large sums of money on all its candidates, including its presidential nominees, without being subject to the contribution limits or reporting requirements of the law. Finally, federal financial support for nominating conventions of the major parties was also increased.[12]

THE IMPACT OF THE LAW

Expenditures

The new legislation has had a significant impact on campaign expenditures. Although it has limited spending by presidential candidates' organizations, it has also stimulated a variety of candidate-inspired mechanisms designed to circumvent these limits. If only expenses reported by campaign organizations are considered, expenditures have remained relatively constant over the years. They have been increased by a cost of living adjustment (COLA) as indicated in Table 2–5, but that adjustment has not kept pace with the actual rise in campaign-related expenses such as those for media, air travel, hotel accommodations, even fund-raising. Between 1980 and 1984 alone, the COLA increased by 37.4 percent, but television advertising costs rose by a hefty 56 percent.[13]

According to Herbert Alexander, a political scientist specializing in campaign finance, the expenditures of the major candidates in nomination contests and general elections, if measured in terms of constant dollars (that is, what they will buy today) have actually declined from 1972 to 1984.[14]

From the perspective of campaign managers, the crunch in expenditures represents a real problem. Today most presidential organizations spend an increasing proportion of their budget on media. In 1984 this amounted to almost two-thirds of both Mondale's and Reagan's total expenditures. In contrast, grass roots activities have tended to be slighted.

The need to mount efforts in the field, however, has increased the importance of nonparty groups, particularly during the nomination period, and also of state and local party organizations during the general election. The expenditures of these groups, which may affect the presidential contest, are not subject to the limits imposed on the candidate committees, so long as the candidate committees do not orchestrate them.[15]

Independent expenditures of individual and nonparty groups have risen significantly in recent years. In 1980, $13.6 million was spent independently on the presidential campaign. In 1984, this figure had risen to $16.7 million, with ideological groups spending the bulk of this money.[16]

Table 2–5 PRESIDENTIAL SPENDING LIMITS AND COLAS, 1976–1984

	Unadjusted Limit 1974 Base Year	1976	1980	1984
COLA*	—	9.1%	47.2%	102%
Primary Election Limit**	$10 million	$10.9 million	$14.7 million	$20.2 million
General Election Limit	$20 million	$21.8 million	$29.4 million	$40.4 million
Party Convention Limit				
1976	$2 million	$2.2 million		
1980	$3 million		$4.4 million	
1984	$4 million			$8.1 million
Party General Election Limit (2¢ × VAP*** adjusted by COLA)	—	$3.2 million	$4.6 million	$6.9 million

Source: Federal Election Commission, "Annual Report 1984," June 1, 1985, pp. 8–9.

*COLA means the cost-of-living adjustment, which the Department of Labor annually calculates using 1974 as the base year.

**Primary candidates receiving matching funds must comply with two types of spending limits: A national limit (listed in the above table) and a separate limit for each state. The state limit is $200,000 or 16 cents multiplied by the state's voting age population, whichever is greater. (Both amounts are adjusted for increases in the cost of living.) The maximum amount of primary matching funds a candidate may receive is half of the national spending limit.

***VAP means Voting Age Population, which was 146.8 million in 1976, 157.5 million in 1980 and 171.4 million in 1984.

The Republican party has benefited disproportionately from independent spending at the presidential level. It has also been advantaged by the 1979 amendment that permits state and local party committees to raise and spend money for voter identification, registration, and turnout. These state and local expenditures have restored the financial advantage that the Republicans enjoyed before the passage of the campaign finance legislation. This advantage is likely to continue.

Revenue

Individuals. One of the most important consequences of the law has been to reduce the influence a small number of large contributors had on the presidential nomination and election. No longer can candidates depend on a few wealthy friends to finance their campaigns. The $1,000 limit on individual donors, which is not subject to a cost-of-living adjustment, the $250 ceiling on matching grants, and the eligibility requirements for federal funds have made the solicitation of a large number of small contributors absolutely essential.

There are some ways to stretch, if not circumvent, the contribution limits, however. Candidates can aid their own campaigns. There is no restriction on their use of personal funds in the years prior to the election, until their candidacy is formally established. At that point a $50,000 personal limit is imposed. Moreover, funds raised but not spent by candidates in campaigns for other offices—such as for the Senate, House of Representatives, or a state governorship—can be tapped in their quest for the presidential nomination. Although $1,000 is the maximum individual gift, voluntary goods and services are unrestricted. Artists and musicians, in particular, can generate considerable revenue for candidates by offering their time and talent. Concerts, and to a lesser extent art sales, have become excellent sources of revenue.

Borrowing money is also possible. Campaigns can obtain loans if they can get them, provided the terms of payment are clear and the loans are made in accordance with regular business practices.

With constraints on the wealthy, to whom can presidential aspirants turn for financial help? Today, there are two principal types of fund-raisers: one is the successful entrepreneur who has a network of well-to-do personal friends and business associates; the other is the direct mailer who owns or has access to computerized lists of individuals organized on the basis of their likely political orientation. The personal fund-raiser, often referred to as a *collector,* taps people directly; the direct mailer sends them a highly crafted letter. Both types of solicitation are essential to a success-ful campaign.

At the outset of a presidential campaign, candidates usually find it necessary to gain the support of a number of collectors. These individuals help finance start-up activities by seeking large contributions (up to $1,000). The collectors are not politicians but are partisans. For them politics is an avocation. Although their motives may vary, most desire access to the candidate as a reward for their political involvement. Some aspire to high government position if their candidate is successful, while others wish to exercise influence, receive social invitations, enjoy the excitement of politics, or help the best person win.[17]

Unlike collectors, direct mailers are professionals. Their task is to solicit contributions from a large number of small donors. Inevitably, their type of fund-raising is slower and more costly, but it can produce huge payoffs. Not only can direct mail generate a lot of money, it can also produce a sympathetic donor list for further solicitation. It is frequently necessary to go back to these donors for additional support during the campaign.

Table 2–6 lists the principal sources of revenue for the presidential nominees in 1984. As the table indicates, there is still some variation in the size of the gifts, with the better-known candidates (the front-runners) enjoying the highest percentage of large donations.

While reducing the impact of personal wealth was a desired conse-quence of the election law, the loss of candidate control over the campaign was not. Yet this too has occurred. The crunch in expenditures has required candidates to seek other ways to supplement their campaigns. In addition to the state and local party activities, they have relied on and benefited from the support of nonparty groups.

Groups. Although the election law prohibits corporations and labor un-ions from making direct contributions to political campaigns, it does allow their employees, stockholders, or members to form political action com-mittees (PACs) and fund them through voluntary contributions.[18] They can directly affect the presidential selection process in three ways: by giving up to $5,000 to a single candidate, by spending an unlimited amount *independently* on the candidate's behalf, and by using their organization to mobilize and register voters.

Direct donations are the least important. Money given directly to candidates by PACs in presidential campaigns rarely exceeds 3 percent of the total amount raised during the election year. In 1984 it constituted 2.8 percent of the total, and much less for the front-runners. Independent

Table 2–6 PRENOMINATION REVENUES OF MAJOR PARTY CANDIDATES, 1984

Candidates	Net Receipts	Individual Contributions	Percent $750 and up	PAC Contributions (Nonparty)	Federal Matching Funds
Democratic					
Askew, Reubin O'D	$3,352,684	1,705,241	27	0	975,898
Cranston, Alan	8,213,496	3,418,233	39	336,063	2,113,731
Glenn, John	14,408,488	6,683,939	45	368,009	3,325,377
Hart, Gary W.	24,284,417	8,919,174	23	0	5,328,463
Hollings, Ernest F.	2,796,252	1,362,663	27	245,859	821,598
Jackson, Jesse L.	10,094,899	5,138,544	8	23,699	3,061,394
Larouche, Lyndon Hermyle, Jr.	4,970,320	2,075,540	15	750	494,142
McGovern, George Stanley	1,847,724	831,599	6	14,040	612,732
Mondale, Walter F.	37,771,529	17,414,611	30	750	9,494,915
Others	503,501	195,993	18	0	0
Total	108,243,310	47,745,537	28	989,170	26,228,250
Republican					
Reagan, Ronald	28,686,520	16,484,796	29	130,680	10,099,998

Source: Federal Election Commission, "Presidential Pre-Nomination Campaigns," Final Report (April, 1986), pp. 1, 4, 6.

expenditures, on the other hand, can be significant. Although they have mushroomed in recent elections, their effect on individual contests is more difficult to evaluate. Groups can be particularly valuable in educating, mobilizing, and turning out voters. The organizing efforts of labor PACs in the 1984 primaries and caucuses helped produce pluralities for Walter Mondale in several key states, and they contributed to Jimmy Carter's victories in the states of Texas and Ohio in the 1976 general election.

Additionally, PACs can contribute money to state and local political parties in their efforts to turn out a large vote in the general election. Corporations and labor unions may also fund these activities, unless prohibited by state law from doing so. Much of this state and local giving is orchestrated by officials of the national parties.

PACs have proven to be so important that presidential candidates now regularly form their own. Known as nonconnected organizations, they have been used primarily to fund organizational activities, build support, and defray travel and other expenses of the candidate in the years between the last election and the actual opening of the current campaign. In addition, some of the budgets of these nonconnected PACs goes into donations to others during the midterm elections. This money is intended to generate reciprocal support from elected officials for the presidential nominee later on. Walter Mondale in 1984 and George Bush, in preparing for the 1988 elections, gained from this support.

A good example of a nonconnected PAC has been the Citizens for the Republic. Started in 1977, this organization had within a year raised $2.5 million and spent $1.9 million on operations. Most of this money was used for fund-raising, travel, and other expenses of the PAC's principal speaker, Ronald Reagan. In the process of raising money, the Citizens developed a list of more than 300,000 contributors. This list was purchased for a nominal fee by the campaign committee for the reelection of President Reagan.

The Reagan PAC became the prototype for other nonconnected organizations. By the end of 1985, PACs established by aspirants for the 1988 Republican nomination had raised over ten million dollars. Of these groups, Vice President George Bush's was by far the most successful if measured in terms of dollars and cents, collecting $9 million in donations by midOctober 1986. Much of this money was used to support a sizable national staff, field coordinators for the early primary and caucus states, and a range of prenomination activities. The PACs of Bush and several other candidates spent sizable sums in Michigan in 1986 to influence the selection of precinct delegates who would help choose the state's convention delegates in 1988.[19]

The Democrats have also used PACs. In 1981 Walter Mondale and Edward Kennedy each formed their own PAC to boost their expected candidacies in 1984. When Kennedy withdrew by 1982, his PAC had already raised $2.5 million. Mondale had a similar amount and a donor list of 25,000 names.

Mondale's use of PACs got him into trouble in 1984. His campaign organization had encouraged the formation of delegate PACs to provide money and support to slates of individuals who were seeking direct election as Mondale delegates to the Democratic nominating convention. A letter from a Mondale official indicated how such PACs could be established, and suggested that any legal question concerning support for them should be referred to the campaign's legal counsel. As a consequence of these efforts, PACs for Mondale delegates were organized and raised money in nineteen states. In several of them funds raised were used to pay the salaries of individuals who had been previously paid by the national campaign organization. There were even transfers of money between PACs of different states. Gary Hart, Mondale's principal opponent, charged that this activity violated the law, which prohibited collusion between the official campaign organization and the PACs. After trying to sidestep the issue, the Mondale campaign was finally pressured to repay the sums his delegate PACs had spent, approximately $400,000.

The Democratic PAC controversy in 1984 led some Democratic aspirants for their party's 1988 nomination to denounce PACs and to seek other ways to fund their prenomination activities. One device used by Hart, Arizona Governor Bruce Babbitt, and others, including Republicans Jack Kemp and Pat Robertson, has been the creation of a tax-exempt foundation. Although foundations cannot provide direct support for candidates for office, they can provide support for their ideas—for research, agenda-building, staff, and travel. They can also produce valuable donation lists. The indirect use of these foundations for political activities that help individual candidates, however, has also generated controversy, not only because it circumvents the election law but because it conflicts with an Internal Revenue Service regulation that these foundations cannot engage in political campaigns on behalf of any candidate.[20]

Matching Funds. In addition to individuals and groups, the third source of money for the nomination process is the government itself. Individual contributions up to $250 can be matched by an equal amount from election funds in the calendar year of the election, if certain conditions are met. Contributions received in the previous year are also eligible for matching in the election year, provided they were given to the candidate's official committee.

While eligibility for matching funds is not difficult to establish and, in fact, has been getting easier, the maintenance of eligibility is harder.[21] Candidates for their party's nomination who fail to receive at least 10 percent of the vote in two consecutive primaries in which they are entered lose their eligibility until such a time as they receive at least 20 percent of the vote in a primary. Twice during the 1984 campaign Jesse Jackson lost his eligibility for matching funds, only to regain it later.

Losing eligibility not only stops the flow of government funds, it also casts doubts on the viability of a candidacy in the eyes of the media, politicians, and potential contributors. For these reasons candidates tend to avoid nonessential contests in which they are not likely to receive the minimum 10 percent of the vote.

There is a catch to accepting matching funds, as noted earlier in this chapter. Candidates are then subject to state and national expenditure limits. This tends to be a problem in the early, small caucus or primary states, such as Iowa and New Hampshire, particularly for lesser-known candidates, who need strong showings to establish their credibility. These spending restrictions led one Republican aspirant, John Connally, to reject matching funds in 1980 so as to be freed of these expenditure limits. Connally's strategy was not successful. Others have chosen to accept the government subsidies despite the expenditure limits because they need the money, because they do not wish their rejection of public funds to become a campaign issue, because they would still be subject to the individual and group contribution limits, and because there are other devices they can use to skirt the expenditure limits in the early states.

On balance, the matching-fund provision has provided greater opportunities for aspirants to seek their party's nomination. However, the law does not completely eliminate the financial advantage that nationally recognized candidates have, especially at the beginning of the process. What it does do, if anything, is to extend fundraising back into the years *before* the election. The need to qualify for funds, the $250 maximum for matching, and the $1,000 contribution limit for individuals require candidates for their party's nomination to build donor lists and solicit personal contributions for several years before the nomination. Conversely, these factors discourage late entrants, even nationally recognized leaders.

Parties and Candidates

The law has and will continue to affect the major parties. Designed to bolster candidates of the two major parties, it discourages minor parties by requiring their candidates to obtain at least 5 percent of the presidential vote to be eligible for public funds. Independent candidate John Anderson qualified in 1980, but only after the election was over. He eventually received $4.2 million, enough to pay off his debts—but not enough to have mounted a vigorous campaign.

Since Anderson was not assured of federal funds, he had difficulty borrowing money. Unable to secure large bank loans, he had to depend on private contributions and loans. He raised $12.1 million, mainly through mass mailings. Ironically, having qualified in 1980, Anderson was automatically eligible for funds in 1984 had he chosen to run. Thus, the law, despite its intent, provides an incentive for the continuation of a third-party candidacy once that candidacy has been successfully launched in the previous election.

The impact of the law on the major parties has also produced unintended consequences. By providing funds directly to individuals who seek the Republican and Democratic nominations, the law facilitates candidacies and candidate organizations within the national parties, thereby factionalizing them. The organization of the successful candidate is not dismantled after the nomination; it is expanded, and often competes with the regular party organizations in the states. On the other hand, the 1979 amendments have encouraged state and local parties to play a large role in the general election.

Finally, the law affects candidates. Once the nomination is won, the incumbent is usually advantaged. Equalizing spending at the national level hurts a challenger more. Presidents make the news simply by being President; challengers have to buy time on television to present themselves as serious presidential candidates.

In 1976 the law also seemed to work to the benefit of the Democratic candidate because it eliminated the fund-raising advantage that Republican nominees had enjoyed over the years. However, in 1980 and again in 1984 Republicans benefited more from independent expenditures and state and local party efforts, an advantage that should continue for some time to come.

SUMMARY

Campaign finance became an important aspect of presidential elections by the end of the nineteenth and the beginning of the twentieth centuries. In recent years, however, it has become even more important as costs have escalated. Expanded use of communications, particularly television, to reach the voters has been primarily responsible for the increase, although other methods of contacting voters and assessing their opinions have also added to the sharp rise in expenditures.

With few exceptions, candidates of both major parties turned to the large contributors, the so-called fat cats, for financial support in the early and mid-twentieth century. Their dependence on a relatively small number of large donors, combined with spiraling costs, created serious problems for a democratic selection process. The 1972 presidential election, with its high expenditures, dirty tricks, and illegal campaign contributions, vividly illustrated some of these problems and generated support from Congress and the public for rectifying them.

In the 1970s Congress enacted and amended the Federal Election Campaign Act. Its purpose in doing so was to bring donors into the open and to prevent their exercising undue influence on elected officials. By placing limits on contributions, controlling expenditures, and subsidizing the election, Congress hoped to make the selection process less costly and more equitable. It established the Federal Election Commission to oversee compliance and prosecute offenders.

The legislation has achieved some but not all of its intended goals. It has reduced the importance of large donors and has increased the importance of having a large number of small contributors during the preconvention period. It has also enhanced the significance of political action committees. Used by presidential nominees to underwrite their preprimary costs, these PACs also help candidates by their contributions in the primaries and by their organizing and educational efforts in both the nomination process and the general election.

The law has not reduced expenditures in the primaries, although it has continued to control candidates' expenditures in the general election. The matching-fund provision has actually encouraged major-party candidacies, thereby increasing spending as well as factionalism within the parties. The limit on contributions, the expenditure ceilings, and the federal subsidies have brought pressure for equity in the prenomination period but have not achieved it.

For the general election, the campaign finance legislation has worked to equalize spending between the major party candidates. The political result of increasing equality has been to deny the Republicans some of their traditional financial advantage, but not to deny the incumbents some of theirs. As a result of the 1979 amendments, however, Republican party organizations at the state and local levels have regained their advantage by outraising and outspending their Democratic counterparts.

Although the law has helped major party candidates, it has not necessarily contributed to the health and vitality of the major parties at the national level. It is the candidates, not the parties, who receive the bulk of the funds. Moreover, the prohibition against private contributions in the general election has made independent expenditures more important, further weakening the national parties' influence on the campaigns of their nominees. Limited funding has forced the candidates themselves to be more prudent, to try to exercise more central control over their finances, and to reach the largest possible audience in the most cost-effective way—usually through television.

Finally, the law has contributed to our knowledge about the conduct of campaigns. Gifts and expenditures of candidates are now part of the public record. This information is used by candidates to develop strategy, by the media to cover the election, and by academicians and other analysts to explain the outcome. The publicizing of actions that violate the letter and spirit of the law has served to discourage such actions. In general, compliance has not been a major problem, although much ingenuity has been spent circumventing restrictions on expenditures and contributions and on making "soft" money available for the presidential campaign.

NOTES

1. Herbert E. Alexander, "Spending on Presidential Campaigns," in Robert E. Hunter (ed.), *Electing the President: A Program for Reform* (Washington, D.C.: The Center for Strategic and International Studies, Georgetown University, 1986), p. 57.

2. Herbert E. Alexander, "Making Sense About Dollars in the 1980 Presidential Campaigns," in Michael J. Malbin (ed.), *Money and Politics in the United States* (Washington, D.C.: American Enterprise Institute/Chatham House, 1984), p. 24.

3. Edward W. Chester, *Radio, Television and American Politics* (New York: Sheed & Ward, 1969), p. 21.

4. Alexander, *Financing Politics* (Washington, D.C.: Congressional Quarterly, 1984), pp. 11–12.

5. Alexander, "Spending on Presidential Campaigns," p. 61.

6. Ibid., p. 198.

7. Michael J. Robinson, "The Power of the Primary Purse: Money in 1984," *Public Opinion,* 7 (Aug./Sept. 1984), 49–51.

8. T. Wayne Parent, Calvin C. Jillson, and Ronald E. Weber, "Voting Outcomes in the 1984 Democratic Party Primaries and Caucuses," *American Political Science Review,* 81 (1987), 80.

9. This brief discussion of the sources of political contributions is based primarily on Alexander's description in *Financing Politics,* pp. 55–59.

10. Henry C. Frick, as quoted in Jasper B. Shannon, *Money and Politics* (New York: Random House, 1959), p. 35.

11. In 1972 the chief fund-raiser for the Nixon campaign, Maurice Stans, and Richard Nixon's private attorney, Herbert Kalmbach, collected contributions, some of them illegal, on behalf of the President. They exerted strong pressure on corporate executives, despite the prohibition on corporate giving. Secret contributions totaling millions of dollars were received, and three special secret funds were established to give the White House and the Committee to Reelect the President (CREEP) maximum discretion in campaign expenditures. It was from these funds that the dirty tricks of the 1972 campaign and the Watergate burglary were financed.

12. The amendment also attempted to limit the amount that nonparty groups could spend on behalf of publicly funded candidates. The Supreme Court subsequently overturned this provision. In a decision that was consistent with the majority opinion in *Buckley v. Valeo,* the Court said that a congressional limit on spending violates rights of free speech and association protected by the First Amendment to the Constitution. *FEC v. National Conservative Political Action Committee* (105 S.Ct. 1459, 1985).

13. Maxwell Glen, "Front-Loading the Race," *National Journal* 18 (1984), 2884.

14. Alexander, "Spending on Presidential Campaigns," p. 57.

15. The expenditures of the exploratory committees and official campaign commit-tees are subject to the $1,000 contribution ceiling, the state and national expenditure limits, and the reporting requirements. Multicandidate PACs have higher contribution ceilings, no expenditure limits except those for contributions to candidate organizations, and less stringent reporting requirements.

16. These figures, however, may exaggerate the importance of certain groups and underestimate that of others. For independent PACs, such as ideological ones, money spent on fund-raising and organizational activities is included in the total campaign expenses that are reported to the FEC. The amount spent on these activities can be considerable—as high as 80 percent of the total budget. In contrast, corporate and labor PACs often charge their administrative costs to other accounts. They spend a higher proportion of their money directly on the campaign. This suggests that the impact of the ideological groups may not be nearly so great as the size of their reported expenditures suggests. Ronald Brownstein, "On Paper Conservative PACs Were Tigers—Look Again," *National Journal,* 17 (1985), 1504–1509.

17. Ronnie Dugger, "The Mating Game for '88," *New York Times Magazine*, part 2 (Dec. 7, 1986), 52–60.

18. Corporations may ask for voluntary contributions from their stockholders and administrative and executive personnel without limit, but may solicit employees only twice a year and only by mail. For labor unions, the provision is reversed. Members may be solicited without limit, but stockholders and executive personnel may be requested to donate only twice a year. The request must be made by mail and sent to a home address. The purpose of these provisions is to prevent coercion in obtaining contributions.

19. These expenditures were challenged on the grounds that they should be subject to the state and national limits applicable to candidates who plan to accept federal funds. The FEC rejected this argument, however, and ruled in 1986 that precinct delegate recruitment did not qualify as campaign activity within the purview of the law.

20. To avoid any appearance of impropriety, Kemp resigned as chairman of his foundation, Fund for an American Renaissance, in June 1986.

21. The amount and distribution of funds required for eligibility has not increased with inflation. It remains $5,000 in twenty states in contributions of $250 or less—a total of $100,000.

Selected Readings

Adamany, David. "Money, Politics and Democracy: A Review Essay," *American Political Science Review*, 71 (1977), 289–304.

Alexander, Herbert E. *Financing Politics*. Washington, D.C.: Congressional Quarterly, 1984.

Drew, Elizabeth. *Politics and Money*. New York: Collier Books, 1983.

Goldstein, Joel. "The Influence of Money on the Prenomination Stage of the Presidential Selection Process: The Case of the 1976 Election," *Presidential Studies Quarterly*, 8 (1978), 164–179.

Heard, Alexander. *The Costs of Democracy*. Chapel Hill: University of North Carolina Press, 1960.

Malbin, Michael J., ed. *Money and Politics in the United States*. Washington, D.C.: American Enterprise Institute, 1984.

———. *Parties, Interest Groups, and Campaign Finance Laws*. Washington, D.C.: American Enterprise Institute, 1980.

Robinson, Michael J. "The Power of the Primary Purse: Money in 1984," *Public Opinion*, 7 (Aug./Sept. 1984), 49–51.

Sabato, Larry J. *PAC Power*. New York: W. W. Norton, 1985.

Chapter 3

THE POLITICAL ENVIRONMENT

Introduction

The nature of the electorate influences the content, images, and strategies of the campaign and affects the outcome of the election—an obvious conclusion, to be sure, but one that is not always appreciated. Campaigns are not conducted in ignorance of the voters. Rather, they are calculated to appeal to the needs and desires, attitudes and opinions, associations and interactions of the electorate.

Voters do not come to the election with completely open minds. They come with preexisting views. They do not see and hear the campaign in isolation. They observe it and absorb it as part of their daily lives. In other words, their attitudes and associations affect their perceptions and influence their behavior. This is why it is important for students of presidential elections to examine the formation of political attitudes and the patterns of social interaction.

Who votes and who does not? Why do people vote for certain candidates and not others? Do campaign appeals affect voting behavior? Are the responses of the electorate predictable? Political scientists have been interested in these questions for some time. Politicians have been interested for even longer.

A great deal of social science research and political savvy have gone into finding the answers. Spurred by the development of sophisticated survey techniques and methods of data analysis, political scientists, sociologists, and social psychologists have uncovered a wealth of information on how the public reacts and the electorate behaves during a campaign. They have examined correlations between demographic characteristics and voter turnout. They have explored psychological motivations, social influences, and political pressures that contribute to voting behavior. This chapter will examine some of their findings.

It is organized into three sections. The first discusses who votes. Describing the expansion of suffrage in the nineteenth and twentieth centuries, the section then turns to recent trends. Turnout is influenced by partisan, economic, and social factors. It is also affected by laws that govern elections and by circumstances of the vote itself, such as the closeness of the contest, interest in the campaign, and even the weather on election day. The impact of these variables on the decision whether or not to cast a ballot is the principal focus of this section.

The second and third parts of the chapter study influences on the vote. First, the *partisan* basis of politics is examined. How do political attitudes affect the ways people evaluate the campaign and shape their actual voting decision? A psychological model of voting behavior is presented and then used to explain contemporary voting patterns.

Next, the *social* basis of politics is analyzed. Dividing the electorate into distinct and overlapping socioeconomic, ethnic, and religious groupings, this section deals with the relationship of these groupings to voting behavior. It places primary emphasis on the formation of party coalitions during the 1930s and their evolution into the 1980s.

The final part of this section looks to the future. Are the two major parties going through a period of realignment or still in a period of dealignment? Are voters becoming more independent in their allegiances and their voting decisions? Recent research helps us answer these questions.

TURNOUT

Who votes? In one sense, this is a simple question to resolve. Official election returns indicate the number of voters and the states, even the precincts, in which the votes were cast. By easy calculation, the percentage of those eligible who actually voted can be determined. In 1980, 52.6 percent of the adult population voted in the presidential election; in 1984, 53.3 percent voted. (See Table 3–1.)

For campaign strategists and political analysts, however, more information is needed. In planning a campaign, it is necessary to design and target appeals to attract specific groups of voters. In assessing the results, it is also essential to understand how particular segments of the electorate responded. By evaluating turnout on the basis of demographic characteristics and partisan attitudes, strategists and analysts alike obtain the information they need to make sophisticated judgments.

Voting turnout has varied widely over the years. In the first national election, in 1788, only about 4 percent of the adult population participated. The presidential vote was even smaller, since most electors were designated by the state legislatures and not chosen directly by the people. The percentage of the population voting rose significantly between 1824 and 1840, leveled off throughout the remainder of the nineteenth century, and then increased dramatically in the twentieth century with the extension of suffrage to women in 1920 and the removal of many racial barriers in the 1960s.

Table 3-1 indicates the number and percentage of adults voting in selected years between 1824 and 1952 and in every presidential election thereafter.

Table 3-1   PARTICIPATION IN PRESIDENTIAL ELECTIONS

Year	Total Adult Population*	Total Presidential Vote	Percentage of Adult Population Voting
1824	3,964,000	363,017	9%
1840	7,381,000	2,412,698	33
1860	14,676,000	4,692,710	32
1880	25,012,000	9,219,467	37
1900	40,753,000	13,974,188	35
1920	60,581,000	26,768,613	44
1932	75,768,000	39,732,000	52.4
1940	84,728,000	49,900,000	58.9
1952	99,929,000	61,551,000	61.6
1960	109,674,000	68,838,000	62.8
1964	114,085,000	70,645,000	61.9
1968	120,285,000	73,212,000	60.9
1972	140,777,000	77,719,000	55.2
1976	152,308,000	81,556,000	53.5
1980	164,473,000	86,515,000	52.6
1984	173,936,000	92,653,000	53.3

Source: Population figures for 1824 to 1920 are based on estimates and early census figures that appear in Neal R. Peirce, *The People's President* (New York: Simon & Schuster, 1968), p. 206. Population figures from 1932 to the present are from the U.S. Department of Commerce, Bureau of the Census, *Statistical Abstract of the United States* (Washington, D.C., 1986), p. 255.

*Restrictions based on sex, age, race, religion, and property ownership prevented a significant portion of the adult population from voting in the nineteenth and early twentieth centuries. Of those who were eligible, however, the percentage casting ballots was often quite high, particularly during the last half of the nineteenth century.

The increasing numbers reflect the expansion of suffrage. Although the proportion of the population who are eligible voters has increased, the turnout of those eligible to vote has actually declined. It dropped in the nation as a whole from 1960 to 1980 and then rose very slightly in 1984, despite the large-scale registration drives undertaken by the major parties. Only in the South, which had a long history of people being excluded from voting on the basis of race, has a larger proportion of adult citizens cast more ballots since 1960. Why has the percentage of voters declined in the last two decades? Some of the reasons have to do with the expansion of suffrage itself, and some with the procedures governing registration and voting.

The Expansion of Suffrage

The Constitution empowers the state legislatures to determine the time, place, and manner of holding elections for national office. While it also gives Congress the authority to alter such regulations, Congress did not do so until the Civil War. Thus, the states were free to restrict suffrage, and most did.[1] In some, property ownership was a requirement for exercising the franchise; in others, a particular religious belief was necessary. In most, it was essential to be white, male, and over twenty-one.

By the 1830s, most states had eliminated property and religious restrictions. The Fifteenth Amendment, ratified in 1870, removed race and color as qualifications for voting. In theory, this enabled all black males to vote. In practice, it enfranchised those in the North and border states, but not those in the South. A series of institutional devices such as the poll tax, literacy tests, and restrictive primaries in which only Caucasians could participate (known as white primaries), combined effectively with social pressure to prevent blacks from voting in the South for another hundred years.

Following the Civil War, both the number of eligible voters and the percentage of actual voters increased. One political scientist estimated the rate of turnout in the 1880s to be as high as 80 percent of those eligible.[2] Close competition between the parties contributed to this higher level of participation, as did the absence of registration procedures and the use of secret ballots in some states.

In the twentieth century, the passage of the Nineteenth, Twenty-fourth, and Twenty-sixth Amendments continued to expand the voting-age population. In 1920, women received the right to vote; in 1964, the collection of a poll tax was prohibited in national elections; in 1971, suffrage was extended to all citizens eighteen years of age and older. Previously, each state had established its own minimum age.

Moreover, the Supreme Court and Congress began to eliminate the legal and institutional barriers to voting. In 1944, the Court outlawed the white primary.[3] In the mid-1960s, Congress, by its passage of the Civil Rights Act (1964) and the Voting Rights Act (1965), banned literacy tests in federal elections for all citizens who had at least a sixth-grade education in an American school. Where less than 50 percent of the population was registered to vote, federal officials were sent to help facilitate registration. No longer was long and costly litigation necessary to ensure the right to vote. Amendments to the Voting Rights Act have also reduced the residence requirement for presidential elections to a maximum of thirty days.

The expansion of suffrage has produced more voters. It has enlarged the electorate but it has also meant that a smaller percentage of that electorate actually votes. Newly enfranchised voters tend to cast ballots less regularly than those who have previously enjoyed the right to vote.

Registration procedures still act as an impediment to voting. These procedures vary from state to state. The period during which people may register, the places where they have to go to do so, even the hours when registration may occur, are controlled by state law. Naturally, the harder the states make it to register, the smaller the vote they can expect. This is a particular problem for a mobile society such as that of the United States. With one-third of the population moving on an average of every two years, the need to reregister in order to vote effectively decreases the size of the vote. Two political scientists, Raymond E. Wolfinger and Steven J. Rosenstone, estimated that turnout could be increased by as much as 9 percent by making modest adjustments in these laws that would ease registration procedures.[4]

Concern has been voiced about the relatively low turnout of voters in the United States as compared with other democratic countries. Recent voting statistics demonstrate that this concern is justified. If the percentage of *eligible* voters in the United States who actually vote is compared to that of twenty-one other democratic countries located primarily in Western Europe, the United States ranks twentieth; if, however, the percentage of *registered* voters who actually vote is the basis for comparison, the United States fares better, ranking eleventh out of twenty-four.[5] And unlike many other countries, the United States does not impose penalties on those who fail to register and vote, nor does it have a national system for automatic registration.

In other words, the comparison is not as bad as it seems. But there is a sizable difference between the proportion of registered voters who actually cast ballots (86.8 percent in 1980) and the proportion of all eligible voters (including those who are not registered) who do so (52.6 percent in 1980). This suggests that registration procedures remain a major obstacle to higher voter turnout in the United States. There are other factors, however, that also contribute.

Psychological and Social Influences on Turnout

In addition to laws and procedures, other influences on whether or not people vote are their interest in the election, concern over the outcome, feelings of civic responsibility, and sense of political efficacy (their belief that their vote really matters).[6] Naturally, people who feel more strongly about the election are more likely to get involved. Those with more intense partisan feelings are more likely to have this interest, more likely to participate in the campaign, and more likely to vote on election day. Voting, in fact, becomes a habit. The more people have done it in the past, the more likely they will do it in the future.

Wolfinger and Rosenstone, who examined turnout in the 1972 presidential election, found that it increases with age until a person reaches the mid-forties, then remains constant until about age seventy, when it begins to decline.[7] Table 3-2 provides empirical support for the proposition that turnout increases with age, at least up to a point.

Other characteristics also related to turnout are education, income, and occupational status. As people become more educated, as they move up the socioeconomic ladder, as their jobs gain in status, they are more likely to vote. Education is the most important of these variables. It has a larger impact than any other single social characteristic.[8] As Table 3-2 demonstrates, the higher the level of education, the greater the percentage voting.

The reason education is so important is that it provides the skills for processing and evaluating information, for perceiving differences between the parties, candidates, and issues, and for relating these differences to personal values and behavior. Education also affects personal success. It increases a person's stake in the system, interest in the election, and concern over the outcome. Since the lesson that voting is a civic responsibility is usually learned in the classroom, schooling may also contribute to a more highly developed sense of responsibility about voting. Finally,

Table 3–2   VOTING TURNOUT BY POPULATION CHARACTERISTICS,
            1968–1984 (IN PERCENTAGES)

	1968	1972	1976	1980	1984
Male	69.8	64.1	59.6	59.1	59.0
Female	66.0	62.0	58.8	59.4	60.8
Age					
18–20		48.3	38.0	35.7	36.7
21–24	51.0	50.7	45.6	43.1	43.5
25–34	62.5	59.7	55.4	54.6	54.5
35–44	70.8	66.3	63.3	64.4	63.5
45–64	74.9	70.8	68.7	69.3	69.8
65 and over	65.8	63.5	62.2	65.1	67.7
Education					
8 years or less	54.5	47.4	44.1	42.6	42.9
9–11	61.3	52.0	47.2	45.6	44.4
12	72.5	65.4	59.4	58.9	58.7
More than 12	81.2	78.8	73.5	73.2	*
Race					
White	69.1	64.5	60.9	60.9	61.4
Black	57.6	52.1	48.7	50.5	55.8
Hispanic origin	NA	37.4	31.8	29.9	32.6

Source: U.S. Department of Commerce, Bureau of the Census, *Statistical Abstract of the United States*
(Washington, D.C., 1986), p. 256.
    *Of those who completed three years or less of college, 67.5 percent said they voted; this percentage
rises to 79.1 for those who completed four years.

education provides the knowledge and confidence to overcome voting
hurdles—to register on time, to file absentee ballots properly, and to mark
the ballot or use the voting machine correctly on election day.[9]

Given the relationship of education to turnout, it may seem surprising that the rate of turnout should decline in the nation as a whole at a
time when the general level of education is rising and the country is
becoming more affluent.[10] Yet there is an explanation for this. The
reasons for the decline seem to be related to the increasing number of
younger and older voters and also to the growth of political cynicism and
apathy, particularly among those in the lower socioeconomic groups.

Young people tend to be more mobile than their parents. Moreover,
they have not developed the habit of voting or even of identifying with
a party. As a consequence, they vote with less regularity than those who
are older.

Similarly, there has been an increase in the number of elderly citizens. They too tend to vote less, primarily for reasons of health. Elderly
women, who were socialized at a time when politics was considered a male
responsibility, vote less often than their male counterparts. That women

outlive men by an average of eight years also contributes to the decreasing proportion of the electorate voting.

The so-called youthing and aging of the electorate has resulted in a lower percentage of voter turnout. It does not, however, explain most of the decline, since all age groups have lower turnout.

One thesis is that the public simply became disillusioned with the electoral and governing processes, primarily from the late 1960s through the 1970s. Political scientist Richard Brody found "a substantial decline in the belief that participation is politically meaningful, that government is responsive, and that the outcome of the election is a matter of concern to the individual voter." This finding led Brody to the conclusion that "abstention flows from the belief—held by an increasingly large segment of the electorate—that voting simply isn't worth the effort."[11]

Although negative feelings toward parties, their leaders, and the government persist, recent surveys suggest a softening of these feelings. The electorate of the mid-1980s seems to have more faith in government responsiveness and a greater sense of political trust than did voters a decade ago.[12] These more positive feelings, however, did not result in a significantly greater turnout in 1984.

There is also a class bias in voting, which appears to be related to negative feelings people have on their own ability to affect events and to the trust they place in political leaders. Between the years 1964 and 1976 Thomas E. Cavanagh found the decline in turnout to be greater among blacks than whites, and greater among those in the lowest socioeconomic groups.[13]

Turnout and Partisanship

The decrease in turnout has hurt the Democrats more than the Republicans, since the Democratic party draws more of its electoral support from those in the lower socioeconomic groups, those with less formal education, and those with few professional opportunities. As a consequence, the Democrats have traditionally sought to bring the "have-nots" into the political process, and especially, to the voting booths. They have generally employed a "sweep" strategy to do so, trying to register as many people as possible. This strategy is based on the assumption that the greater the turnout, the more Democratic candidates will benefit.

In 1984, with polls showing a substantial Reagan advantage among registered voters, the Democrats launched their most ambitious registration drive to date. They hoped to capitalize on the enthusiasm generated among minorities by Jesse Jackson's campaign for the party's nomination. Unable to finance the effort from its treasury, the party relied heavily on independent, nonpartisan organizations to enlist new voters.[14]

The Republicans responded with a registration campaign of their own, one that was more expensive, more sophisticated, and more centralized than the Democrats'. Believing only a minority of nonvoters could be expected to join the party, the Republicans chose a "targeting" approach. They utilized a variety of lists and a "merge and purge" technique, and depended on elaborate communications technology to pinpoint unregistered Republicans and Reagan supporters among nonvoters. The party was careful not to register persons sympathetic to the Democrats.[15] As a result of this stratagem, record numbers of people were registered.

By most estimates, the Republicans registered more new voters than the Democrats. Why was the Republican effort more successful than that of the Democrats in 1984? The GOP's stronger organization and larger financial base were obviously factors. So were the resurgent economy, the popularity of the incumbent, and the optimism he generated. But the Republicans also appealed to those who were more likely to vote, those in the higher socioeconomic groups. In other words, the Republicans registered more people who probably would have registered anyway.

The Republican experience in 1984 indicates that there may be a point of diminishing returns in registration drives, beyond which party efforts simply substitute for individual decisions to register and vote. This point tends to be lower for the Republicans than for the Democrats.[16]

The new Republican registrants voted at a higher rate than did the new Democratic registrants. But despite the addition of twelve million people to the registration rolls in 1984, only four million more went to the polls that year than in the previous election. Turnout remained ten percentage points below its 1960 level.

THE PARTISAN BASIS OF POLITICS

In addition to who votes, the partisan basis of politics affects why people vote as they do. Considerable research has been conducted on the attitudes and behavior of the American voter. Much of it has been done under the direction of the Center for Political Studies at the University of Michigan. Beginning in 1952, the Center began conducting nationwide surveys during presidential elections.[17] The object of these surveys was to identify the major influences on voting behavior.

A random sample of the electorate was interviewed before and after

THE POLITICAL ENVIRONMENT

the election. Respondents were asked a series of questions designed to reveal their attitudes toward the parties, candidates, and issues. On the basis of the answers, researchers constructed a model to explain voting behavior and presented it in a book entitled *The American Voter*.[18] Published in 1960, this very important work contains both theoretical formulations and empirical findings. Both the model and the findings were generally accepted by politicians and political scientists throughout the 1960s.

A Model of the American Voter

The model constructed by the Michigan researchers assumes that individuals are influenced by their partisan attitudes and social relationships, in addition to the political environment in which an election occurs. In fact, it is these attitudes and those relationships that condition the impact of that environment on individual voting behavior.

According to the theory, people develop attitudes early in life, largely as a consequence of interacting with their families, particularly their parents. These attitudes, in turn, tend to be reinforced by neighborhood, school, and religious associations. The reasons they tend to be reinforced lie in the psychological and social patterns of behavior. Psychologically, it is more pleasing to have beliefs and attitudes supported than challenged. Socially, it is more comfortable to associate with "nice," like-minded people, those with similar cultural, educational, and religious experiences, than with others. This is why the environment for most people tends to be supportive much of the time.[19]

Attitudes mature and harden over the years. Older people become less amenable to change and more set in their ways. Their behavior is more predictable.[20]

Political attitudes are no exception to this general pattern of attitude formation and maintenance. They too are developed early in life; they too are reinforced by association; they too grow in intensity over time; they too become more predictable with age.

Of all the factors that contribute to the development of a political attitude, an identification with a political party is one of the most important. It affects how people see the campaign and how they vote. Party identification operates as a conceptual mechanism. Identifiers tend to evaluate the campaign within a partisan framework. Political attitudes provide cues for interpreting the issues, for judging the candidates, and for deciding whether and how to vote. The stronger these attitudes, the more compelling the cues; conversely, the weaker the attitudes, the less likely they will affect perceptions during the campaign and influence voting on election day.[21]

The amount of information known about the candidates also affects the influence of partisanship. In general, the less known, the more likely that people will follow their partisan inclinations when voting. Since presidential campaigns normally convey more information than other elections, the influence of party is apt to be weaker in these higher-visibility contests.

When identification with party is weak or nonexistent, other factors, such as the personalities of the candidates and their issue positions, will be correspondingly more important. In contrast to party identification, which is a long-term stabilizing factor, candidate and issue orientations are short-term, more variable influences that differ from election to election. Of the two, the image of the candidate has been more significant.

Candidate images turn on personality and policy dimensions. People tend to form general impressions about candidates on the basis of what is known about their leadership capabilities, decision-making capacity, and personal traits. For an incumbent President seeking reelection, accomplishments in office provide much of the criteria for evaluation. Other characteristics, such as trustworthiness, integrity, and candor, are also important. For the challenger, it is the potential for office as demonstrated by experience, knowledge, confidence, and assertiveness, plus a host of personal qualities.[22]

The candidate's position on the issues, however, seems less critical than does his or her partisanship and performance in similar positions. Candidates themselves often contribute to this effect by fudging their stands during the general election campaign so as to broaden their appeal and not alienate potential supporters. The effort to stay in the mainstream tends to place the major party candidates close to one another on a variety of issues.

The low level of information and awareness that much of the electorate possesses also tends to downgrade the impact of issues on voting behavior. To be important, issues must stand out from campaign rhetoric. They must attract attention; they must hit home. Without personal impact, they are unlikely to be primary motivating factors in voting. To the extent that issue positions are not discernible, the evaluation of the candidate's performance or potential becomes a stronger influence on the vote.

Ironically, that portion of the electorate which can be more easily persuaded, weak partisans and independents, tends to have the least information.[23] Conversely, the most committed tend to be the most informed. They use their information to support their partisanship.

The relationship between degree of partisanship and amount of information has significant implications for a democratic society. The traditional view of a democracy holds that information and awareness are necessary in order to make an intelligent judgment on election day. However, the finding that those who have the most information are also the most committed, and that those who lack this commitment also lack the incentive to acquire information, has upset some of the assumptions about the motivation for acquiring information and the importance of that information in rendering a voting decision in a democratic society.

Considerable debate has turned on the question, how informed and rational is the electorate when voting? One well-known political scientist, the late V.O. Key, even wrote a book dedicated to "the perverse and unorthodox argument . . . that voters are not fools."[24] Key studied the behavior of three groups of voters between 1936 and 1960: switchers, stand-patters, and new voters. He found those who switched their votes to be interested in and influenced by their own evaluation of policy, personality, and performance. In this sense, Key believed that they exercised intelligent judgment when voting.[25]

Others have pointed to an increasing issue awareness in recent elections as evidence that voters are making more informed and rational judgments based on their ideological preferences and policy views.[26]

If these findings are correct, they may suggest that the initial model propounded by *The American Voter* has become time-bound. But this is far from clear. Just how informed voters are and how important issues and ideology have become remain matters of considerable controversy in political science today.

To summarize, *The American Voter* suggests that partisans vote habitually, not necessarily rationally or irrationally. Instead of coming to the election with open minds, most of them come with preexisting partisan attitudes that affect their perceptions and influence their judgment. The campaign provides the stimuli that act on these attitudes and perceptions to trigger appropriate responses. For those who think of themselves as partisan, their party identification provides a ready mechanism for evaluating the campaign and for acting in a prescribed manner on election day. Moreover, the identification of much of the electorate with political parties acts to stabilize the system. It provides a hedge against a volatile electoral response.

To the extent that voters are informed about the personal qualifications of candidates' and their positions on issues, they have a basis for deviating from partisan voting patterns if they wish. Knowledge about the presidential candidates tends to be greater than that about other candidates seeking office.

Partisan Voting Patterns

The Michigan model of the American voter was based on research conducted in the 1950s. In each subsequent national election, nationwide surveys have been conducted in order to understand shifts in voting behavior. While the basic psychological explanation of voting behavior has not been changed, empirical findings point to shifts in the identification and intensity of partisan beliefs.

Two major trends stand out. First, there has been a reduction in the number of people who identify with a party, and conversely, an increase in the number of self-proclaimed independents. Second, there has been a decline in the strength of partisan identities. Each of these changes has important long- and short-term implications for American electoral politics.

Table 3–3 lists the percentage of party identifiers and independents. The table indicates that there was a 9 percent decline in people who identify with a political party, and a 13 percent increase in the number of self-proclaimed independents, between 1952 and 1984. Most of the shift occurred after 1964. The table also suggests that the decline was principally in the strong partisan category. The increase in strong party identifiers, particularly among younger voters, beginning in the 1980s, however, may augur a reversal of this trend.

In general, partisanship has weakened among most population groups. Many strong partisans have become weak partisans, and many weak partisans now consider themselves independent. How independently they behave on election day is another matter. Truly independent voting has increased far less rapidly than independent identification.[27] In other words, a sizable portion of self-proclaimed independents continues to vote for candidates of the same party.

According to the theory, the decline in partisanship and the growth of independents should have produced a more variable and manipulatable electorate. With weaker partisan allegiances and more independent identifiers, the candidates and issues should, in themselves, be more important influences on the vote. Both these expectations have materialized, al-

Table 3–3 PARTY IDENTIFICATION, 1952–1984* (IN PERCENTAGES)†

Party Identification	1952	1954	1956	1958	1960	1962	1964	1966	1968	1970	1972	1974	1976	1978	1980	1982	1984
Strong Democrat	22	22	21	23	21	23	26	18	20	20	15	17	15	15	16	20	17
Weak Democrat	25	25	23	24	25	23	25	27	25	23	25	21	25	24	23	24	20
Independent Democrat	10	9	7	7	8	8	9	9	10	10	11	13	12	14	11	11	11
Independent Independent	5	7	9	8	8	8	8	12	11	13	13	15	14	14	12	11	11
Independent Republican	7	6	8	4	7	6	6	7	9	8	11	9	10	10	12	8	13
Weak Republican	14	14	14	16	13	16	13	15	14	15	13	14	14	13	14	14	15
Strong Republican	13	13	15	13	14	12	11	10	10	10	10	8	9	8	10	10	13
Apoliticals: Don't know	4	4	3	5	4	4	2	2	1	1	2	3	1	2	2	2	2

Source: Center for Political Studies, University of Michigan.
*The survey question was, "Generally speaking, do you usually think of yourself as a Republican, a Democrat, an Independent, or what? (If Republican or Democrat), Would you call yourself a strong (R) (D) or a not very strong (R) (D)? (If Independent), Do you think of yourself as closer to the Republican or Democratic party?"
†Percentages may not equal 100 due to rounding.

though they seem more related to the weakening intensity of partisan feelings than to the increasing number of self-identified independents.

Partisan Deviations

There has been a dramatic rise in split-ticket voting. According to Arthur H. Miller and Martin P. Wattenberg, about three times as many people divide their vote today as did in the 1950s.[28] The defections come primarily from weak partisans. Figure 3–1 presents the rates of defection among party identifiers from 1952 to 1984.

Defections from partisan voting patterns have helped the Republicans more than the Democrats. Without votes from Democratic defectors, the GOP could not have won six presidential elections since 1952.

Figure 3–1   DEFECTION RATES AMONG PARTY IDENTIFIERS, 1952–1984

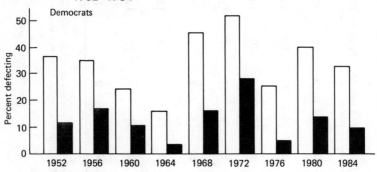

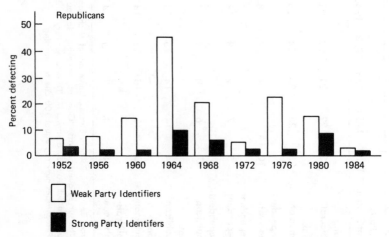

Source: Survey Research Center/Center for Political Studies University of Michigan

The help, however, has been short-term. The Republicans have won few permanent converts, although the increase in Republican partisanship in 1984 suggests that this too may be changing.

With partisanship weaker than in the past, alternative cues to voters have become more important. Television has contributed to the focus on candidate images. Shifts in the electoral coalitions have also produced more issues that divide parties. In the 1930s, when economic concerns were dominant, ideology and partisanship dovetailed; in the late 1960s and early 1970s, when social and foreign-policy issues were dominant, they have not. Political attitudes and partisanship have continued to diverge in the 1980s.

In short, since *The American Voter* was written, partisan ties have become weaker. More people feel less strongly about political parties. This, in turn, has produced more candidate voting and, to a lesser extent, more issue voting, especially at the presidential level. The increasing importance of these short-term factors has contributed to a more manipulatable and volatile electorate, one that decides later in the campaign whether and how to vote.[29]

Voting behavior has become more personalized. Partisanship, although still relevant, has decreased in importance. Why?

The events of the late 1960s and early 1970s, the decline in the age of the electorate, and, most particularly, the impact of television on campaigning have all contributed to the declining influence of party.

The reaction to Vietnam and Watergate, to the credibility gaps and political abuses of the so-called imperial Presidents, undoubtedly generated feelings of mistrust of and hostility to politicians and, particularly among the young during this period, less willingness to identify with a political party. Moreover, the salience of social and cultural issues rendered the traditional partisan alliances, which had been built on economic ties, much less relevant.

A second reason for the drop in partisan identification has been the lowering of the voting age to eighteen and the increased proportion of the population that has reached that age. Over the last thirty years, the percentage of the electorate twenty-four years of age and under has nearly doubled. Since party identification tends to develop and harden over time, the youthing of the electorate has undoubtedly contributed to the decline in partisanship and growth of independents. This trend may now be changing, with the electorate getting older and younger voters becoming more partisan.

A third factor has to do with contemporary modes of campaigning and the declining role of the party in that capacity. In the past, the political party came between the voter and the candidate. Political parties provided the organization, planned the campaign, and made the sales appeal. In doing so, they trumpeted their own cause. Today, much of the information comes directly from the candidate's organization via television. The party no longer mediates as it did in the pretelevision age.

THE SOCIAL BASIS OF POLITICS

There is another way of explaining and evaluating voting behavior. Instead of focusing directly on the political attitudes of the electorate, it is possible to examine people's associations with one another. To the extent that individuals see themselves as members of particular groups, and to the extent that these groups have developed and articulated a position on the parties, candidates, or issues, the group becomes a focal point for helping the individual decide how to evaluate the campaign and what to do on election day. In this way, it affects perceptions of the campaign and influences voting.

While most associations, especially those that are voluntary, work to reinforce preexisting dispositions and attitudes, some do not. Instead, they create cross-pressures that counter the mind-set at least some of the electorate brings to the campaign. For example, the blue-collar laborer who is Catholic might desire a candidate who is liberal on economic issues and conservative on social ones. How does such a voter react to a liberal Democrat such as George McGovern or Walter Mondale? The voter may decide not to cast a presidential ballot, to vote Republican, or eventually to vote Democratic but with little enthusiasm. What cross-pressures do is increase the propensity for not voting or for voting against partisan inclinations.

Over the years certain economic, social, and geographic groupings have been evident in the coalitions that make up the two major parties. These contemporary coalitions, which coalesced during the New Deal period, provided the parties with a core of supporters to whom campaigns were directed and appeals fashioned.

The Democrats have the larger of the two coalitions. It consists primarily of overlapping minorities. Jews, blacks, Hispanics, and, to a lesser extent, Catholics have been particularly supportive of Democratic candidates. The Republican coalition, on the other hand, consists primarily of the dominant group in the country—white Anglo-Saxon Protestants.

The New Deal Realignment[30]

Political coalitions develop during periods of partisan realignment. The last time this occurred was in the 1930s. Largely as a consequence of the Great Depression, the Democrats emerged as the dominant party. Their coalition, held together by a common economic concern that the government play a more active role in dealing with the nation's economic problems, supported Franklin Roosevelt's New Deal program. Those who saw government involvement as a threat to the free-enterprise system opposed much of Roosevelt's domestic legislation. They remained Republican in attitude and voting behavior.

The Democrats became the majority party during this period by expanding their coalition. Since the Civil War, the Democrats had enjoyed southern support. White Protestants living in rural areas dominated the southern electorate. Blacks were largely excluded from it. Only in the election of 1928, when Al Smith, the Catholic governor of New York, ran as the Democratic candidate, was there a sizable southern popular and electoral vote for a Republican candidate at the presidential level. Being a Catholic and an opponent of Prohibition made Smith unacceptable to many white Protestant fundamentalists who lived in the South.

Roosevelt maintained and expanded southern support across the socioeconomic spectrum. Poor as well as wealthy southerners backed his candidacy. In each of his four presidential races, Roosevelt received well over two-thirds of the southern vote.[31]

Another group that voted Democratic before the 1930s was Catholics. Living primarily in the urban centers of the North, Catholics became increasingly important to the Democrats as their numbers grew. Poor economic and social conditions, combined with the immigrant status of many Catholics, made them dependent on big-city bosses, who were able to deliver a sizable Democratic vote. In 1928, for the first time, a majority of the cities in the country voted Democratic. Catholic support for Smith and the Democratic party figured prominently in this vote.

The harsh economic realities of the Depression enabled Roosevelt to expand Democratic support in urban areas still further, particularly to those in the lower socioeconomic strata. Outside the South, Roosevelt's political coalition was differentiated along class lines. It attracted people with less education and income and those with lower-status jobs.[32] Organized labor, in particular, threw its support to Roosevelt. Union members became a core group in the Democratic coalition.

In addition to establishing a broad-based, lower-class party, Roosevelt also lured specific racial and ethnic groups, such as blacks and Jews, from their Republican affiliation. Blacks voted Democratic primarily for economic reasons, while Jews supported Roosevelt's liberal domestic programs and his anti-Nazi foreign policy. Neither of these groups provided the Democratic coalition of the 1930s with a large number of votes, but their loyalty to the party and long-term impact on it has been significant.

In contrast, during the same period, the Republican party shrank. Not only were Republicans unable to attract new groups to their coalition, but they were unable to prevent the defection of some supporters whose economic situation affected their partisan loyalties and influenced their vote. Although the Republicans did retain the backing of a majority of business and professional people, they lost the support of much of the white Protestant working class. Republican strength remained concentrated in the Northeast, particularly in the rural areas.[33]

Evolving Political Coalitions

The coalition that formed during the New Deal held together, for the most part, until the 1960s. During this period, blacks and Jews increased their identification with and support of the Democratic party and its candidates. Catholics tended to remain Democratic, although they fluctuated more in their voting behavior at the presidential level. Non-southern white Protestants continued to support the Republicans.

There were some changes, however, mainly along socioeconomic lines. Domestic prosperity contributed to the growth of a larger middle class. Had such a class identified with the Republicans for economic reasons, the Democratic majority would have been threatened. This did not occur, however. Those who gained in economic and social status did not, as a general rule, discard their partisan loyalties. The Democrats were able to hold on to the allegiance of a majority of this group and improve their position with the professional and managerial classes, which had grown substantially during this period. The Republicans continued to maintain their advantage with those in the upper socioeconomic strata. The economic improvement in the country had the effect of muting the class distinctions that were evident during the 1930s and 1940s.[34]

Finally, changes were occurring in the South. White southerners, particularly those who first voted after 1940, began to desert their party at the presidential level, largely over civil-rights issues. In 1948, Harry Truman won 52 percent of the southern vote, compared with Roosevelt's 69 percent four years earlier. While Stevenson and Kennedy carried the

South by reduced margins, in 1960 the southern white Protestant presidential vote went Republican for the first time.[35] If it had not been for the growth of the black electorate in the South and its overwhelming support for Democratic candidates, the defection of the southern states from the Democratic camp would have been even more dramatic.

Major shifts in the national electorate began to be evident in the mid-1960s, and have continued into the 1980s. (See Table 3–4.)

One of the most significant and enduring of these changes has been the continued defection of southern white Protestants to the Republicans at the presidential level. This shift has occurred at other levels as well. In 1940, Roosevelt won 80 percent of the southern white Protestant vote. Thirty-six years later Jimmy Carter, a southern white Protestant himself, was not able to carry the southern white Protestant vote. In 1984, Walter Mondale gained the support of only one-quarter of this group.

Party identification of southern whites has changed as well. Since 1952 there has been a substantial decline in the partisan loyalty that the Democrats have enjoyed. In that year 85 percent of southern whites considered themselves Democrats; in 1984 that proportion had shrunk to 46 percent. The ratio of Democrats to Republicans went from six-to-one to almost even.[36]

Catholic allegiance to the Democratic party has also weakened. The Democratic vote of this group has declined from its high of 78 percent in 1960 to a low of 39 percent in 1984—the same level of support that Protestants gave Mondale. (See Table 3–4) Further, the proportion of Catholics identifying with the Republican party has doubled in the past decade. From the Democrats' perspective, the best that can be said is that a plurality of Catholics still consider themselves Democrats.

The Democrats have lost support from members of labor union families as well. In seven of the eight presidential elections between 1952 and 1980, this group favored the Democratic candidate by an average of nearly thirty percentage points. In 1980, however, the result was closer—50 percent to 43 percent in favor of Carter. Four years later, Mondale carried this group by only four percentage points, despite the endorsements of most labor leaders. Although there has been some movement in the partisan identification of members of union households toward the Republican party, the Democrats still enjoy a large advantage.

Another potentially important shift has been the movement of new voters, particularly youth, to the Republican party. After being more Democratic than their elders in the five previous presidential contests, younger voters (ages 18–29) supported Reagan in his reelection bid just

Table 3–4   VOTE BY GROUPS IN PRESIDENTIAL ELECTIONS, 1952–1984
(IN PERCENTAGES)

	1952		1956		1960		1964	
	Stevenson	Eisenhower	Stevenson	Eisenhower	Kennedy	Nixon	Johnson	Goldwater
National total sex	44.6	55.4	42.2	57.8	50.1	49.9	61.3	38.7
Male	47	53	45	55	52	48	60	40
Female	42	58	39	61	49	51	62	38
Race								
White	43	57	41	59	49	51	59	41
Nonwhite	79	21	61	39	68	32	94	6
Education								
College	34	66	31	69	39	61	52	48
High school	45	55	42	58	52	48	62	38
Grade school	52	48	50	50	55	45	66	34
Occupation								
Professional and business	36	64	32	68	42	58	54	46
White collar	40	60	37	63	48	52	57	43
Manual	55	45	50	50	60	40	71	29
Age (years)								
Under 30	51	49	43	57	54	46	64	36
30–49	47	53	45	55	54	46	63	37
50 & older	39	61	39	61	46	54	59	41
Religion								
Protestant	37	63	37	63	38	62	55	45
Catholic	56	44	51	49	78	22	76	24
Politics								
Republican	8	92	4	96	5	95	20	80
Democrat	77	23	85	15	84	16	87	13
Independent	35	65	30	70	43	57	56	44
Region								
East	45	55	40	60	53	47	68	32
Midwest	42	58	41	59	48	52	61	39
South	51	49	49	51	51	49	52	48
West	42	58	43	57	49	51	60	40
Members of labor union families	61	39	57	43	65	35	73	27

Source: "Gallup Opinion Index," November, 1984, p. 32. Reprinted with permission.
*Less than 1 percent

as strongly as did those over thirty. Their approval of Reagan's leadership as President, Walter Mondale's lack of appeal to this group, and the increasing economic concerns of younger people all contributed to their Republican vote. If this age group continues to vote and identify with the Republican party, the long-term implications would be significant and could affect the balance between the major parties.

Although the Democrats have lost support from southern whites, Catholics, union families, and the young, they have retained the allegiance of other groups of their New Deal coalition. In recent decades,

Table 3–4   VOTE BY GROUPS IN PRESIDENTIAL ELECTIONS, 1952–1984 (IN PERCENTAGES) (Continued)

1968			1972		1976			1980			1984	
Humphrey	Nixon	Wallace	McGovern	Nixon	Carter	Ford	McCarthy	Carter	Reagan	Anderson	Mondale	Reagan
43.0	43.4	13.6	38	62	50	48	1	41	51	7	41	59
41	43	16	37	63	53	45	1	38	53	7	36	64
45	43	12	38	62	48	51	*	44	49	6	45	55
38	47	15	32	68	46	52	1	36	56	7	34	66
85	12	3	87	13	85	15	*	86	10	2	87	13
37	54	9	37	63	42	55	2	35	53	10	39	61
42	43	15	34	66	54	46	*	43	51	5	43	57
52	33	15	49	51	58	41	1	54	42	3	51	49
34	56	10	31	69	42	56	1	33	55	10	34	66
41	47	12	36	64	50	48	2	40	51	9	47	53
50	35	15	43	57	58	41	1	48	46	5	46	54
47	38	15	48	52	53	45	1	47	41	11	40	60
44	41	15	33	67	48	49	2	38	52	8	40	60
41	47	12	36	64	52	48	*	41	54	4	41	59
35	49	16	30	70	46	53	*	39	54	6	39	61
59	33	8	48	52	57	42	1	46	47	6	39	61
9	86	5	5	95	9	91	*	8	86	5	4	96
74	12	14	67	33	82	18	*	69	26	4	79	21
31	44	25	31	69	38	57	4	29	55	14	33	67
50	43	7	42	58	51	47	1	43	47	9	46	54
44	47	9	40	60	48	50	1	41	51	7	42	58
31	36	33	29	71	54	45	*	44	52	3	37	63
44	49	7	41	59	46	51	1	35	54	9	40	60
56	29	15	46	54	63	36	1	50	43	5	52	48

blacks have increased their loyalty to the Democratic party. Few Republican identifiers are left among black voters, in contrast to the late 1950s, when almost 25 percent considered themselves Republican. In presidential elections since 1964, over 85 percent of the black vote has gone to the Democratic candidate. (See Table 3–4.) In 1984 one out of every four Mondale voters was black.

Jewish voters have evidenced a small decline in their partisan sympathies. They have become more independent in their voting behavior. However, they remain predominantly Democratic. Carter received 72 percent of the Jewish vote in 1976 but only 47 percent in 1980—the first election since World War II when a majority of Jews did not vote Democratic. Dissatisfaction with Carter led Jews to give John Anderson 14 percent of their vote in that election. In 1984, however, Jews returned to their traditional voting patterns, with approximately two-thirds of this group supporting the Democratic candidate, Walter Mondale.

In the light of these shifts, how then can the party coalitions be described today? The Democrats still receive overwhelming support from blacks, those with the lowest incomes, and those who live in the central cities. However, the relatively small size of the latter two groups compared to the general population, and their lower turnout, make them less important a part of the total electorate than they were in the past. On the other hand, the larger Democratic-oriented groups, union families, southerners, and Catholics, have weakened in their backing of Democratic candidates at the presidential level. Finally, young voters in the 1980s have not identified with the Democratic party in anywhere near the proportion that they did a decade or two ago.

The Republicans have become more white, middle-class, and suburban. They have gained support in the south and southwest, the so-called Sunbelt. They have maintained their Protestant support but have also become more Catholic. And they have made inroads among the young.

With the social basis of the parties eroding, the old coalitions have become frayed. While class, religion, and geography are still related to party identification and voting behavior, they are not as strongly related as they were in the past. Voters are less influenced by group cues. They exercise a more independent judgment on election day, a judgment that is less predictable. That is why the Republicans' chances have improved. Although they have not become a majority of the electorate, the GOP has reduced the Democrats' advantage.

Realignment or Dealignment?

Are Republican gains evidence of a new realignment of voters? Will that party soon emerge as the partisan majority? The answer is still unclear.[37]

Several trends, however, are apparent.

1. The GOP has consistently won an electoral majority at the presidential level. It has been victorious in six of the last nine elections, winning three of the last four in landslides. Of the three the Republicans lost, two were very close. Only in 1964 and 1976 did a Democratic

candidate win a majority of the total presidential vote. In fact, since World War II, the Republican candidates have received 365.8 million votes for President compared with 327.1 million for Democratic candidates—a difference of more than 38 million.

2. Republican candidates for the Presidency have increasingly attracted more support from traditional Democratic voters than have Democratic candidates from Republican voters. Not only has there been more defection to rather than from the Republican party, but a majority of certain Democratic groups (white southerners, Catholics, and new voters) have voted Republican in recent presidential elections. If this practice were to continue, it is likely members of these groups would begin to think of themselves as Republicans.

3. Population shifts in the South and Southwest seem to give the Republicans an advantage in the Electoral College. Twenty-three states have voted for the Republican candidate in each of the last five presidential elections. These states have 202 electoral votes, nearly three-quarters of the number needed for victory. By contrast, only the District of Columbia has given its support to all of the recent Democratic nominees. Thus, the Democratic candidate begins the campaign with a considerably smaller base of support in the Electoral College than does the Republican.

4. Finally, the Republicans have attracted large numbers of male voters in recent years. Reagan won almost two-thirds of the male vote in 1984. Today a plurality of men consider themselves Republicans. Women, on the other hand, have maintained and even increased their identification with the Democratic party.

While these trends have benefited the Republicans at the expense of the Democrats, they have not as yet produced a Republican plurality, much less a Republican majority. More people still think of themselves as Democrats than Republicans (see Table 3–3). Moreover, the Democrats continue to control the House of Representatives (by sizable numbers), the Senate, two-thirds of the state legislatures, and a majority of the governorships.[38]

The persistence of a Democratic plurality in the light of Republican presidential voting suggests the continuation of the dealignment that began in the late 1960s and early 1970s. By dealignment is meant a weakening in the attachment that people feel toward political parties. In other words, their partisan attitudes are less firm than in the past. For many, split-ticket voting has become the rule, not the exception. Today's electorate is more likely to move from one party's candidate to the other party's candidate from one election to the next. Contemporary voters are more likely to base their voting decisions on their evaluation of the candidates, rather than simply on their party loyalties.

The evidence also points to the emergence of a two-tier system. At the presidential level, the Republicans seem to have an advantage; at other levels, the Democrats are still dominant.

SUMMARY

The electorate is not neutral. People do not come to campaigns with completely open minds. Rather, their preexisting loyalties and experiences color their perceptions and affect their judgment.

Of these attitudes, partisanship has had the strongest impact on voting behavior. It is a mechanism for placing oneself within the political world, for evaluating the campaign, and for deciding whether and how to vote. It is also a motive for being informed, for being concerned, and for turning out on election day.

Since the 1960s there has been a substantial decline in the proportion of the population casting ballots. This can be partially attributed to the weakening of party ties, to the increasing size of the under-thirty and over-seventy age groups within the electorate, and to the cynicism and apathy generated by the events of the late 1960s and the 1970s. This cynicism and apathy has been particularly evident among those in the lower socioeconomic groups, those with the least formal education.

Partisan attitudes have also eroded since the 1960s. The percentage of people identifying with a party, and, most particularly, the strength of that identification, have declined. One consequence has been the increasing importance of short-term factors in campaigning. A second has been the enhanced impact of the media. A third has been the uncertainty of election outcomes, especially at the presidential level.

Since larger numbers of voters are less strongly affected by partisan cues, new importance has been placed on their perception of the images that candidates attempt to project, and, to a lesser extent, on the policy stances they take. For a candidate's image to have an impact, it must seem authentic and convey desirable attributes for the office. For a candidate's issue positions to have an effect, they must be clearly identifiable and personally meaningful to the voters.

With candidate images and issue stands more likely to influence the electorate's decision, the media's role in the political process has been enhanced. Media now provide the critical link between the candidates and the voters. For the most informed and committed, media exposure works to reinforce attitudes; for the least informed, whether committed or uncommitted, it has little effect. For weak partisans and independents, however, even moderate exposure can alter perceptions and affect voting.

Finally, the weakening of partisan ties has produced a vote that either party can win. It has produced a presidential vote that has less carryover to congressional and state elections. And it has produced an electorate that is more volatile and less predictable at the presidential level.

The parties' coalitions have also shifted. The Democratic party, which became dominant during the New Deal period, has lost the support of a majority of southern whites in presidential elections and has suffered defections from labor and Catholics. But it has also maintained its support from other minority groups such as Jews, blacks, and Hispanics. Its coalition has weakened but not disintegrated.

The Republican party is more homogeneous than the Democratic party, although less so than it has been in the recent past. Retaining backing from the upper socioeconomic strata, the Republicans have gained in the South, benefited from the increased social conservatism of a growing middle class, and made potentially significant strides among the young. The party has been able to win presidential elections, but has not thus far been able to expand its electoral coalition to a partisan plurality, much less majority.

These changes have important implications for the political system. The decline in turnout, the weakening of partisan attitudes, and the splintering of the parties' electoral coalition may augur a new era in electoral politics. It is unclear, however, whether this is an era of dealignment or realignment. What is clear is that the parties have lost power. A smaller portion of the electorate identify with them and feel strongly about them. Parties still nominate the candidates, but, ironically, have less influence over who is chosen; they still provide the essential labels, but have less effect on who gets elected President. They still take positions, but seem to have less influence on what the policies of the country will be.

NOTES

1. The one specification the Constitution makes is that "the electors in each state shall have the qualifications requisite for electors of the most numerous branch of the state legislature." Article 1, Section 2.

2. V.O. Key, Jr., *Politics, Parties and Pressure Groups* (New York: Thomas Y. Crowell, 1958), p. 624.

3. In 1944 the Supreme Court in the case of *Smith v. Allwright* (321 U.S. 649, 1944), declared the white primary unconstitutional. In its opinion the Court rejected the argument that parties were private associations and thus could restrict participation in their selection process.

4. They projected a 9.1 percent increment in 1972 if the states eliminated closing dates for registration, kept registration offices open during business hours and in the evening or on Saturday, and permitted absentee registration for those who could not register in person. Raymond E. Wolfinger and Steven J. Rosenstone, *Who Votes?* (New Haven: Yale University Press, 1980) p. 73. See also Peverill Squire, Raymond E. Wolfinger, and David P. Glass, "Residential Mobility and Voter Turnout," *American Political Science Review*, 81 (1987), 45–65.

5. In addition to the countries of Western Europe, the other nations included in the study were Australia, Canada, Israel, Japan, New Zealand, and the United States. David Glass, Peverill Squire, and Raymond Wolfinger, "Voter Turnout: An International Comparison," *Public Opinion*, 6 (Dec./Jan. 1984), 49–55.

6. Angus Campbell, Philip E. Converse, Warren E. Miller, and Donald E. Stokes, *The American Voter* (New York: John Wiley, 1960), p. 102.

7. Raymond E. Wolfinger and Steven J. Rosenstone, *Who Votes?*, p. 38.

8. Ibid., pp. 13–26.

9. Ibid., pp. 18–20, 35–36.

10. In nonpresidential elections, turnout has been even lower. Clearly, the attention and excitement of the presidential campaign contribute to more participation and voting. The competitiveness of the election also affects turnout, with closer contests attracting more voters.

11. Richard A. Brody, "The Puzzle of Political Participation in America," in Anthony King (ed.), *The New American Political System* (Washington, D.C.: American Enterprise Institute, 1978), pp. 305–306.

12. Paul R. Abramson, John H. Aldrich, and David W. Rhode, *Change and Continuity in the 1984 Elections* (Washington, D.C.: Congressional Quarterly, 1986), pp. 117–118.

13. Thomas E. Cavanagh, "Changes in American Voter Turnout, 1964–1976," *Political Science Quarterly*, 96 (1981), 53–65.

14. Ann Cooper, "Turnout May Be Higher on Nov. 6, But for the Parties, It May Be a Wash," *National Journal*, 16, (1984), 2068–2073.

15. Ibid., p. 2072.

16. Bruce E. Cain and Ken McCue, "Do Registration Drives Matter: The Realities of Partisan Dreams" (paper delivered at the annual meeting of the American Political Science Association, New Orleans, August 29–September 1, 1985).

17. Actually, a small interview-reinterview survey was conducted in 1948, but the results were never published. In contrast to the emphasis on political attitudes of the large-scale interview projects in the 1950s, the 1948 project had a sociological orientation.

18. Campbell et al., *The American Voter*.

19. Ibid., pp. 146–152.

20. Ibid., pp. 163–165.

21. Ibid., pp. 133–136. Party identification is determined by asking the following question: "Generally speaking, do you usually think of yourself as a Republican, a Democrat, an Independent, or what?" To discern the strength of the identification, a second question is asked: "(If Republican or Democrat), Would you call yourself a strong (R) (D) or a not very strong (R) (D)? (If Independent), Do you think of yourself as closer to the Republican or Democratic party?" In examining the concept of party identification, the University of Michigan analysts have stressed two dimensions—its direction and strength. Others, however, have criticized the Michigan model for overemphasizing party and underemphasizing other factors such as social class, political ideology, and issue positions. For a thoughtful critique, see Jerrold G. Rusk, "The Michigan Election Studies: A Critical Evaluation" (paper delivered at the annual meeting of the American Political Science Association, New York, September 3–6, 1981).

22. For a more extensive discussion of desirable presidential images, see Chapter 7, pp. 204–237, and Benjamin I. Page, Choices and Echoes in Presidential Elections (Chicago: University of Chicago Press, 1978), pp. 232–265.

23. Campbell et al., The American Voter, pp. 143 and 547. Independents who lean in a partisan direction tend to be better informed than those who do not. These independent leaners have many of the characteristics of party identifiers, including loyalty to the party's candidates. They do not, however, identify themselves as Republicans or Democrats.

24. V.O. Key, Jr., The Responsible Electorate (Cambridge: Harvard University Press, 1966), p. 7.

25. The switchers, however, constituted only a small percentage of the total electorate. Stand-patters were a larger group. For them, policy preferences reinforced their partisan loyalties. The beliefs and behavior of the stand-patters confirmed the basic thesis that partisanship influences voting for most people most of the time. Ibid., p. 150.

26. See, for example, David E. RePass, "Issue Salience and Party Choice," American Political Science Review, 65 (1971), 389–400; John E. Jackson, "Issues, Party Choices, and Presidential Votes," American Journal of Political Science, 19 (1975), 161–185; Arthur H. Miller and Warren E. Miller, "Issues, Candidates and Partisan Divisions in the 1972 American Presidential Election," British Journal of Political Science, 5 (1975), 393–433; Arthur H. Miller, Warren E. Miller, Alden S. Raine, and Thad A. Brown, "A Majority Party in Disarray: Policy Polarization in the 1972 Election," American Political Science Review, 70 (1976), 753–778; Norman H. Nie, Sidney Verba, and John R. Petrocik, The Changing American Voter (Cambridge, Mass.: Harvard University Press, 1976), p. 166.

27. Hugh L. LeBlanc and Mary Beth Merrin, "Independents, Issue Partisanship and the Decline of Party," American Politics Quarterly, 7 (1979), 240–256.

28. Arthur H. Miller and Martin P. Wattenberg, "Policy and Performance Voting in the 1980 Election," (paper delivered at the annual meeting of the American Political Science Association, New York, September 3–6, 1981).

29. In the 1950s the authors of The American Voter had discovered that a majority of voters made their voting decision before the general election campaign. In 1984 the old trend reappeared—at least at the presidential level. However, it was not due to partisan identification but to the popularity of the President who was seeking reelection. Voters reached an easy and early decision that they wanted to keep Ronald Reagan in the White

House. The absence of a popular incumbent running in 1988 should once again increase the difficulty of the voting decision for much of the electorate, causing them to reserve their judgment until later in the campaign.

30. This description of the New Deal realignment is based primarily on the discussion in Everett Carll Ladd, Jr., with Charles D. Hadley, *Transformation of the American Party System* (New York: W.W. Norton, 1974), pp. 31–87.

31. Ibid., p. 43.

32. Ibid., p. 69.

33. Ibid., pp. 55–57.

34. Ibid., pp. 93–104.

35. Ibid., p. 158.

36. Ray Wolfinger and Michael C. Hagen, "Republican Prospects: Southern Comfort," *Public Opinion*, 8, (Oct./Nov. 1985), p. 9.

37. For an extended discussion of this issue, see Everett Carll Ladd, "On Mandates, Realignments, and the 1984 Presidential Election," *Political Science Quarterly*, 100 (1985), 1–25; Seymour Martin Lipset, "The Elections, The Economy and Public Opinion: 1984," *PS*, 18 (1985), 28–38; Laurily K. Epstein, "The Changing Structure of Party Identification," *PS*, 18 (1985), 48–52; David W. Brady and Patricia A. Hurley, "The Prospects for Contemporary Partisan Realignment," *PS*, 18 (1985), 63–68; James A. Barnes and John C. Weicher, "Urban Blight: The Democrats' Eroding Metropolitan Base," *Public Opinion*, 8 (Feb./Mar. 1985), 49–51; Richard Scammon and James A. Barnes, "Republican Prospects: Southern Discomfort," *Public Opinion*, 8 (Oct./Nov. 1985), 14–17; Paul R. Abramson et al., *Change and Continuity in the 1984 Elections*, pp. 254–258 and 286–301.

38. The Democratic party has been aided in its control of the House of Representatives by its dominance at the state legislative level. It is the state legislatures that draw the districts for state representatives and members of Congress. Naturally, the party in power does this drafting to its own advantage. The Republicans have begun a major program designed to improve the party's representation in the state legislatures. One of the objectives of this effort is to exercise greater influence over the redistricting that will occur after the 1990 census.

Selected Readings

Brody, Richard A. "The Puzzle of Political Participation in America," in Anthony King (ed.), *The New American Political System.* Washington, D.C.: American Enterprise Institute, 1978, 287–324.

Campbell, Angus, Philip E. Converse, Warren E. Miller, and Donald E. Stokes. *The American Voter.* New York: John Wiley, 1960.

Carmines, Edward G., and James A. Stimson. "The Racial Reorientation of American Politics," in John C. Pierce and John L. Sullivan (eds.), *The Electorate Reconsidered.* Beverly Hills, Calif.: Sage Publications, 1980. 199–218.

Cavanagh, Thomas E. "Changes in American Voter Turnout, 1964–1976," *Political Science Quarterly*, 96 (1981), 53–65.

Edsall, Thomas B. *The New Politics of Inequality.* New York: W. W. Norton, 1984.

Fishel, Jeff, ed. *Parties and Elections in an Anti-Party Age.* Bloomington: Indiana University Press, 1978.

Kirkpatrick, Jeane J. "Changing Patterns of Electoral Competition," in Anthony King (ed.), *The New American Political System.* Washington, D.C.: American Enterprise Institute, 1978, 249–285.

Ladd, Everett Carll. "On Mandates, Realignments, and the 1984 Presidential Election," *Political Science Quarterly,* 100 (1985), 1–25.

Ladd, Everett Carll, Jr., with Charles D. Hadley. *Transformations of the American Party System.* New York: W. W. Norton, 1975.

Nie, Norman H., Sidney Verba, and John R. Petrocik. *The Changing American Voter.* Cambridge, Mass.: Harvard University Press, 1976.

Reichley, A. James. "Religion and Political Realignment," *The Brookings Review,* 3 (1984), 29–35.

Wolfinger, Raymond E., and Steven J. Rosenstone. *Who Votes?* New Haven: Yale University Press, 1980.

PART II

THE
NOMINATION

Chapter 4

DELEGATE SELECTION

Introduction

Presidential nominees are selected by the delegates to their party's national convention. The way those delegates are chosen can influence the choice of nominees. It can also affect the influence of the state and its party leadership.

Procedures for delegate selection are determined by state law. Today, these procedures also have to conform to general guidelines and rules established by the national party. In the past, they did not. Rather, statutes passed by the state legislature reflected the needs and desires of the political leaders who controlled the state. Naturally, these laws were designed to buttress that leadership and extend its influence.

Primary elections in which the party's rank and file chose the delegates were discouraged, co-opted, or even circumvented. Favorite son candidates, tapped by the leadership, prevented meaningful contests in many states. Other states held primaries but made them advisory, with the actual selection of the delegates left to caucuses, conventions, or committees, which were more easily controlled by party officials. There were also impediments to potential delegates' getting on the ballot: high fees, lengthy petitions, early dates for filing. Winner-take-all provisions gave a great advantage to the organization candidate, as did rules requiring delegates to vote as a unit.

Not until the 1970s was popular participation in the selection of convention delegates encouraged. It was a national party, the Democrats, who took the lead by adopting a series of reforms that affected the period during which delegates could be selected, the procedures for choosing them, and ultimately their behavior at the convention. While these rules limited the states' discretion, they did not result in uniform primaries and caucuses. Considerable variation still exists in how delegates are chosen, how the vote is apportioned, and who participates in the selection.

This chapter will explore these rules and their consequences for the nomination process. It is organized into four sections. The first details the changes in party rules. The second considers the legal challenges to these rules and the Supreme Court's decisions on these challenges. Part three examines the impact of the rules changes on the party and the electorate, while part four discusses how they have affected the candidates and their campaigns.

REFORMING THE NOMINATION PROCESS

Historically, states enacted their own rules for delegate selection with relatively little guidance from the national party. Some discouraged popular participation; others encouraged it but made no effort to fairly reflect rank-and-file opinion of the candidate with the delegate support that candidate received. In very few states was the delegation as a whole reflective, demographically or ideologically, of the party's electorate within that state.

Democratic party reforms have attempted to change this. The party had two primary objectives in altering its rules: to encourage greater rank-and-file participation and to select delegates who were representative of the rank and file. The problem has been how to do this and still win elections. Judging by the Democrats' lack of success at the presidential level since 1968, they have not as yet found a satisfactory solution.

The Democratic party has gone through two fairly distinct periods in reforming its delegate selection procedures. During the first, 1968–1980, it adopted a highly structured set of national rules and sought to impose them on the states. In stage two, from 1981 to the present, the party has permitted its state affiliates greater flexibility in determining how their delegations are to be chosen. Throughout these two periods, the Republican party has not mandated national rules, although its state parties have been affected by Democratic reforms, particularly in those states whose legislatures are controlled by the Democrats.

Democratic Rules, 1968–1980

The catalyst for the rules changes was the tumultuous Democratic convention of 1968, in which Senator Hubert Humphrey won the nomination although he had not entered one single primary. Yet the primaries of that year were very important. They had become the vehicle by which Democrats could protest the Johnson administration's conduct of the war in Vietnam.

Senator Eugene McCarthy, the first of the antiwar candidates, had challenged Lyndon Johnson in the New Hampshire primary. To the surprise of many political observers, McCarthy received 42.4 percent of the vote, almost as much as the President, who got 49.5 percent. Four days after McCarthy's unexpectedly strong showing, Senator Robert Kennedy, brother of the late President and political rival of Johnson, declared his candidacy for the nation's highest office. With protests against the war increasing and divisions within the Democratic party intensifying, Johnson bowed out, declaring that he did not want the country's involvement in Southeast Asia to become a political issue.

Johnson's withdrawal cleared the way for Hubert Humphrey, the Vice President, to become a candidate. Humphrey, however, waited almost a month to announce his intentions. His late entrance into the Democratic nomination process precluded his running in the primaries. Like Johnson, Humphrey did not want to become the focal point of antiwar protests. Nor did he have the grass-roots organization to match McCarthy's and Kennedy's. What he did have was the support of many Democratic leaders, including the President.

The last big-state primary was in California. Kennedy scored a significant victory, but during the celebration that followed, he was assassinated. This left McCarthy as the principal antiwar candidate, but one who was far short of a convention majority. Despite the last-minute entrance of Senator George McGovern, who hoped to rally Kennedy delegates to his candidacy, Humphrey won the nomination easily. To make matters worse for those who opposed Humphrey and the administration's war efforts, a platform amendment calling for an unconditional end to the bombing of North Vietnam was defeated. McCarthy and Kennedy delegates felt victimized by the process and the product. They were angry. They demanded reform.

Compounding the divisions within the convention were demonstrations outside of it. Thousands of youthful protestors, calling for an end to the war, congregated in the streets of Chicago. The police, under orders from Mayor Richard Daley to maintain order, used strong-arm tactics to disperse the crowds. Clashes between police and protestors followed. Television filmed these confrontations, and showed them during its convention coverage. The spectacle of police beating demonstrators further inflamed emotions and led to calls for reform, not only from those who attended the convention but from those who watched it.

After the election, the Democratic party responded to these protests. A commission, chaired initially by Senator George McGovern, was appointed to study procedures for selecting and seating convention delegates and to propose ways of improving them. The commission recommended that delegate selection be tuned more closely to popular sentiment within the state and, implicitly, less to the wishes of state party leaders. Rules to make it easier for individuals to run as delegates, to limit the size of the districts from which they could be chosen, and most important to require proportional voting within the district, were approved by the party.

Additionally, Democrats tried to prevent independents and, especially, partisans of other parties, from participating in the selection of their delegates. The difficulty, however, was to determine who was a Democrat, since some states did not require or even permit registration by party. In implementing this rule, the party adopted a very liberal interpretation of Democratic affiliation. Anyone identifying himself or herself as a Democrat at the time of voting, or who simply requested a Democratic ballot, was viewed as a Democrat. This effectively permitted crossover voting, although theoretically it precluded so-called open primaries, in which voters are given the ballots of both major parties, discard one, and vote the other.

In addition to better translating public preferences into delegate selection, the other major objective of the reforms was to better equalize representation on the delegations themselves. Three groups in particular—blacks, women, and youth—had protested their underrepresentation on party councils and at the conventions. Their representatives and others who were sympathetic to their plight pressed hard for more power and better representation for minorities. The reform commission reacted to these protests by proposing a rule requiring that all states represent blacks, women, and youth in reasonable relationship to their presence in the state population. Failure to do so was viewed as *prima facie* evidence of discrimination. In other words, the party established quotas.

Considerable opposition to the application of this rule during the 1972 nomination process developed, and it was subsequently modified to require that states implement affirmative action plans for those groups that had been subject to past discrimination.[1] The party went one step further with respect to women. It required that, beginning with its 1980 nominating convention, each state delegation be equally divided between the sexes.

One consequence of these Democratic rules was to make primaries the preferred method of delegate selection. Moreover, primary voting became more closely tied to delegate selection than it had been in the past. The number of advisory primaries, in which the popular vote is not tied to the selection of delegates, declined, while the number of binding primaries, in which it is tied, increased.[2] This gave the party's electorate a more direct voice in choosing the nominee.

Caucuses were still permitted, but they too were redesigned to encourage rank-and-file participation. No longer could a state party leader cast a large number of proxies for the delegates of his choice. Caucuses had to be publicly announced with adequate time given for campaigning. Moreover, they had to be conducted in stages, and three-fourths of the delegates had to be chosen in districts no larger than those for members of Congress.

Another consequence, not nearly so beneficial to the goal of increased participation, was a lengthening of the process, escalating its costs, fatiguing its candidates, boring the public, and dividing the party. Since the contests at the beginning received the most attention from the media, candidates, and public alike, states moved their primaries forward, front-loading the process and forcing candidates to start their campaigns even earlier than in the past.

Primaries and caucuses affected the type of delegate selected as well. They made it more difficult for elected officials and party leaders to automatically attend the nominating conventions. The absence of these members of the party's governing elite generated and extended cleavages between the nominees and their electoral coalitions and the party's organization and its leadership.

These cleavages created serious problems for the Democrats. Put simply, they adversely affected the chances of its nominees winning the general election, and if successful, of governing. During the presidential campaign, the divisiveness impaired a unified organizational effort, tarnished the images of party candidates, and increased defections from straight partisan voting.[3] After the election, it delayed agenda- and coalition-building.

In short, party reforms produced unintended consequences. These consequences—the proliferation of primaries, the lengthening of the process, the divisiveness within the party, the poor representation of elected leaders, and, most important, the failure to win elections and govern successfully—led the Democrats to reexamine and modify their rules for delegate selection in the 1980s.

Democratic Rules, 1981–Present

Two commissions, one appointed in 1981 and the other in 1985, both composed of a cross section of party officials, interest group representatives, and supporters of leading candidates for the nomination, proposed a series of rule changes to rectify the negative effects of past reforms. The new reforms were designed to strengthen the party and improve the chances of its nominees without at the same time undermining the goals of *fair reflection* and *equal representation.*

The rule modifications fall into three categories: those that affect the time frame and procedures of the selection process, those that affect the representation of public officials and party leaders, and those that govern the behavior of delegates at the convention itself.

The objective of the original reforms was to encourage participation by the rank and file and to reflect its sentiment in the allocation of delegates. Three problems in particular impeded the achievement of these objectives.

1. The states that held their primaries and caucuses early seemed to exercise disproportionate influence. This led to a tendency by states to front-load the process, by candidates to expend most of their resources at the beginning or as soon as they got them, and by participants to turn out more regularly in March than in May.

2. The relatively small percentage of the vote needed to receive delegates (known as a threshold) encouraged candidacies. Not only did the low threshold factionalize the party, it provided an incentive for those without national experience, reputation, and even party ties, to run. By obtaining the votes of as little as 15 percent of those who participated in a primary or caucus, relatively unknown candidates could win delegates, and—more important during the early period—gain recognition. They could use this recognition, in turn, to build constituencies and become national figures.

3. The application of the proportional voting rule tended to discourage campaigning in competitive districts, and fostered it in noncompetitive ones. The rule in effect undercompensated the winner in districts in which there were an even number of delegates. A win by less than 20 percent resulted in an even split of delegates. As a consequence, candidates were discouraged from investing resources in districts in which they

could reach the minimum necessary to gain delegates but not enough to clearly dominate. This adversely affected turnout and representation.

To modify the first of these problems, the party has tried to impose a window period, when primaries and caucuses could be held, from the second Tuesday in March to the second Tuesday in June. What to do with those states, such as Iowa and New Hampshire, whose laws require that they choose their delegates before others, has been the critical issue.

Believing that it could not conduct its own selection process in these states, the national party decided that the best it could do was establish the window and grant these states an exception, but require them to hold their contests closer to the designated period than in the past. In 1984 Iowa and New Hampshire were permitted to schedule their contests fifteen and seven days before the window opened. However, when Vermont decided to hold a nonbinding presidential popularity vote on the day of its town meetings, in early March, Iowa and New Hampshire each moved their contest one week earlier, and the national party reluctantly acquiesced.

The 1988 exemptions were based on the 1984 experience. According to Democratic rules, Iowa's caucuses may occur approximately three weeks before the window opens, New Hampshire's primary two weeks before, and the Maine and Wyoming caucuses no earlier than nine and four days before. However, the states of Iowa and New Hampshire moved their contests one week earlier than Democratic rules permitted when South Dakota scheduled its primary for February 23. Vermont also planned a preference primary prior to the window period. As in 1984 there is little the party can do to compel compliance with its rules other than refusing to seat delegates who are chosen before its selection process officially begins. (See Appendix C for a schedule of the caucuses and primaries in 1988.)

Front-loading also remains a problem, more so now than ever.[4] In 1984, 6 percent of the delegates were chosen in primaries or caucuses before March, and 36 percent during that month. In 1988 the percentage chosen during the first official month will be much higher, with the southern regional primaries on the first Tuesday, southern caucuses on the first weekend, a mini-midwestern regional primary the second week, and other states moving their contests earlier. After the polls close on Super Tuesday (March 8th), approximately 40 percent of the delegates of both parties will have been chosen. By the end of the following week, this figure will exceed 50 percent.

Another change has been the modifications to the so-called fair reflection rule. One modification affects the minimum percentage of the vote necessary to be eligible for delegates; the other pertains to the methods by which the primary vote is converted into delegates.

Thresholds were controversial in 1984. Democratic rules for that year raised the minimum vote needed to obtain delegates to 20 percent in caucuses and up to 25 percent in primaries. This disadvantaged minority candidates such as Jesse Jackson. With his supporters concentrated in heavily black areas, Jackson was unable to reach the minimum percentage needed in many predominantly white districts. Although he received 19 percent of the vote in primaries, he obtained only 10 percent of the delegates selected in them.

Bending to pressure from Jackson and others, the Democrats have lowered the threshold in 1988 to 15 percent in primaries and caucuses. This will help lesser-known and minority candidates win delegates, but could also factionalize the Democratic vote.

While the principle of proportional voting has been retained, the new rules give states greater flexibility in determining how their vote will be allocated. Two allocation formulas, prohibited in previous years, are now acceptable. One permits the direct election of delegates within districts; the other allows a bonus of one delegate to be awarded to the candidate who receives the most popular votes within a district.

Both of these variations on the proportional voting theme advantage front-runners. The first is often referred as the winner-take-all primary because it creates the possibility that the popular vote leader could get all the delegates within a district by winning only a plurality of the votes (as few as 35–45 percent, depending on the number of other candidates running). Losing candidates, on the other hand, could be shut out entirely, even though their delegates received a substantial portion of the vote.

In 1980 only two states conducted winner-take-all primaries within electoral districts. In 1984, after the rules were changed, seven elected to do so. The incentive for states is that it tends to produce a more cohesive delegation, thereby maximizing the state's influence on the nominees and the platform.

Walter Mondale was the principal beneficiary of this rule change, which his supporters backed, in 1984. He won six of the seven winner-take-all primaries, received 40 percent of the popular vote in these contests, but won 53 percent of the delegates. In Pennsylvania he got 45 percent of the vote but 80 percent of the pledged delegates. In New Jersey his delegate victory was even more lopsided, winning 45 percent of the popular vote and 95 percent of the delegates. Were it not for the winner-take-all primary in California, where Hart's popular vote was magnified by his delegate totals, Mondale's advantage would have been even greater.

Similarly, the other type of acceptable formula for allocating delegates, known as winner-take-more, also benefits the front-runner. Here too

Mondale did much better than his rivals in 1984. Winning four of the five winner-take-more primaries, he was able to convert 41 percent of the popular vote in these five states into 53 percent of the delegates.

In contrast, Hart was comparably stronger in those states in which delegates were chosen in direct proportion to the popular vote. (See Table 4–1.)

The rules for allocating delegates preserved the nomination for Walter Mondale in 1984. He would not have had a majority going into the convention without them. Political scientist Gary R. Orren calculates that Mondale would have been almost 400 votes short of the nomination had the delegates been allocated strictly in proportion to the popular vote. Hart would have been about 660 short. Under these circumstances Jackson, who should have had the support of 645 delegates on the basis of his popular vote, would have held the key to the choice between them.[5]

If the past is any indication, the rules for apportioning delegates will affect the results in 1988 as well. To put it simply, they help those in a position to take advantage of them—well-known candidates with in-depth organizations.

Another reform in the 1980s has been the addition of new leadership delegates. The party had been unhappy with the decreasing number of its elected officials who attended the convention as delegates in the 1970s. The absence of these officials, it was thought, contributed to the lack of support that the nominees received during the campaign and after the election. Jimmy Carter's difficulties in dealing with Congress were cited as evidence of the need for closer cooperation between party leaders and the presidential standard-bearer.

In order to facilitate closer ties, the Democrats established two new categories of delegates: (1) party leader and elected official delegates and (2) superdelegates. Those in the first category, equal to 15 percent of the state's delegation, were to be pledged and allocated to candidates on the same

Table 4–1 PROPORTIONAL VOTING AND DELEGATE ALLOCATION, 1984

	Percentage of Primary Vote			Pledged Delegates Won		
	Mondale	Hart	Jackson	Mondale	Hart	Jackson
Winner-take-all (loophole)	40	36	18	53	32	7
Winner-take-more (bonus)	41	32	21	53	33	14
Proportional representation	32	39	17	38	45	11
Total	39	36	19	49	36	10

Source: Gary R. Orren, "The Nomination Process: Vicissitudes of Candidate Selection," in Michael Nelson (ed.), *The Election of 1984* (Washington, D.C.: The Congressional Quarterly, 1985), p. 39. Reprinted with the permission of the Congressional Quarterly Inc.

basis as the rest of the delegation. Those in the second category were to be officially unpledged. Chosen from a group consisting of all the Democratic governors, all the members of the Democratic National Committee, four-fifths of the Democratic members of Congress, and a small number of distinguished elected officials, these superdelegates could hold the balance of power in a divided convention. In 1984 there were 568 superdelegates; in 1988 there will be 644, 15.5 percent of the convention total.

The principal difference between the 1984 and 1988 superdelegates, other than their increased number in 1988, is the time when the members of Congress may be chosen. In 1984 they were selected in January, before any caucus or primary was held. This very early date gave front-runner Walter Mondale a tremendous advantage in influencing their selection and winning their support.[6] Complaints that the popular vote had been preempted and that nonestablishment candidates were disadvantaged by the early selection of members of Congress led the party to move the selection for 1988 to the middle of the nomination cycle, between April 19th and May 7th.

Finally, the Democrats have reversed the rule adopted by the convention in 1980 that delegates, who are publicly committed, must vote for the candidate to whom they are pledged. Democratic delegates today can vote their consciences, although their initial selection as delegates must still have the approval of the candidate to whom they are committed. It is unlikely under the circumstances that many delegates will change their minds at the convention, unless their candidate encourages them to do so.

On balance, the Democratic reforms for 1984 and 1988 permit states to exercise greater flexibility in delegate selection. Rather than rigidly imposing guidelines, the party has chosen the path of least resistance, granting exemptions to states that oppose particular rules or allowing them greater discretion in applying these rules. The beneficiaries of this flexibility are apt to be those states whose rules produce a more cohesive delegation and those candidates who have the resources to win these blocs of delegates. The more front-loaded the process the more difficult it will be for candidates to use the early contests as stepping-stones to the nomination.

Republican Rules

Unlike the Democrats, the Republicans have not changed their rules after each recent national convention. Nor can they. It is the Republican convention itself that approves the rules for choosing delegates for the next Republican convention. Under normal circumstances, these rules cannot be altered by the Republican National Committee, nor by special commissions the party creates.

Also unlike the Democrats, the Republicans have not chosen to mandate national guidelines for their state parties. Whereas the Democrats impose some form of proportional voting, the Republicans do not. In 1980, the year in which the Republicans last had a contested nomination, only about one-third of states allocated Republican delegates in direct proportion to the popular vote within that state. Whereas the Democrats have designated a window period, the Republicans have not. The first stage in the Michigan and Arizona selection process for the 1988 Republican convention occurred in the summer of 1986, and the first round of the Michigan caucuses is scheduled for January 1988, well before the Iowa and New Hampshire contests. Whereas the Democrats have superdelegates, the Republicans do not, although state and national Republican leaders have attended their conventions in greater proportion than their Democratic counterparts (see Table 4–5). Nor do the Republicans require that 50 percent of each state delegation be women. Until recently, women have constituted less than one-third of the delegates at Republican conventions.

Republicans, however, have been affected by the Democratic rules changes. Since state legislatures enact laws governing party nominations, and since the Democrats have controlled most of these legislatures, they have literally forced some of their reforms on the Republicans. Moreover, the Republicans have also made changes of their own. A Committee of Delegates and Organizations, appointed in 1969, recommended that delegate selection procedures encourage greater participation in states that used conventions to pick their delegates; that more information about these procedures be promulgated to the party's electorate; and, that voting by proxy be prohibited. These recommendations, adopted by the 1972 Republican convention, took effect in 1976.

THE LEGALITY OF PARTY RULES

As previously mentioned, party reforms, to be effective, must be enacted into law. Most states have complied with the new rules. A few have not, resulting in confrontation between these states and the national party. When New Hampshire and Iowa refused to move the dates of their respective primary and caucuses into the Democrats' window period in 1984, the national party backed down. But when Illinois chose its 1972 delegates in a manner that conflicted with new Democratic rules, the party sought to impose its rules on the state.

In addition to the political controversy this generated, it also presented an important legal question: which body, the national party or state, was the higher authority? In its landmark decision, *Cousins* v. *Wigoda* (419 U.S. 477, 1975), the Supreme Court sided with the party. The Court stated that political parties were private organizations with rights of association protected by the Constitution. States could not abridge these rights unless there were compelling constitutional reasons to do so. While states could establish their own primary laws, the party could determine the criteria for representation at its national convention.

The *Cousins* v. *Wigoda* decision provided an additional incentive for states to change their laws when they conflicted with party rules. The number of challenges declined. They were not, however, eliminated entirely. The issue of crossover voting as practiced in the open primary prompted another court test and decision in favor of the party.

Democratic rules prohibited open primaries. Four states had conducted this type of election in 1976. Three voluntarily changed their law for 1980. The fourth, Wisconsin, did not. The national party's compliance review commission ordered the state party to design an alternative process. It refused. The case went to court.

Citing the precedent of *Cousins* v. *Wigoda,* the Supreme Court held in the case of *Democratic Party of the U.S.* v. *Wisconsin ex. rel. La Follette* (450 U.S. 107, 1981) that a state had no right to interfere with the party's delegate selection process unless it demonstrated a compelling reason to do so. It ruled that Wisconsin had not demonstrated such a reason; hence, the Democratic party could refuse to seat delegates who were selected in a manner that violated its rules.

A more recent decision by the Supreme Court, also involving open primaries, has further enhanced the power of parties, in this case state parties, to establish rules for nominating candidates. In December 1986 the Supreme Court, in the case of *Tashjian v. Republican Party of Connecticut* (107 S. Ct. 544, 1986), voided a Connecticut law that prohibited open primaries. Republicans, who were in the minority in Connecticut, had favored such a primary as a means of attracting independent voters. Unable to get the Democratic-controlled legislature to change the law, the state Republican party went to court, arguing that the statute violated First Amendment rights of freedom of association. In a 5 to 4 ruling, the Supreme Court agreed, and struck down the legislation.

Although these Court decisions have given the political parties the legal authority to design and enforce their own rules, the practicality of doing so is another question. Other than going to court if a state refuses to change its election law, a party, particularly a national party, has only two viable options: require the state party to conduct its own delegate selection process in conformity to national rules, or grant the state party an exemption so that it can abide by the law of the state. In 1984 the Wisconsin Democratic party was forced by the national Democratic party to adopt a caucus mode of selection. Turnout declined accordingly. In 1988 the Democrats have given Wisconsin and Montana, the only other state with a tradition of open primaries, exemptions to the closed-primary rule. Other states are still precluded from switching to an open primary.

While the procedures for choosing convention delegates have not engendered major political or legal controversies within the Republican party, the formula for apportioning the delegates has. The Republicans determine the size of each delegation on the basis of three criteria: statehood (6 delegates), House districts (3 per district), and support for Republican candidates elected within the previous four years (1 for a Republican governor, 1 for each Republican senator, 1 if the Republicans win at least half of the Congressional districts in one of the two congressional elections, and a bonus of 4.5 delegates plus 60 percent of the electoral vote if the state voted for the Republican presidential candidate in the last election).

This apportionment formula effectively discriminates against the larger states in two ways. First, it awards many of the bonus delegates to a state without regard to its size. Thus, the voting strength of the larger states is proportionally reduced by the bonuses, while that of the smaller states is increased. Secondly, since the larger states are more competitive, they are less likely to be awarded bonus delegates on a recurring basis. Particularly hard hit are states in the Northeast and Midwest, such as New York, Pennsylvania, and Ohio.

The Ripon Society, a moderate Republican organization, has continually challenged the constitutionality of this apportionment rule, but it has not been successful. The first of these challenges, initiated in the form of a lawsuit, was declared moot when a decision was delayed until after the 1972 Republican convention. A second case, begun in 1975, challenged the formula on the grounds that it violated the Supreme Court's "one person-one vote" rule. This argument was rejected by the U.S. Court of Appeals for the District of Columbia, and the Supreme

Table 4–2   DELEGATE APPORTIONMENT IN 1984 AND 1988

Democratic Party			Republican Party		
State	1984	1988	State	1984	1988
Alabama	62	61	Alabama	38	38
Alaska	14	17	Alaska	18	19
Arizona	40	40	Arizona	32	33
Arkansas	42	43	Arkansas	29	27
California	345	336	California	176	175
Colorado	51	51	Colorado	35	36
Connecticut	60	59	Connecticut	35	35
Delaware	18	19	Delaware	19	17
District of Columbia	19	24	District of Columbia	14	14
Florida	143	146	Florida	82	82
Georgia	84	86	Georgia	37	48
Hawaii	27	25	Hawaii	14	20
Idaho	22	23	Idaho	21	22
Illinois	194	187	Illinois	93	92
Indiana	88	85	Indiana	52	51
Iowa	58	58	Iowa	37	37
Kansas	44	43	Kansas	32	34
Kentucky	63	60	Kentucky	37	38*
Louisiana	69	71	Louisiana	41	41*
Maine	27	27	Maine	20	22
Maryland	74	78	Maryland	31	41
Massachusetts	116	109	Massachusetts	52	52
Michigan	155	151	Michigan	77	77
Minnesota	86	86	Minnesota	32	31
Mississippi	43	45	Mississippi	30	31*
Missouri	86	83	Missouri	47	47
Montana	25	25	Montana	20	20
Nebraska	30	29	Nebraska	24	25

Court has refused to intervene. The Society has continued to contest the rules within the party, but to no avail.

The Democratic apportionment formula has also been subject to some controversy. Under the plan used since 1968 and modified in 1976, the Democrats have allotted 50 percent of each state delegation on the basis of the state's electoral vote, and 50 percent on the basis of its average Democratic vote in the last three presidential elections. The rule for apportionment was challenged in 1971 on the grounds that it did not conform to the "one person-one vote" principle, but the Court of Appeals asserted that it did not violate the equal-protection clause of the Fourteenth Amendment. The Democratic formula results in even larger conventions than the Republican. Table 4–2 lists the apportion-

Table 4–2   DELEGATE APPORTIONMENT IN 1984 AND 1988 (Continued)

Democratic Party			Republican Party		
State	1984	1988	State	1984	1988
Nevada	20	21	Nevada	22	20
New Hampshire	22	22	New Hampshire	22	23
New Jersey	122	118	New Jersey	64	64
New Mexico	28	28	New Mexico	24	26
New York	285	275	New York	136	136
North Carolina	88	89	North Carolina	53	54
North Dakota	18	20	North Dakota	18	16
Ohio	175	174	Ohio	89	88
Oklahoma	53	51	Oklahoma	35	36
Oregon	50	51	Oregon	32	32
Pennsylvania	195	193	Pennsylvania	98	96
Rhode Island	27	26	Puerto Rico	14	14
South Carolina	48	48	Rhode Island	14	21
South Dakota	19	19	South Carolina	35	37
Tennessee	76	77	South Dakota	19	18
Texas	200	198	Tennessee	46	45
Utah	27	27	Texas	109	111
Vermont	17	19	Utah	26	26
Virginia	78	85	Vermont	19	17
Washington	70	72	Virginia	50	50
West Virginia	44	44	Virgin Islands	4	4
Wisconsin	89	88	Washington	44	41
Wyoming	15	18	West Virginia	19	28
American Samoa	6	4	Wisconsin	46	47
Democrats Abroad	5	9	Wyoming	18	18
Guam	7	4	Guam	4	4
Latin America	5		Totals	2,235	2,277
Puerto Rico	53	56			
Virgin Islands	6	4			
Unassigned Super-delegates†		253			
Totals	3,933	4,160			

*May be increased by 1 if a Republican governor is elected in 1987.
†Members of Congress to be chosen between April 19 and May 7, 1988.

ment of Republican and Democratic convention delegates for 1984 and 1988.

THE IMPACT OF THE RULES CHANGES

The new rules have produced some of their desired effects. They have opened up the nomination process by allowing more people to participate. They have increased minority representation at the conventions. But they have also decreased the influence of state party leaders over the selection of delegates and ultimately weakened the power of party leaders in the presidential electoral process.

Turnout

One objective of the reforms was to involve more of the party's rank and file in the delegate selection process. This has been achieved. Turnout has increased. In 1968, before the reforms, only 12 million people participated in primaries. In 1972, the first nomination contest after changes were made, that number rose to 22 million. These figures have continued to rise: 1976—29 million; 1980—32 million; and 1984, with only one party having a contested nomination—26 million.

Turnout in Democratic primaries in 1984 was greater than it was in 1980. The competitiveness of the nomination, the appeal of Jesse Jackson to those who have lower rates of participation, and the absence of a Republican contest that attracted independent voters, all contributed to the increase.

While more people have participated in their party's nomination, the level of participation has not been uniform. It has been greater in primaries than in caucuses, greater in the states that hold early contests than in those that hold later ones, and greater in states where delegates were tied to candidates than in states where they were not. Media coverage, candidate appeals, and campaign expenditures have also affected turnout.

There have been variations among groups within the electorate as well. The better-educated, higher-income, older members of the society vote more often in these nomination contests than do those who lack these characteristics. One study of the 1976 and 1980 primary electorates found the demographic differences between the primary voter and average party identifier to be greater for the Democrats than for the Republicans, perhaps reflecting the Democratic party's heavier reliance on those at the lower end of the socioeconomic scale, those with less education, and until recently, those in the younger age group.[7] The same study did not find attitudinal differences, however. Those who participated in the primaries were not more ideologically conscious or consistent than the average partisan or the average voter in the general election.[8]

There were, however, some changes in the composition of the Democratic electorate in 1984. Jesse Jackson's candidacy stimulated a higher black turnout than in previous years (see Table 4-3). Gary Hart's appeal to younger voters contributed to a larger than usual vote from those

Table 4–3   THE DEMOCRATIC PRIMARY ELECTORATE, 1984

		Primary Voters	Group as Percent of All Democrats	Group as Percent of Total Population
Sex	Men	46%	46%	48%
	Women	54	54	52
Race	White	78	75	84
	Black	18	22	12
	White men	37	35	40
	White women	41	40	44
	Black men	8	10	5
	Black women	11	12	6
Age	18–29	17	25	30
	30–44	31	26	28
	45–59	24	24	21
	60 and older	28	25	21
	Men under 45	21	24	28
	Men 45 and older	25	22	20
	Women under 45	26	27	30
	Women 45 and older	28	26	22
Family income	Under $25,000	54	61	55
	$25,000 and over	46	39	45
	Men under $25,000	24	27	26
	Men $25,000 and over	23	20	23
	Women under $25,000	30	33	28
	Women $25,000 and over	23	19	22
Education	Less than high school	14	32	27
	High school graduate	33	41	40
	Some college	27	16	17
	College graduate	26	11	16
Ideology	Liberal	27	21	18
	Moderate	47	47	44
	Conservative	21	25	31
Union household		33	30	25

between the ages of thirty and forty-five. The proportion of women also increased. Table 4–3 summarizes the demographic characteristics of those who participated in the Democratic primaries in 1984.[9]

Representation

A principal goal of the reforms was to make the national nominating convention more representative of those who identify with the party. Before 1972, the delegates were predominantly white, male, and well educated. Mostly professionals whose income and social status placed them considerably above the national mean, they were expected to pay their own way to the convention. Large financial contributors, as well as elected officeholders and party officials, were frequently in attendance.

In 1972 the demographic profile of convention delegates began to change. The proportion of women rose substantially. Youth and minority participation, especially in Democratic delegations, also increased. Since 1976, when that party changed from a quota system to an affirmative-action commitment to increase participation of certain minority groups, the representation of these specified groups has remained fairly constant. Representation of women has increased, largely as a consequence of the initiation of a quota of 50 percent. But attendance by youth, who have been eliminated from the specified minorities, has declined.

Despite the changes in composition of the delegates, their income and educational levels have remained well above the national average. In 1984, 42 percent of the Democratic delegates had family incomes over $50,000, compared to 5 percent of the nation as a whole. Twenty percent of the Republican delegates had incomes of over $100,000, compared to 3 percent for the nation. Similarly, the delegates had much more formal education than did their party's rank and file. Thirty-five percent of the Republicans and slightly over 50 percent of the Democrats had undergraduate degrees and had completed some postgraduate work. Clearly the 1984 convention delegates enjoyed a much higher standard of living and much greater educational opportunities than did most Americans. This was reflected to some extent by a greater emphasis on middle-class issues and less attention to the concerns of the poor and the less educated.

Another significant change in the composition of the conventions has been the increase in first-time participants. In 1972, 83 percent of the Democrats and 78 percent of the Republicans were attending their first convention. By 1980, these figures rose to 87 percent and 84 percent respectively. They declined in 1984.

Table 4–4 THE DEMOGRAPHY OF THE DELEGATES, 1968–1984

| | National Convention Delegates | | | | | | | | | | Public | |
	1968 Dem.	1968 Rep.	1972 Dem.	1972 Rep.	1976 Dem.	1976 Rep.	1980 Dem.	1980 Rep.	1984 Dem.	1984 Rep.	Dem.	Rep.
Women	13%	16%	40%	29%	33%	31%	49%	29%	50%	44%	55%	53%
Blacks	5	2	15	4	11	7	15	3	18	4	20	2
Under thirty	3	4	22	8	15	15	11	5	8	4	20	22
Median age (years)	(49)	(49)	(42)		(43)	(48)	(44)	(49)	(43)	(51)	(44)	(44)
Lawyers	28	22	12		16	15	13	15	17	14		
Teachers	8	2	11			4	15	4	16	6		
Union members			16		21	3	27	4	25	4	30*	20*
Attended first convention	67	66	83	78	80	78	87	84	74	61		
College graduate	19		21		21	27	20	26	20	28	16	22
Postgraduate†	44	34	36		43	38	45	39	51	35		
Protestant			42		47	73	47	72	49	71	61	68
Catholic			26		34	18	37	22	29	22	32	26
Jewish			9		9	3	8	3	8	2	2	2
Liberal					40	3	46	2	48	1	23	12
Moderate					47	45	42	36	42	35	48	41
Conservative					8	48	6	58	4	60	25	43

Source: CBS News Delegate Surveys, 1968 through 1980. Characteristics of the public are average values from seven CBS News/New York Times polls, 1980. Warren J. Mitofsky and Martin Plissner, "The Making of the Delegates, 1968–1980," Public Opinion (Dec./Jan. 1980), 43. Reprinted with permission of American Enterprise Institute. 1984 data for delegates and public supplied by CBS News from its delegate surveys and reprinted with permission of CBS News.

*Households with a union member.
†Includes those in the category of college graduates.

Table 4–5   REPRESENTATION OF MAJOR ELECTED OFFICIALS AT
NATIONAL CONVENTIONS, 1968–1984* (IN PERCENTAGES)

	1968	1972	1976	1980	1984
Democrats					
Governors	96	57	44	74	91
U.S. senators	61	28	18	14	56
U.S. representatives	32	12	14	14	62
Republicans					
Governors	92	80	69	68	93
U.S. senators	58	50	59	63	56
U.S. representatives	31	19	36	40	53

Source: Hugh L. LeBlanc, *American Political Parties* (New York: St. Martin's, 1982), p. 220. LeBlanc derived the data in this table from Warren J. Mitofsky and Martin Plissner, "The Making of the Delegates, 1968–1980," *Public Opinion* (Dec./Jan. 1980), p. 43. Reprinted with permission. 1984 figures provided to author by the Republican and Democratic National Committees.
*Figures represent the percentages of Democratic or Republican officeholders from each group who served as delegates.

The reason for the relatively large proportion of first-time attendees is the selection process itself. In the 1970s, the only effective way to become a delegate was to run in the primaries or caucuses and win. Party leaders, elected officials, and wealthy donors were no longer assured of attending by virtue of their position or the size of their contribution. As a consequence, the proportion of these VIPs who became delegates, particularly at Democratic conventions (see Table 4–5), declined sharply. To offset this decline, the new superdelegates were created by the Democrats, substantially increasing the representation of elected officials. That representation will be even higher in 1988.

It is more difficult to determine the extent to which ideological and issue perceptions of recent delegates differed from those of their predecessors and from the electorate as a whole. In general, convention delegates have been found to be more conscious of issues than their party's rank and file. Moreover, they have tended to display a greater degree of ideological consistency in their attitudes than other party sympathizers. Republican delegates have been found to be more conservative than Republicans as a whole, and Democrats more liberal than Democrats as a whole (see Table 4–4).[10]

Surveys of the ideological perspectives of convention delegates at recent conventions reveal clear distinctions between Republicans and Democrats. Most of the delegates who considered themselves conservative were Republicans. Most of those who considered themselves liberal were Democrats. Moreover, the issue stands of the delegates confirm their ideological cleavage. Republican and Democratic delegates consistently took conservative and liberal positions, respectively, on a range of policy matters.[11] If these positions were plotted on an ideological continuum, they would be more consistent (or ideologically pure) than the electorate they represented, and much more consistent (or pure) than the general public.

The delegate selection process seems to have contributed to the purity of these perspectives by encouraging activists, who have less of a tie to the party and more of a tie to a candidate and his or her issue positions, to get involved. To the extent that this has resulted in the election of more issue purists and fewer partisan pragmatists, compromise has become more difficult and party unity more elusive. One object of the creation of superdelegates by the Democrats was to reverse this trend.

In short, despite the reforms, there continue to be differences between the ideological and demographic characteristics of convention delegates and those of the electorate as a whole. Convention delegates reflect some demographic characteristics of their party's rank and file more accurately than in the past, but this does not necessarily make them more ideologically representative. In fact, delegates have tended to exaggerate the differences between the beliefs and attitudes of Republicans and Democrats. Whether this makes contemporary conventions more or less representative is difficult to say. One thing is clear: it is difficult to achieve representation, reward activism, maintain an open process, unite the party, and win elections, all at the same time.

Party Organization and Leadership

While increasing turnout and improving representation were two desired effects of the reforms, weakening the state party structures and their leadership were not. Yet these two developments seem to have been an initial consequence of the increasing number of primaries. By promoting internal democracy, the primaries helped devitalize party organizations already weakened by new modes of campaigning and party leadership already weakened by the loss of patronage opportunities and growth of social services.[12]

In contrast, the growth of participatory caucuses may have actually strengthened parties by enlarging the pool of citizens who by virtue of their attendance at the caucuses were more likely to engage in other party activities.

Another consequence of the rules changes is that seeking the nomination has become a self-selection process. When combined with government subsidies during the primaries, the reforms have encouraged the proliferation of candidates. This proliferation, in turn, has led to the creation of separate electoral organizations to seek delegate support. Composed largely of activists devoted to the election of a particular candidate, and often to that candidate's policy orientation, these organizations rival the regular party organization in the general election and pose additional problems for it when the election is over.

They also undercut the power of elected party leaders. No longer able to control their state's delegation, much less guarantee themselves and their supporters a place in it, these party officials have to compete with the supporters of the successful candidate for influence over the campaign, and, if successful, for recognition by the new administration. Winning candidates who did not owe their victory to the regular party organization have less reason to depend on it once the election is over and, conversely, more reason to try to take it over.

The addition of party leader and elected official delegates and super-delegates, has begun to reverse this trend. Moreover, the increasing importance of state and local committees in providing funds and organizational support for the general election has benefited state party officials.

Winners and Losers

Rules changes are never neutral. They usually benefit one group at the expense of another. Similarly, they tend to help certain candidates and hurt others. That is the reason candidates have tried to influence the rules, and why the rules themselves have been changed so frequently. Candidate organizations and interest groups have put continuous pressure on the Democratic party to amend the rules, to increase their own clout in the selection process.

Clearly, the prohibition of discrimination, the requirement for affirmative action, and the rule requiring an equal number of men and women in state delegations has improved representation for women and minorities. These changes also have reduced the proportion of white, male, and older delegates who attend. For candidates seeking the party's nomination, this has necessitated that slates of delegates supporting a candidate be demographically balanced to ensure that a multitude of groups are included.

The openness of the process and the greater participation by the party's rank and file has encouraged those who have not been party activists to become involved. This has forced aspirants for the nomination to depend more on the organizing capacities of their own campaign supporters and less on the energies, endorsements, and organizations of state party leaders.

The requirement of proportional voting by the Democrats has also been profound. Not only has it fragmented the party, but initially, it weakened the clout of the larger, more heterogeneous states and increased that of the less competitive, more homogeneous ones. However, the acceptability of the winner-take-all and winner-take-more formulas for apportioning delegates within districts has reversed although not eliminated some of these power shifts within the party.

The proliferation of primaries and the elongation of the prenomination process has also benefited certain states at the expense of others. The early prewindow contests have received disproportionate attention. All of these changes have forced candidates to adjust their strategies accordingly.

CAMPAIGNING FOR DELEGATES

The rules changes, new finance laws, and television coverage have all affected nomination seeking. In the past, entering primaries was optional for leading candidates, and required only for those who did not enjoy party support or national recognition. Today, it is essential for everyone, even an incumbent President. No longer can a front-runner safely sit on the sidelines and wait for the call. The winds of a draft may be hard to resist but, more often than not, it is the candidate who is manning the bellows.

In the past, candidates carefully chose the primaries they would enter and concentrated their efforts where they thought they would run best. Today, they have much less discretion. By allocating delegates on the basis of a proportional primary vote or multistage convention system, the nomination process now provides incentives for campaigning in a larger number of states.

Strategy and tactics have naturally changed. There are now new answers to the old questions: when to declare, where to run, how to organize, what to claim, and how to win. Before 1972, it was considered wise to wait for an opportune moment in the spring of the presidential election year before announcing one's candidacy. Adlai Stevenson did not announce his intentions until the Democratic convention. John F.

Kennedy made his announcement two months before the New Hampshire primary. It was considered wise to restrict primary efforts, obtain the backing of the state party leaders, and work through their organizations. The successful candidates were those who could unify the party. They took few chances. The object of their campaign was to maintain a winning image.

Basic Strategic Guidelines

Plan Far Ahead. Much of this conventional wisdom is no longer valid. Today, it is necessary, especially for lesser-known candidates, to plan their campaigns early. Whether or not candidates choose to make a formal public declaration, they must create an organization, devise a strategy, and raise money well in advance of the first caucuses and primaries. These needs prompted George McGovern to announce his candidacy for the 1972 presidential nomination in January 1971, almost a year and a half before the Democratic convention, and Jimmy Carter to begin his quest in 1974, two years before the 1976 Democratic convention. The earliest official announcement for a 1988 nomination was by Republican Pierre Du Pont IV of Delaware, who formally declared his intention to run in September 1986.[13]

Regardless of the date the official announcement is made, it is now common practice to begin campaigning three to four years before the nomination. Republicans George Bush, Jack Kemp, and Pat Robertson had field organizations contesting for delegates in the first stage of the Michigan caucuses in the summer of 1986, two full years before the Republican convention. Democrat Richard Gephardt had already made twenty-five trips to Iowa and spent forty-one days in the state one year before the initial round of the caucus selection process. Other hopefuls of both parties were busy raising funds, hiring consultants, establishing organizations, and planning their initial forays into those states that held their contests first. By the end of 1986 most had made frequent trips to Iowa and New Hampshire, designated their coordinators for both states, begun to build their state organizations, get their endorsements, and prepare their initial fund-raising efforts.

Do Better Than Expected. Doing well in the initial caucuses and primaries and qualifying for matching grants are the principal public aims of most candidates today. The early contests are particularly important for lesser-known aspirants, less for the number of delegates they can win than for the amount of publicity they can generate and the recognition they can gain as a consequence.

The initial round of the Iowa caucuses has received extensive coverage in recent years. As the first "official" contest for convention delegates, it has assumed importance far beyond the numbers of people who participate or number of delegates who are chosen. Carter in 1976, Bush in 1980, and Hart in 1984 got great boosts from their unexpected showings in this state. Conversely, Ronald Reagan (1980) and John Glenn (1984) were seriously hurt by their performances in Iowa.

To see the impact of Iowa on particular candidates, look at what happened to Gary Hart in 1984. He received only 16.5 percent of the Democratic vote, compared to Mondale's 48.9 percent, George McGovern's 10.3 percent, and John Glenn's 3.5 percent.[14] But Mondale's victory was expected; Hart's second-place finish was not. As a consequence, he shared the media spotlight with Mondale, but profited from more laudatory coverage.

A similar thing had happened to George Bush four years earlier. A straw poll of the participants at the Republican caucuses in Iowa gave him a 6 percent lead over Ronald Reagan. His small lead was big news. Bush quadrupled his media coverage.[15] He quickly moved in the public-opinion polls from support of less than 10 percent among the Republican rank and file to 28 percent, almost as much as his principal opponent, Reagan.[16]

Media coverage can have a negative effect as well. In Bush's case, his upset of Reagan in Iowa in 1980 and a subsequent victory in Puerto Rico enhanced expectations for his performance in later contests. When he lost the New Hampshire primary to Reagan, his defeat was magnified by his two previous wins.

Before 1980, New Hampshire, traditionally the first state to hold a presidential primary, ranked first in the amount of attention it received. Naturally, candidates who did surprisingly well in this primary benefited enormously. Eugene McCarthy in 1968, George McGovern in 1972, and Jimmy Carter in 1976 all gained visibility and credibility from their New Hampshire performances, even though none had a majority of the vote and only Carter had even a plurality.

Winning New Hampshire after his Iowa performance propelled Gary Hart onto the front page and into the nightly news. He became a topic of intense interest. He gained recognition. Before Iowa less than half the electorate had ever heard of him and only 3 percent of the Democrats wanted him as their nominee. After New Hampshire, 90 percent had heard of him and 33 percent wanted him to be the Democratic candidate.

In addition to visibility, Hart also received serious scrutiny for the first time. In the days that followed his New Hampshire win, questions about his change of name, his age, and his family began to tarnish his image. He discovered, as George Bush had four years earlier, that winning unexpectedly in the early contests is a mixed blessing. The reason is that the media treat viable candidates more seriously. There is more investigative reporting and more explicit criticism of them. In general, front-runners receive more negative coverage than do non–front-runners.[17]

Nonetheless, for the non–front-runner, there is no option. These early contests provide a chance to gain national recognition and establish credentials as a viable candidate. With less money, a smaller organization, and fewer volunteers and partisan supporters, the non–front-runner has no choice but to compete. The stakes are great but the odds are not good. The failure to stand out may force the non–front-runner to drop out. On the other hand, winning is no guarantee of future success; it is simply an opportunity to continue.

For the front-runner the needs and opportunities are different. The initial caucuses and primaries present a situation in which superior resources can be used to eliminate or preclude competition, demonstrate electibility, perhaps even invulnerability, and build a delegate lead. Winning confirms the front-runner's status; losing jeopardizes it, but recovery is possible, as Reagan showed in 1980 and Mondale in 1984.

Raise and Spend Big Bucks Early. The candidates who plan far ahead and do better than expected can reap significant fund-raising advantages. Walter Mondale pursued an early big bucks strategy in 1984 with considerable success. He desired to raise as much as possible as early as possible to "max his match," to outspend his opponents, and to pay for his large organization.

Mondale was the first Democrat to qualify for government matching funds in 1984. He did so within 48 hours! So quickly did his staff seek contributions of $250 or less that several of the checks that had been collected had not even been signed by the donors and had to be returned for signature. In January 1984 Mondale received the first check from the FEC, which the media dutifully reported.

Mondale's second objective was to appear financially dominant, to outraise and outspend his potential opponents, to secure the maximum gifts possible from principal Democratic contributors, and, he hoped, to dry up potential funds for others. The Mondale organization operated on the principle that big money is smart money and goes primarily to the candidate contributors believe will win.

Third, Mondale needed money to compete, to fund his strategy of contesting every straw vote, caucus, and primary. This required a large national office, field representatives, and appropriate "educational" efforts in the early states. By the end of February, after only one set of caucuses and one primary had been held, he had spent one-half of the total permitted during the entire nomination process! (See Figure 4–1.)

Mondale's early expenditure of funds points to the problem today's aspirants for their party's nomination face: how to stay within the legal spending limits, particularly in the small early states. A variety of techniques have been utilized. Campaign workers sleep and, if possible, eat in neighboring states. Some are even paid from out-of-state budgets. Candidates and their staffs take interstate flights with stopovers in the critical states so that the air fares will not be subject to the state ceilings. Nonetheless, Mondale exceeded the limits in both Iowa and New Hampshire.

To overcome the spending limits problem, John Connally had gone a step further in 1980. Believing that he could not defeat Ronald Reagan if he could not outspend him, Connally refused federal matching funds so as not to be bound by the restrictions on expenditures. Reverend Pat Robertson has indicated that he may not accept matching funds in 1988.

The principal risk with heavy up-front spending is lack of funds later if they are needed. Mondale faced this difficulty in 1984. He was forced to cut back on his staff and reduce their salaries while his opponent, Gary Hart, was adding to his staff and increasing his expenditures. Figure 4–1

Figure 4–1   CANDIDATE EXPENDITURES AND DELEGATE
SELECTION

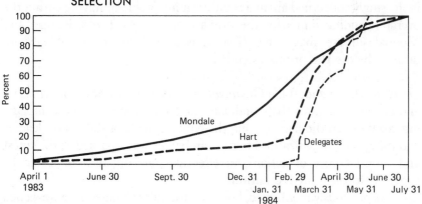

Excludes Fund-Raising Expenditures

Source: Gary R. Orren, "The Nomination Process: Vicissitudes of Candidate Selection," in Michael Nelson (ed.), *The Elections of 1984* (Washington, D.C.: Congressional Quarterly, 1985), p. 48. Orren uses data provided by the Federal Election Commission. Reprinted with permission of the Congressional Quarterly Inc.

traces the expenditures of Mondale and Hart during the 1984 nomination, as well as the accumulation of delegates during this period.

For a non–front-runner, such as Hart in 1984, the problem was just the opposite: how to raise sufficient money to mount a serious effort in the beginning. Hart's campaign was so short of funds in the winter of 1984 that he had to take out a second mortgage on his home to pay for staff and media. Once he did better than expected in Iowa and won the New Hampshire primary, the donations began to flow and credit was extended to his campaign. This resulted in a $4 million debt when he lost, a debt that plagued his abortive 1988 quest for the Democratic nomination.

The need to have large sums early will be exacerbated in 1988 by the southern regional primaries and the movement of other caucuses and primaries toward the beginning of the nomination cycle. To take advantage of any boost that Iowa or New Hampshire may provide, it will be necessary to fund simultaneous media campaigns in a number of states. At a minimum, Democrats estimate they will need about eight million dollars and Republicans, ten to twelve million, to do so.

Two principal consequences follow from the need for early money; the financial campaign in the years before the nomination has assumed greater importance than in the past, and non–front-runners are disadvantaged even more than they were previously. The odds against a little-known outsider using Iowa and New Hampshire as a stepping stone to the nomination have lengthened in recent years. Candidates also have to be increasingly concerned about a countervailing problem, staying within the overall spending limits for the primary period. As it was, Reagan and Mondale almost "maxed-out" (that is, used all of their permissible expenditures) before the primaries ended.

Develop a Deep and Wide Organization. The concentration of primaries and caucuses requires that candidates create a deep and wide campaign organization. In the past, getting the endorsements of state party leaders and using their organizations to run campaigns was regarded as the surest and easiest course of action. An effective state organization could be expected to turn out the faithful.

As previously mentioned, however, the rules changes have weakened the ability of state party leaders to deliver the votes. This fact, along with the need to run in many primaries during a fairly short period of time, has required the creation of separate candidate organizations. The Republicans have generally established separate units within each state, while the Democrats have usually opted for more centralized structures that hopscotch from state to state. Both types of organizations are large and costly, numbering several hundred paid staffers and thousands of volunteers.

In 1984 Mondale's organization was clearly superior to his opponents'. With a large Washington staff in place in 1983, he was able to mount effective field operations. In the large caucus states, in particular, Mondale won primarily because of his organization. In the primary states Mondale's principal advantage was in delegate recruitment and slating. He had many more pledged delegates running for him than did Hart or Jackson.

The major task of any organization is to mobilize voters. Telephone banks must be established, door-to-door canvassing undertaken, and appropriate material mailed or hand delivered. It is also necessary to create the impression of public support and generate excitement. Doing all this involves a large volunteer effort.

Eugene McCarthy and George McGovern recruited thousands of college students to help in 1968 and 1972. Jimmy Carter had his "Peanut Brigade," a group of Georgians who followed him from state to state, in 1976. Mondale benefited from the support of organized labor in 1984. Union members distributed his literature, identified potential voters, and helped get them to the polls on primary day. Labor PACs rented offices and telephones for Mondale's efforts and made them available to his paid staff. Halls of the United Automobile Workers were actually used for the initial round of voting in the Michigan caucuses. No wonder Mondale did well in that state.

Monitor Public Opinion. With intentions clear, money in hand, and an organization in place, it is necessary to ascertain public sentiment, appeal to it, and perhaps manipulate it. To achieve the first step, polling is essential.

The use of polls by candidates is fairly recent. Thomas E. Dewey was the first to have private polling data available to him when he tried unsuccessfully to obtain the Republican nomination in 1940. John F. Kennedy was the first candidate to engage a pollster in his quest for the nomination. Preconvention surveys conducted by Louis Harris in 1960 indicated that Hubert Humphrey, Kennedy's principal rival, was vulnerable in West Virginia and Wisconsin. On the basis of this information, the Kennedy campaign decided to concentrate time, effort, and money in these Protestant states. Victories in both helped demonstrate Kennedy's broad appeal, thereby improving his chances for the nomination enormously.

Today, all major presidential candidates commission polls. These private surveys are important for several reasons. They provide information about the beliefs and attitudes of voters, their perceptions of the candidates, and the kinds of appeals that are apt to be most effective.

In the winter of 1983 Democratic pollster Patrick Caddell discerned a desire for new, younger, innovative leadership among Democratic voters in Iowa. He presented these findings to Gary Hart, whose campaign had not generated much enthusiasm or even much notice to that point. Hart redesigned his appeal along the lines recommended by Caddell, with favorable results. (See the box for Caddell's poll.)

Polling is not only important for designing an appeal. It is important for monitoring it over the course of the campaign. By noting shifts in perceptions and attitudes, candidates can adjust their appeals, and to some extent their positions, accordingly.

Poll results are also used to build momentum, increase morale, raise money, and affect media coverage. By indicating who can win and who should be taken seriously, polls affect the amount of attention candidates receive. In general, the more coverage they have, particularly during the early months, the more volunteers they can attract and the more money they can raise.

The benefits of appearing to be popular and electable suggest why candidates have also used their private polls for promotional purposes. Releasing favorable surveys is a standard stratagem.[18] Nelson Rockefeller, in fact, tied his quest for the Republican nomination in 1968 to poll data. Since he did not enter the primaries, Rockefeller's aim was to convince Republican delegates that he, not Richard Nixon, would be the strongest candidate. Private surveys conducted for Rockefeller in nine large states, five important congressional districts, and the nation as a whole one month before the Republican convention indicated that he would do better against potential Democratic candidates than Nixon. Unfortunately for Rockefeller, the final Gallup preconvention poll, fielded two days after former President Dwight Eisenhower endorsed Nixon, did not support these findings. The Gallup results undercut the credibility of Rockefeller's polls as well as of another national poll that had Rockefeller in the lead, and thus effectively ended his chances for the nomination.

While polls directly affect a candidate's strategy and tactics, their impact on the general public is less direct. Despite the fear of many politicians, there are few empirical data to suggest that polls create a bandwagon effect. There is, however, some evidence of a relationship between a candidate's standing in the polls, success in the primaries, and

CADDELL'S NEW LEADERSHIP POLL

Some people say that different styles of Presidents are needed at different times. Which one of the following styles do you think the country needs in its President now?

1. A President who would be moderate, calm, and keep America strong and on an even keel—say, like Dwight Eisenhower. 6%
2. A President who supports an active government in areas such as education, the environment and the economy, while protecting the unemployed, needy, and poor—say, like Hubert Humphrey had he been President. 21
3. A President who would be a new, youthful leader, who would inspire the country with bold ideas and programs for a better future—say, like John Kennedy 49

All of them 3
None of them 2
Choices 1 & 2 2
Choices 1 & 3 3
Choices 2 & 3 12
Don't know 2

I'd like to read you some descriptions of three imaginary candidates. We'll call them candidates A, B and C.

Candidate A is a liberal in his mid-fifties who has a generation of political experience and federal service in Washington. He is supported by many of the party's establishment leaders and is strongly anti-Reagan. He advocates a return to proven Democratic policies and programs, and a strong, active government.

Candidate B is a moderate in his early sixties who has had several successful careers and is now a Senator. He is more conservative than many Democratic candidates, particularly on defense spending and revitalizing business. He agrees with many of the assumptions behind Reagan's policies, but thinks Reagan has been too extreme and would adjust those programs.

Candidate C is a moderate-liberal Senator in his early forties who has served for a decade in the Senate. He supports bold, innovative solutions for the future and the nation's problems, rather than the past policies of either party. He calls for the emergence of a new generation of leadership which will restore a sense of shared sacrifice and national spirit, and puts the national interest ahead of the demands of any special group.

> With all other things being equal, which of these imaginary candi-
> dates would you be most likely to vote for in next year's caucus?
>
> Candidate A   25%
> Candidate B   24%
> Candidate C   45%
> Undecided/don't know   6%
>
> Source: Patrick Caddell, "Senator Smith Poll," conducted November, 1983 as appears in
> Peter Goldman and Tony Fuller, et al., *The Quest for the Presidency 1984* (Toronto: Bantam
> Books, 1985), pp. 398–399.

winning the nomination. Whether the public-opinion leaders win because they are more popular or whether they are more popular initially because they are better known and ultimately because they look like winners is unclear.

Target a Personalized Appeal. The information obtained from polls is used to create and shape leadership images and to target these images to sympathetic voters. In designing an appeal, both substance and style must be considered. Candidates must refer to general and specific policy problems and how they would deal with them. They must try to project a broad orientation as well as some issue specificity, depending on the audience.

In 1984 Walter Mondale pointed to Democratic values, his experience in government, and his support of his traditional policy positions to demonstrate his capacity to lead the Democratic party. In contrast, Gary Hart emphasized new ideas, new directions, and a new leadership style. As shown in his new agenda appeal (see the box), he presented himself as the candidate of the future and Mondale as the candidate of the past.

John Glenn, the former astronaut who was the first American to orbit the earth, pointed to his scientific achievements and political experience as a U.S. senator as evidence of his leadership potential.

In the last contested Republican nomination, in 1980, Ronald Reagan emphasized his ideological and policy perspectives, George Bush his various legislative, executive, and diplomatic positions, and Representative John Anderson his moderate approach and independent mind. All three stressed their distinctive leadership styles.

Designing an image, both general and specific, is only the first step. Potential constituencies must be identified and appeals directed to them. The problem Anderson had in 1980 was identifying a specific Republican constituency. Reagan appealed to conservatives within the party; Bush

HART'S NEW AGENDA APPEAL

I am seeking the presidency in 1984 because I believe this election is a watershed in our history—when we decide as a nation whether we will go forward to claim the future or sink in the quicksand of the past—when we decide as a people whether we will recapture our mission and our destiny or let it slip from our grasp.

I'm here today to reaffirm our need for new leadership, to describe what that leadership involves, and to explain why both the incumbent president and the current Democratic frontrunner cannot provide it.

The election of 1984 is, at its heart, not a choice between Democrats and Republicans, or liberals and conservatives, but a choice between the past and the future.

It must not become a choice between two different forms of reaction—between those in the Republican Party who have taken us back to William McKinley and those in the Democratic Party who would return to the old programs, old patterns and outworn appeals.

The issue in 1984 is not whose recent record is the worst, but whose proposals are the best.

The issue in 1984 is not who seems the lesser of evils but who has the courage to make the great decisions.

The issue in 1984 is not who has the right public relations or who has the right endorsements or who has the right stuff—but who has the right answers for America.

In 1984, we cannot afford to rerun the last election. We have already held it—and we lost.

projected himself as the alternative, appealing to moderates. Without a discernible liberal constituency within the Republican party, Anderson had no natural group of supporters to whom to turn. He ended up splitting the moderate Republican vote with Bush.

Targets were clearer in 1984 for the principal Democratic candidates. Only one aspirant, Alan Cranston, directed his appeal primarily to liberals. Mondale focused on party regulars, older Democratic identifiers, and traditional support groups such as labor, educators, and even women. Hart spoke to the younger generation, the better educated, and the more affluent. He also appealed to independents, who could participate in the Democratic primaries in some states. John Glenn fashioned a middle-of-

Table 4-6   THE 1984 PRIMARY VOTE

	Mondale	Hart	Jackson
Sex:			
Men	38%	36%	17%
Women	39	35	20
Race:			
White	42	43	5
Black	19	3	77
Age:			
18–29	26	39	26
30–44	30	38	23
45–59	41	34	18
60 & over	52	31	10
Income:			
Under $25,000	40	32	22
$25,000 & over	36	40	15
Education:			
Less than high school	51	26	18
High school graduate	43	34	16
Some college	33	38	21
College graduate	31	41	20
Party:			
Democrat	42	33	20
Independent	28	44	16
Ideology:			
Liberal	34	36	25
Moderate	41	37	15
Conservative	37	34	16
Union household	45	31	19
Total Primary Vote	38.2	35.6	18.6

Source: Adam Clymer, "The 1984 National Primary," *Public Opinion,* 7 (Aug./Sept. 1984), p. 53, reprinted with the permission of the American Enterprise Institute.

the-road message to more conservative Democrats, particularly those living in the South, while Jesse Jackson directed his campaign primarily to minorities, particularly to blacks.

Surveys taken during the primaries indicate that these targets did in fact provide the candidates with much of their support. Table 4–6, utilizing data from a computer model of the electorate designed by the *New York Times,* lists the percentages of the primary vote each of the three principal Democratic candidates received from various demographic groups.

Hart did best among white, affluent, nonunion voters. Mondale's strength was his labor support, while Jackson's vote came primarily from blacks.[19]

Once images are created and constituencies targeted, the appeal must be communicated. The mass media have become the principal mechanism through which this is accomplished. In the nomination period candidates tend to concentrate on the local press—making themselves available to reporters and editors, timing speeches and announcements to receive maximum press coverage, buying advertisements to be broadcast on the radio during rush hours and on television during the evening's prime time. Financial factors limit their use of the national media.

Recent nominations have seen their share of creative sloganing. Bush criticized Reagan's economic proposals in 1980 as "voodoo economics." Mondale attempted to reveal the emptiness of Hart's "new agenda" with the line, "Where's the beef?" Offhanded comments, magnified by the media, have also become campaign issues. In 1984 it was Jackson's reference to Jews as "Hymies" in an informal conversation with a black reporter that created a stir and forced Jackson to deny repeatedly that he was anti-Semitic.

All of these factors—timing, finance, organization, and communications—affect the quest for delegates. They help shape the candidates' strategies and tactics for the nomination. Generally speaking, there have been two successful contemporary prototypical strategies, one for the lesser-known aspirant, the other for the front-runner. Jimmy Carter, George Bush, and Gary Hart utilized the first of these strategies in their initial quests for the nomination. In 1980 Carter and Reagan both adopted the second, as did Walter Mondale four years later.

The Non–Front-Runner Strategy.

The Carter strategy in 1976 was to run hard and fast at the outset. Stress was placed on the early caucuses and primaries. Since Carter had a name recognition problem, a major objective of his early campaign was to attract the media.

Hamilton Jordan, Carter's campaign manager, designed the basic game plan two years before the election. He described the early preconvention strategy as follows:

> The prospect of a crowded field coupled with the new proportional representation rule does not permit much flexibility in the early primaries. No serious candidate will have the luxury of picking or choosing among the early primaries. To pursue such a strategy would cost that candidate delegate votes and increase the possibility of being lost in the crowd. I think that we have to assume that everybody will be running in the first five or six primaries.

A crowded field enhances the possibility of several inconclusive primaries with four or five candidates separated by only a few percentage points. Such a muddled picture will not continue for long as the press will begin to make "winners" of some and "losers" of others. The intense press coverage which naturally focuses on the early primaries plus the decent time intervals which separate the March and mid-April primaries dictate a serious effort in all of the first five primaries. Our "public" strategy would probably be that Florida was the first and real test of the Carter campaign and that New Hampshire would just be a warm-up. In fact, a strong, surprise showing in New Hampshire should be our goal which would have tremendous impact on successive primaries.[20]

The goal was achieved. Dubbed the person to beat after his victories in the Iowa caucuses and New Hampshire primary, Carter with his defeat of George Wallace in Florida overcame a disappointing fourth place in Massachusetts a week earlier and became the acknowledged front-runner.

The efficiency of the Carter organization, the effectiveness of his personal style of campaigning, and the lack of strong opposition helped Carter to win eight of the next nine primaries. These victories gave him approximately 35 percent of the delegates selected by early May, more than double that of his nearest competitor. Although Carter lost ten out of the last seventeen primaries, he was able to continue to build a delegate lead over the field. By the end of the primaries, his nomination had become a foregone conclusion.

The Carter effort in 1976 became the model for George Bush in 1980 and Gary Hart in 1984. Concentrating their efforts in Iowa and New Hampshire, both campaigned vigorously and used media to increase their name recall. Both visited the states frequently. Bush also built an impressive organization in both states; Hart did not. Rather, he projected his appeal primarily through radio and television.

Their activities paid off, at least initially. Bush's victory and Hart's surprising second-place finish in Iowa elevated them overnight to serious contenders. New Hampshire, however, burst Bush's bubble. He was unable to meet heightened expectations and unable to eliminate John Anderson to become *the* alternative to Reagan. Bush's lackluster style of campaigning and de-emphasis of substantive issues contributed to his difficulties.

For Hart, New Hampshire had precisely the opposite effect. It propelled him to the position of front-runner. Lacking Mondale's organizational and financial base, however, he was not in a position to take advantage of his newly won status on Super Tuesday. During the time it took him to develop that base, he encountered critical media coverage, which was reinforced by his opponents. That criticism plus tactical errors in several of the large industrial states tarnished Hart's image. This made it difficult for him to reduce Mondale's delegate lead even though he had finally obtained the resources to do so.

To summarize, for lesser-known aspirants, the non–front-runner strategy offers an opportunity to increase their recognition by the public and, at the same time, to demonstrate their effectiveness as candidates. A win, no matter how slight, confounds the odds, surprises the media, embarrasses the front-runner, and energizes the non–front-runner's candidacy. Media coverage expands; fund-raising is made easier; volunteers join the organization; endorsements become more likely; and momentum can be generated, at least in the short run.[21] In the 1988 campaign most of the candidates except for George Bush can be expected to try to follow this route to the nomination.

Another Non–Front-Runner Approach

Jesse Jackson was not a typical non–front-runner in 1984. He did not employ the prototypical strategy. He announced his candidacy later than most. He did not have a large organization nor extensive paid media. He raised money in ways very different from traditional candidates. Nor did he have a realistic chance of winning. Why then did he seek the nomination?

Jackson's objectives were threefold: to promote the interests of those who were not well represented in the Democratic party, to exert influence on the composition of the ticket and the platform, and to use the campaign as a pulpit for his own ideas and a vehicle for mobilizing his own constituency. To achieve these objectives, Jackson had first and foremost to remain a candidate. He needed the campaign.

Jackson did not appeal to a cross section of the party. His support was primarily black and predominantly young, although he tried to put together a "rainbow coalition" consisting of blacks, Hispanics, women, and others he viewed as disadvantaged. He personally appealed for money at his rallies, not at fancy dinners or in sophisticated computerized mailings. He ran only one commercial, yet maintained the media spotlight. Jackson was news. What he said, how he said it, what effect his words had on others, both supporters and opponents, kept him visible.

Others have also used the campaign as a pulpit for focusing attention on themselves and their ideas. Ellen McCormick ran as an antiabortion candidate for the Democratic nomination in 1976. Lyndon LaRouche has used the Democratic primaries in 1980 and 1984 as a pretext for expanding his philosophy. George McGovern entered the 1984 nomination sweepstakes in large part to participate in the public forum generated by the campaign. The likelihood of the Reverend Jesse Jackson along with the Reverend Pat Robertson using the nomination process to extend their beliefs, mobilize their supporters, and enhance their political influence looms large again in 1988.

The Front-Runner Strategy

Front-runners have more flexibility in designing their strategy. They do not need to gain recognition nor establish their credentials. They do need to maintain and extend their constituencies. And like everyone else, they need to acquire delegates.

The principal advantages front-runners have occur at the beginning. A key element of their strategy must be to maximize these advantages. They need to utilize the benefits of a superior organization, financial base, media coverage, political endorsements, and volunteer efforts to overwhelm their opposition. The front-loading of the primaries provides added impetus to strike a knockout blow in the early rounds, when the lesser-known opponents are least able to compete with them. Here's how Carter strategist, Hamilton Jordan, saw it in 1980:

> It is absolutely essential that we win the early contests and establish momentum. If we win the early contests, it is difficult to see how anyone could defeat us for the nomination. Conversely, if we lose the early contest[s], it is difficult to see how we could recoup and win the nomination.[22]

Walter Mondale pursued a similar strategy in 1984. He not only threw as many resources as he could into Iowa and New Hampshire, but he and his staff devoted considerable attention and finances to the nonbinding straw votes that preceded them. It is likely that George Bush will take a similar tack in 1988.

Once the initial rounds have been completed, the key for the front-runner is to amass as many delegates as possible by using an already established field organization and coordinated media efforts. The proportional voting rules dictate that almost all primaries and caucuses be entered, regardless of the prospects of winning. The same rules, however, encourage unequal resource allocation, roughly in proportion to the number of delegates who can realistically be won.

For the front-runner the name of the game is delegates. Winning is nice, momentum is helpful, but delegates ensure continued coverage, credibility, and convention votes. It is the acquisition of delegates that provides a hedge against future losses and a mechanism for maintaining current position within the party and among its electorate. In 1980 both Carter and Reagan easily survived large-state losses by virtue of their big delegate lead and the proportion of delegates they gained even in defeat. In 1984 Mondale held on to his position as front-runner despite Hart's victories in both large and small states, because with each contest the former Vice President got closer and closer to the magic number.

SUMMARY

The delegate selection process has changed dramatically since 1968. Originally dominated by state party leaders, it has become more open to the party's rank and file as a consequence of the reforms initiated by the Democratic party. These reforms, designed to broaden the base of public participation and increase the representation of the party's electorate at its nominating convention, have affected the Republicans as well, even though the GOP has not chosen to mandate national guidelines for its state parties, as the Democrats have. Supreme Court decisions that give the national parties the authority to do so, new state laws that conform to these rules, and public pressure to reflect popular sentiment and improve representation have led to a greater number of primaries and of delegates selected in them for both parties.

More primaries and open caucuses have resulted in greater public participation, although turnout levels have varied with the date of the contest, the level of intraparty competition, the amount of money spent, and other candidate-related factors. The delegates have been demographically more representative than those of the prereform era. Larger percentages of women, minorities, and first-time attendees have been chosen. Attitudinally, however, the delegates remain more ideologically conscious, consistent, and extreme in their views than rank-and-file partisans.

There have been other effects not nearly so beneficial to the parties. Candidacies have proliferated. Opportunities for outsiders have increased. The parties, particularly the Democrats, have become more factionalized at the national level, with personalized organizations, issue activists, and caucus groups developing, receiving recognition, and exerting influence within them. These unintended consequences, which affected the Democrats more than the Republicans, have generated still other reforms (imposition of a window period, creation of new delegates; formulas for proportional voting) designed to produce more cohesiveness within the party without abolishing the original goals. They have also been designed to strengthen the influence of party leaders.

The strategy for seeking delegates has also been affected by the rules changes. Since primaries have become more important, they can no longer be avoided by front-runners, even incumbent Presidents. The days of the power brokers are over. To some extent they have been replaced by pollsters who monitor public opinion, by consultants who project and target appeals, and by those who design and reinforce leadership images.

Given the more broadly based mode of delegate selection, it is now necessary for all candidates to develop a preconvention strategy that maximizes their public appeal. The basic tenets of this strategy include:

1. Plan far ahead.
2. Do better than expected.
3. Raise and spend big bucks early.
4. Create a deep and wide organization.
5. Monitor public opinion.
6. Target a personalized appeal.

Tactical decisions on how to mobilize and allocate sufficient resources to build and maintain delegate support depend on the particular circumstances of individual candidates.

In general, there have been two successful prototypes: the come-from-nowhere approach of the non–front-runner and the early knockout strategy of the leading candidates.

For the non–front-runner, the initial goal is to establish credibility as a viable candidate. Publicly announcing one's intentions, establishing a campaign headquarters, qualifying for matching funds, and obtaining political endorsements are necessary but not sufficient. At the outset, the key is recognition. Over the long haul, it is momentum. Recognition is bestowed by the media on those who do well in the early primaries and caucuses; momentum is achieved through a series of prenomination victories. Together they compensate for what the non–front-runner lacks in reputation and popular appeal. That is why non–front-runners must concentrate their time, efforts, and resources in the first few contests. They have no choice. Winning will provide them with opportunities; losing will confirm their secondary status.

For the front-runners, the task is different. They have to maintain their electability, not establish it. This provides them with a little more flexibility at the outset. Their candidacy may be announced later, although their organization must still be in place early. Particular primaries and caucuses may be targeted, but the first ones still have to be contested. A broad-based campaign may be planned, but the major resources still have to be raised and spent early. Front-runners must take advantage of their organizational and financial base to build a quick and insurmountable lead.

In the end, it is the ability to generate a broad-based public appeal that is likely to be decisive. Only one person in each party can amass a majority of the delegates, and that is the individual who can build a broad coalition. While specific groups may be targeted, if the overall constituency is too narrow, the nomination cannot be won. That is why candidates tend to broaden and moderate their appeal over the course of the prenomination process.

NOTES

1. The groups that were initially singled out were Native Americans, blacks, and youth. Subsequently, the list of affected groups has been altered by the addition of Hispanics, Asian/Pacific Americans, and women, and by the deletion of youth.

2. Some states hold a presidential preference vote with a separate election of convention delegates by a convention. Others connect the presidential vote and delegate selection on an at-large or district basis. By voting for a particular candidate and/or delegates pledged to that candidate, voters may register their presidential choice and delegate selection at the same time and by the same vote. The number of these primaries has increased as a consequence of the rules changes. A third alternative is to cast separate votes for President and for convention delegates.

3. For a recent discussion of the impact of divisiveness in the nomination process on the general election, see Patrick J. Kenney and Tom W. Rice, "The Effects of Primary Divisiveness in Presidential Elections" (paper delivered at the annual meeting of the American Political Science Association, New Orleans, La., August 29–September 1, 1985).

4. The extent of front-loading over the years can be seen in the increasing percentages of delegates selected by the first Tuesday in April: 1968 (7%), 1972 (17%), 1976 (33%), 1980 (42%), and 1984 (52%). Front-loading makes it more difficult to use the early contests as building blocks to the nomination. Today, candidates must wage many more simultaneous campaigns much sooner in the process. George McGovern in 1972 and Jimmy Carter in 1976 did not have to campaign in more than two primaries on the same day until May. Gary R. Orren, "The Nomination Process: Vicissitudes of Candidate Selection," in Michael Nelson (ed.), *The Elections of 1984* (Washington, D.C.: The Congressional Quarterly, 1985, pp. 41–42).

5. Ibid, p. 41.

6. In five primary states that Hart won, the support of the unpledged superdelegates gave Mondale a plurality of each delegation. For a discussion of the impact of these

superdelegates on the 1984 Democratic nomination, see Priscilla L. Southwell, "The 1984 Democratic Nomination Process: The Significance of Unpledged Superdelegates," *American Politics Quarterly*, 14 (1986), 75–88.

7. John G. Geer, "The Representativeness of Presidential Primary Electorates" (paper delivered at the annual meeting of the American Political Science Association, New Orleans, La., August 29–September 1, 1985), 8–11.

8. Ibid., pp. 16–25.

9. It is questionable to what extent demographic characteristics, individually or collectively, motivate people to participate and vote. According to Barbara Norrander, structural characteristics such as those resulting from party rules and state laws, the type of primary, the time when it is held, and the procedures governing the election and voter eligibility also affect turnout. Barbara Norrander, "Selective Participation: Presidential Primary Voters as a Subset of General Election Voters," *American Politics Quarterly*, 14 (1986), 35–53.

Norrander and Gregg W. Smith have found that these factors have differing impacts depending on which party controls the White House. For the party in power, the amount of money spent and the educational level of the state seem most important. For the party out of power, more candidates, more money, and more media attention have produced more votes. Barbara Norrander and Gregg W. Smith, "Type of Contest, Candidate Strategy, and Turnout in Presidential Primaries," *American Politics Quarterly*, 13 (1985), 28–50.

10. A study of delegates at the 1956 Republican convention claimed that they were so conservative that most Republican party identifiers were actually closer to the Democratic delegates' positions on a range of issues than they were to those of the Republican delegates. Herbert McCloskey et al., "Issue Conflict and Consensus Among Party Leaders and Followers," *American Political Science Review*, 54 (1960), 406–427.

In 1972, Jeane Kirkpatrick discovered that the pattern was reversed. Democratic rank-and-file party identifiers had beliefs that conformed more closely to those of the Republican delegates than to those of the Democratic delegates. Jeane Kirkpatrick, "Representation in the American National Conventions: The Case of 1972," *British Journal of Political Science*, 5 (1975), 313–322.

Subsequently, the views of Democratic delegates have moderated somewhat, although they are still more liberal than are those of the average Democratic voter.

11. Warren J. Mitofsky and Martin Plissner, "The Making of the Delegates, 1968–1980," *Public Opinion*, 3 (Oct./Nov. 1980), 40–42; John S. Jackson, Barbara Brown, and David Bositis, "Herbert McCloskey and Friends Revisited: 1980 Democratic and Republican Party Elites Compared to the Mass Public," *American Politics Quarterly*, 10 (1982).

12. Howard L. Reiter maintains that the reforms routinized and legitimized long-term changes that were occurring to the party system. Of these changes he mentions "the advent of the electronic media, civil service reforms which undercut the patronage system, the rise of the educated middle class and assimilation of immigrants, government social welfare programs, new campaign techniques, and the nationalization of politics." Howard L. Reiter, "The Limitations of Reform: Changes in the Nominating Process," *British Journal of Political Science*, 15 (1985), 399–417.

13. It is now even customary to withdraw early. Kennedy surprised political pundits by announcing in December 1982 that he would not seek the 1984 Democratic nomination. Similarly he announced in 1986 that he would not be a candidate in 1988.

14. The vote itself was small. Only 85,000 people attended the caucuses, out of 500,000 who usually can be expected to vote for the Democratic candidate in the presidential election. Hart received the votes of 12,500 of this group. See William C. Adams, "Media Coverage of Campaign '84: A Preliminary Report," *Public Opinion*, 7 (Apr./May 1984), 11.

15. Michael J. Robinson and Margaret Sheehan, *Over the Wire and on TV: CBS and UPI in Campaign '80* (New York: Russell Sage Foundation, 1983), p. 80.

16. Thomas E. Patterson, "Television and Election Strategy," in Gerald Benjamin (ed.), *The Communications Revolution in Politics* (New York: Academy of Political Science, 1982), p. 26.

17. Robinson and Sheehan, *Over the Wire and on TV*, p. 243.

18. This tactic can border on the unethical if conclusions based on unrepresentative samples are presented or if parts of surveys that distort the general findings are released. This occurred in 1967 after the publication of Gallup and Harris polls of New Hampshire voters showed President Johnson running behind several Republican contenders. A private poll, commissioned by the Democratic National Committee, was leaked to columnist Drew Pearson. The poll had Johnson still in the lead. What was not immediately apparent was that the poll consisted of a relatively small sample of people taken in only one county of the state, a Democratic county. When these facts became known, the poll lost its significance as a barometer of New Hampshire opinion.

19. For an interesting aggregate-level analysis of state characteristics that affected the Democratic primary vote in 1984, see T. Wayne Parent, Calvin C. Jillson, and Ronald E. Weber, "Voting Outcomes in the 1984 Democratic Party Primaries and Caucuses," *American Political Science Review*, 81 (Mar. 1987), 67–83.

20. Hamilton Jordan, "Memorandum to Jimmy Carter, August 4, 1974," in Martin Schram, *Running for President, 1976* (New York: Stein & Day, 1977), pp. 379–380.

21. According to Larry M. Bartels, momentum is a product of personal preferences that are projected onto expectations. Bartels argues that momentum can best be achieved by a little-known candidate who scores unexpected successes in situations where there is no clear front-runner. What happens is that people who have little substantive information about this candidate project their own desires for an ideal candidate onto this new winner. This increases expectations and contributes to momentum. Larry M. Bartels, "Expectations and Preferences in Presidential Nominating Campaigns," *American Political Science Review*, 79 (1985), 804–815.

22. Hamilton Jordan, quoted in Martin Schram, "The President's Campaign," *Washington Post* (June 8, 1980), A 16.

Selected Readings

Adams, William C. "Media Coverage of Campaign '84," *Public Opinion* 7 (Apr.–May 1984), 9–13.

Aldrich, John H. *Before the Convention.* Chicago: University of Chicago Press, 1980.

Crotty, William, and John S. Jackson III. *Presidential Primaries and Nominations,* Washington, D.C.: The Congressional Quarterly, 1985.

Epstein, Leon D. "Political Science and Presidential Nominations," *Political Science Quarterly*, 93 (1978), 177–195.

Fleishman, Joel L., ed. *The Future of American Political Parties.* Englewood Cliffs, N.J.: Prentice-Hall, 1982.

Jackson, John S., Barbara Brown, and David Bositis. "Herbert McCloskey and Friends Revisited, 1980 Democratic and Republican Party Elites Compared to the Mass Public," *American Politics Quarterly,* 10 (1982), 158–180.

Kirkpatrick, Jeane J. *The New Presidential Elite: Men and Women in National Politics.* New York: Russell Sage Foundation, 1976.

Lengle, James, and Byron Shafer. "Primary Rules, Political Power, and Social Change," *American Political Science Review,* 70 (1976), 25–40.

Mitofsky, Warren J., and Martin Plissner, "The Making of the Delegates, 1968–1980," *Public Opinion,* 3 (Oct./Nov. 1980), 37–43.

Nakamura, R.T. "Beyond Purism and Professionalism: Styles of Convention Delegate Fellowship," *American Journal of Political Science,* 24 (1980), 207–232.

Orren, Gary R. "The Nomination Process: Vicissitudes of Candidate Selection," in Michael Nelson (ed.), *The Election of 1984.* Washington, D.C.: The Congressional Quarterly, 1985, pp. 27–82.

Polsby, Nelson W. *The Consequences of Party Reform.* New York: Oxford University Press, 1983.

Price, David E. *Bringing Back the Parties.* Washington, D.C.: Congressional Quarterly, 1984.

Ranney, Austin. "Delegate Selection," in David Butler, Howard E. Penniman, and Austin Ranney (eds.), *Democracy at the Polls,* Washington, D.C.: American Enterprise Institute, 1981, 75–106.

Reiter, Howard L. "The Limitations of Reform: Changes in the Nominating Process," *British Journal of Political Science,* 15 (1985), 399–417.

Shafer, Byron. *Quiet Revolution: The Struggle for the Democratic Party and the Shaping of Post-Reform Politics.* New York: Russell Sage Foundation, 1983.

Chapter 5

THE
CONVENTION

Introduction

Theoretically, national conventions perform four basic functions. As the party's supreme governing body, they determine its rules and regulations; they choose its presidential and vice presidential nominees; they decide on its platform; and, they provide a forum for unifying the party and for launching its presidential campaign. In practice, however, conventions often ratify previously made decisions. The choice of a presidential candidate is frequently a foregone conclusion, and the selection of a running mate is, in reality, the presidential nominee's. Similarly, drafts of party platforms are formulated before the convention and are either accepted by the delegates with little or no change or shape the character of the debate at the convention.

A variety of factors have reduced the convention's decision-making capabilities. The way in which most of the delegates are selected enhances the prospects that they will be publicly committed to a candidate and that their votes for the nominee will be known long before they are cast. In fact, the major television networks, newsmagazines, and newspapers regularly conduct delegate counts during the preconvention stage of the nomination process, and forecast the results.

The broadcasting of conventions has also detracted from the delegates' ability to bargain and cajole. It is difficult to compromise before a television camera, especially during prime time. Public exposure has forced negotiations off the convention floor and even out of "leaky" committee rooms.

Size is another factor that has affected the proceedings. Conventions used to be relatively small. In 1860, 303 delegates nominated Democrat Stephen Douglas, while 466 chose Republican Abraham Lincoln. Today, the participants run into the thousands. Table 5–1 lists the number of delegate votes at Democratic and Republican conventions since 1940. When alternates and delegates who possess fractional votes are included, the numbers grow even more. In 1988 the Republicans, swelled by the bonus given states that went for the GOP in 1984, will have 2,277 delegates, while the Democrats, augmented by the bonus delegates of elected and party officials, will have 4,160 delegates.

Because of the large number of delegates, divisions within the party have been magnified. There is more pressure from minorities to be heard. These pressures, in turn, have produced the need for more efficient organizations, both within the groups desiring recognition and by party officials and candidate representatives seeking to maintain order and to create a unifying image. For the party leaders and the prospective nominee, the task has become one of orchestration, and the goal is to conduct a huge pep rally replete with ritual and pomp—a made-for-television production.

Table 5–1 DELEGATE VOTES AT NOMINATING CONVENTIONS, 1940–1988*

Year	Republicans	Democrats
1940	1,000	1,100
1944	1,059	1,176
1948	1,094	1,234
1952	1,206	1,230
1956	1,323	1,372
1960	1,331	1,521
1964	1,308	2,316
1968	1,333	2,622
1972	1,348	3,016
1976	2,259	3,008
1980	1,994	3,331
1984	2,234	3,933
1988	2,277	4,160

Source: Richard C. Bain and Judith H. Parris, *Convention Decisions and Voting Records*, 2nd ed. (Washington, D.C.: Brookings Institution, 1973), Appendix C. Updated by author.
*The magic number, the number of votes needed for nomination, equals one more than half.

This chapter explores some of these aspects of modern conventions. The first section describes the formal structure—the agenda and the speeches. The next section focuses on the media—specifically, on how they have covered conventions and how the parties have reacted to that coverage. Illustrations from recent conventions are used to highlight the drama and trauma of television reporting.

Subsequent portions of the chapter deal with the politics of choice—namely, procedural and substantive issues and presidential and vice presidential selection. The third section examines rules fights, credentials challenges, and platform debates as barometers of the party's cohesiveness. These disputes indicate the relative strength of different groups within the party and the importance they attach to prizes other than the nomination. They also provide a perspective on the inner workings of the party, sometimes forecasting the amount of support the nominees can expect to receive from their own party in the general election.

The fourth section of the chapter explores the selection of the presidential candidates. It looks at candidate organizations as they strive to win the convention and then unify the party. Finally, it examines the characteristics of the nominees chosen in recent years.

OFFICIAL PROCEEDINGS

Preliminary decisions on the convention are made by the party's national committee, usually on the recommendation of its chair and the appropriate convention committees. An incumbent President normally exercises considerable influence over many of these decisions: the choice of a convention city, the selection of temporary and permanent convention officials, and the designation of the principal speakers. These decisions are rarely challenged by the convention. Both the Democrats and the Republicans traditionally have turned to national party leaders, primarily members of Congress, to fill many of the positions.

Organizing the Meeting

Over the years, a standard agenda has been followed by both parties. (See Table 5–2.) The first day is devoted to speeches. Short addresses by party officials and state and local leaders begin the meeting. In 1984 the Republicans added sex to the criteria for choosing their first-day speakers.

PLANNING FOR THE CONVENTION

The city where the convention is to be held is usually chosen a year and a half in advance of the convention. A number of factors are usually considered when deciding upon the best possible site. They include the size and availability of the convention hall, its suitability for television, the number of hotel rooms, local transportation to and from the hall, the political atmosphere of the city, its symbolic value, and most importantly, the financial concessions it makes to host the meeting.

The size of modern conventions requires huge halls to seat the delegates and alternates and to accommodate the thousands of others who wish to attend. For 1988 the Republicans specified that their convention hall seat 17,000, the Democrats 20,000. Each party has also required the host city to have 20,000 first-class hotel rooms, including 2,000 suites, plus adequate transportation and press facilities for the conventioneers.

In recent years security has also become a major concern. The 1968 demonstrations at the Democratic convention in Chicago have led leaders of both parties to take elaborate precautions to prevent potentially disruptive activities.

The cost of preparing the hall for the convention can be extremely high. While cities cannot pay the parties directly for the privilege of hosting a convention, they can provide services in kind. Thus, for 1984 San Francisco spent approximately $4 million in constructing facilities for the Democratic party at its new Moscone Center, assumed the costs for much of the added security, about $3 million, and spent another million on other convention-related activities. In return, San Francisco expected to reap approximately $65 million that delegates, alternates, media, and others would spend while they were in the city attending the meetings.

The services that are provided by the host city supplement the federal government's subsidy to the major parties for holding their conventions. In 1984 this subsidy amounted to $8.1 million.

The political atmosphere has also been important in selecting a convention site. Parties and their prospective nominees prefer to launch their campaign among supporters. Being nominated in Chicago in 1860 helped Lincoln almost as much as it hurt Humphrey 108 years later.

Cities can have symbolic significance as well. The Democrats ruled out such cities as Atlanta and Chicago for 1980 because their states had not ratified the Equal Rights Amendment (ERA). After the deadline for the amendment had passed, the Democrats chose Atlanta for their 1988 convention, indicating the party's desire to appeal to southern voters. Similarly, the Republicans' selection of Detroit for 1980 was intended to demonstrate the party's efforts to broaden its coalition to include organized labor, while its choice of New Orleans in 1988 was designed to reemphasize its new southern base.

Four of the six major addresses were given by prominent women, in an obvious attempt to offset the appeal a female vice presidential candidate gave the Democrats. Race, geography, and ideological perspective have also been considered when selecting principal speakers.

The major address on the first day is traditionally the keynote. Given during prime viewing hours to a large home and convention audience, this

Table 5–2 AGENDA OF NATIONAL NOMINATING CONVENTIONS

First Day

Opening ceremonies (prayer, Pledge of Allegiance, National Anthem)
Welcoming speeches (governor of host state and mayor of host city)
Election of convention officers
Treasurer's report (treasurer of the national committee)
Chairman's report (chairman of the national committee)
Keynote address

Second Day

Opening ceremonies
Credentials Committee report*
Rules Committee report*
Platform Committee report*

Third Day

Opening ceremonies
Nominations of presidential candidates
Roll call for presidential nomination

Fourth Day

Opening ceremonies
Nominations of vice presidential candidates
Roll call for vice presidential nomination
Acceptance speeches:
 Vice presidential nominee
 Presidential nominee
Adjournment

*These reports are often interspersed with short speeches by party and public officials.

speech is designed to unify the delegates, smoothing over the divisions that may have occurred during the preconvention campaign, and to rouse them and the public for the coming election. The address ritually trumpets the achievements of the party, eulogizing its heroes and severely criticizing the opposition for its ill-conceived programs, inept leadership, and general inability to cope with the nation's problems.

The keynoter for the party that does not control the White House sounds a litany of past failures and suggests in a not-so-subtle way that the country needs new leadership. If a popular President is seeking reelection, however, it is often difficult to make a convincing case for throwing him out. Mario Cuomo, the Democratic keynoter in 1984, faced this dilemma. He dealt with it by distinguishing between the salesman (Ronald Reagan) and his product (Reaganomics), to the delight of the delegates but without lasting impact on the electorate.

Naturally, the keynoter for the party in office reverses the blame and praise. Noting the accomplishments of the administration, and its unfinished business, the speaker urges a continuation of the party's effective leadership.[1] Katherine D. Ortega, the treasurer of the United States and coincidentally a Hispanic American, gave the Republican keynote speech in 1984.

On the second day, reports are presented by the chairs of the major committees (rules, credentials, and platform).[2] Often the product of lengthy negotiations, these reports to the convention represent the majority's voice on the committees. In order for a minority to present its views, 25 percent of the committee in question must concur in the minority report.

In recent conventions, the Democrats have also allowed unsuccessful candidates to make major policy addresses on the evening of the second day. The deal given Ted Kennedy in 1980 and Jesse Jackson in 1984 was prime time exposure in exchange for their support of the national ticket in the fall. In contrast, ex-President Jimmy Carter, who was not deemed an asset to the 1984 presidential election campaign, was given an early slot on the first day to address the convention.

The third day is devoted to the presidential nomination and balloting. In an evenly divided convention, this is clearly the most exciting period. Much ritual has surrounded the nomination itself. In early conventions, it was customary for a delegate simply to rise and place the name of a candidate in nomination without a formal speech. Gradually, the practice of making a nomination became more elaborate. Speeches were lengthened. Ritual required that the virtues of the candidate first be extolled, before his identity was revealed. Today, with public speculation beginning months before and the selection of the nominee a foregone conclusion, the practice of withholding the name has been abandoned. The achievements of the prospective candidate are still lauded, however.

Demonstrations normally follow the nomination. The advent of television, however, has changed the character of these demonstrations. No longer spontaneous, they are now carefully staged to create the impression of significant support.[3] Signs and posters almost magically appear in the hands of supporters as they march around the floor after the candidate's name has been placed in nomination.

Since 1972, the Democrats have tried to tone down demonstrations. Their convention procedures designate a specific amount of time for nominating and seconding speeches. The period during which demonstrations occur is deducted from this amount.

Once all nominations have been made, the balloting begins. The secretary of the convention calls the roll of states in alphabetical order, with the chairman of each delegation announcing the vote. A poll of the delegation may be requested by any member of that delegation.

Vice presidential selection, followed by the nominees' acceptance speeches, are the final order of business. They occur on the last day of the convention. In their early years, nominating conventions evidenced some difficulty in getting candidates to accept the vice presidential nomination. Because of the low esteem in which the office was held, a number of prominent individuals, including Henry Clay and Daniel Webster, actually refused it. In Webster's words, "I do not propose to be buried until I am really dead and in my coffin."[4]

Today, the Vice Presidency is coveted. Its increased significance, especially as a stepping stone to the Presidency, has generated a desire to win nomination to this office. In the twentieth century five Vice Presidents have become President through succession (either death or resignation); one, Richard Nixon, has been elected to the Presidency (although not directly from the Vice Presidency); and two others, Hubert Humphrey and Walter Mondale, have been presidential candidates.

Despite the appeal of the Vice Presidency, it is almost impossible to run for it directly. There are no vice presidential primaries and no government matching funds for vice presidential candidates. Only one "vote" really counts—the presidential nominee's. Although the convention normally accepts the recommendation of its presidential standard-bearer, recent years have seen a sprinkling of protest votes for others.

Only once in recent history has the convention had to make more than a pro forma decision on the vice presidential nomination. In 1956, Democrat Adlai Stevenson professed to have no personal preference. He allowed the convention to choose between Estes Kefauver and John Kennedy. The convention chose Kefauver, the most popular Democrat in the public opinion polls at the time of his nomination.

Since the choice of a vice presidential nominee is usually not difficult or particularly controversial, a great deal of time is not set aside for it. Moreover, the convention vote on the nomination is frequently made on the afternoon of the last day, in order to leave the prime viewing hours for the acceptance speeches of the vice presidential and presidential candidates. These speeches are intended to be the crowning event of the convention. They are the time for displays of enthusiasm and unity. They mark the beginning of the party's presidential campaign.

Articulating the Campaign Themes

The custom of giving acceptance speeches was begun in 1932 by Franklin Roosevelt. Before that time, conventions designated committees to inform the presidential and vice presidential nominees of their decisions. Journeying to the candidate's home, the committees would announce the selection in a public ceremony. The nominee, in turn, would accept in a speech stating his positions on the major issues of the day. The last major party candidate to be told of the nomination in this fashion was Republican Wendell Willkie in 1940.

Today, acceptance speeches can be occasions for great oratory: they are both a call to the faithful and an address to the country. They articulate the principal themes for the general election.

Harry Truman's speech to the Democratic convention in 1948 is frequently cited as one that helped to fire up the party. Truman chided the Republicans for obstructing and ultimately rejecting many of his legislative proposals and then adopting a party platform that called for some of the same social and economic goals. He then electrified the Democratic convention by challenging the Republicans to live up to their convention promises and pass legislation to achieve these goals in a special session of Congress which he announced he was calling. When the Republican-controlled Congress failed to enact the legislation, Truman was able to pin a "do-nothing" label on it and make that the basic theme of his successful presidential campaign.

In 1984 Reagan reiterated the basic goals and achievements of his administration in his acceptance speech. In contrast, Walter Mondale looked past current conditions to future problems. Focusing on the deficit, he sought to distinguish himself from the President:

> I mean business. By the end of my first term, I will cut the deficit by two-thirds.

> Let's tell the truth. Mr. Reagan will raise taxes, and so will I. He won't tell you. I just did.[5]

Democratic delegates cheered his candor, his directness, and boldness; the public did not. Mondale subsequently found he had made a mammoth political blunder, one from which he could not easily escape because he had made it so clearly and so forcefully, before such a large audience, on national television.

DRAMA AND STAGING

Television broadcasting of national conventions began in 1952. Almost immediately, a sizable audience was attracted. Between 1952 and 1968, it is estimated that 20 to 30 percent of the potential viewers watched the conventions, with the number swelling during the most significant events. In 1980 and again in 1984 an estimated 150 million people saw part of the conventions on one of the major networks.

The major networks have provided almost continuous prime-time coverage. In fact, conventions regularly receive more airtime than does the entire general election on the evening news. In 1984 it took almost 15,000 correspondents, technicians, producers, and support staff, at a cost of $15 million, to produce their convention extravaganzas.

Is it worth it? Are conventions that important? What impact does such coverage have? Does it affect what goes on at the convention? Does it influence how the electorate perceives the candidates and their messages in the general election?

The news networks, the parties, and the viewers would probably answer these questions with a qualified "yes." Conventions are part of the

American political tradition. Not to cover them borders on the unpatriotic. When ABC News reduced its coverage to a 90-minute evening format, it was widely criticized for doing so.

Conventions can be interesting. They do attract the country's political leadership, past and present. They make or at least ratify important personnel and policy decisions. These decisions affect governance.

Watching the conventions can affect viewers' opinions and attitudes. In the short run, the convention almost always boosts the popularity of the nominees and decreases that of their opponents. Only George McGovern in 1972 did not gain as a consequence of the Democratic

Table 5–3　IMPACT OF CONVENTIONS ON CANDIDATE POPULARITY, 1976–1984

1976	Before Both Conventions	Post– Democratic Convention	Pre– Republican Convention	Post– Republican Convention
Survey Dates	June 25–28	July 16–19	August 6–9	August 20–23
Carter	53%	62%	57%	50%
Ford	36	31	32	37
Other/ Undecided	11	7	11	13

1980	Before Both Conventions	Post– Republican Convention	Post– Democratic Convention	
Survey Dates	July 11–14	August 1–4	August 15–18	
Carter	37%	29%	39%	
Reagan	41	45	38	
Anderson	15	14	13	
Other/ Undecided	7	12	10	

1984	Before Both Conventions	Post– Democratic Convention	Pre– Republican Convention	Post– Republican Convention
Survey Dates	July 13–16	July 19–20	August 10–13	Sept. 7–10
Mondale	39%	46%	41%	37%
Reagan	53	48	52	56
Other/ Undecided	8	6	7	7

Source: Gallup Polls taken before and after conventions in 1976, 1980, and 1984 as published in *The Gallup Poll* (Wilmington, Del.: Scholar Resources, 1977, 1981, 1985). Published with permission.

convention coverage. The boost, however, is usually short-lived. Several months afterward, the impact is more difficult to discern. Table 5–3 indicates the levels of support for recent nominees before and after the Democratic and Republican nominating conventions.

Political scientists have suggested three major effects of conventions on voters: (1) they heighten interest, thereby increasing turnout; (2) they arouse latent feelings, thereby raising partisan awareness; (3) they color perceptions, thereby affecting personal judgments of the candidates and their issue stands.[6] Studies have also shown that convention watchers tend to make their voting decisions earlier in the campaign.[7]

Politicians assume that the more unified the convention, the more favorable its impact. This assumption has persuaded party leaders to take television coverage into account when planning, staging, and scheduling national party conventions. The choice of a convention site, the decoration of the hall, the selection of speakers, and the instructions to the delegates are all made with television in mind. More often than not, the result is pure theater.

Movie stars regularly make appearances. Color guards, marching bands, and an orchestra amuse the delegates and television audiences alike. Films about the party and its recent Presidents are shown. Entertaining while they inform, the films provide an additional benefit for the party: the darkened hall makes it more difficult for the networks to interview the unhappy delegates. The newspeople are forced to carry the movie on their networks or to talk from the quiet of anchor booths. This minimizes the divisiveness that a variety of opinions often suggests and the turmoil that thousands of people milling about on the convention floor can convey.

Conventions have also become faster-paced than in the past. Tedious reports and roll calls have been reduced. There are fewer candidates placed in nomination, and the speeches themselves are shorter. The length of the meetings has also been reduced. In 1952 the Democratic and Republican conventions each had ten sessions which lasted over forty hours. By 1968 the number of sessions had been cut to five and the number of hours to less than thirty for the Democrats and twenty-five for the Republicans. Afternoon sessions, when held, no longer receive gavel-to-gavel television coverage.

Major addresses are scheduled during prime viewing hours in order to maximize the size of the audience. A 10:30 P.M. (eastern) daylight saving time acceptance speech is considered ideal. Most nominees try to give their address about this time. In 1972, however, a debate over party rules, and the nomination of several candidates for the Democratic vice presidential nomination, delayed McGovern's speech until 2:48 A.M., prime time only in Hawaii and Guam!

While major unifying events are timed to increase the number of viewers, potentially disruptive and discordant situations are scheduled to minimize them. Raucous debates, likely to convey the image of a divided party, are delayed, if possible, until after prime time. In the 1964 Republican convention, for example, when Goldwater partisans got wind of a series of minority platform amendments favored by Nelson Rockefeller and George Romney, they arranged to have the majority report read in its entirety in order to postpone the amendments until the early morning hours in the East, when most potential supporters of the minority position would not be watching. In the 1964 Democratic convention, President Johnson rescheduled a movie paying tribute to President John Kennedy until after the vice presidential nomination, to preclude any bandwagon effect for Robert Kennedy for that position. In 1984 the Democrats scheduled debate on four minority platform planks, introduced by Jesse Jackson, for the afternoon, before the networks were to begin their continuous prime time coverage.

Party officials try to present a united front, but television does not. In order to generate and maintain viewer interest, television tends to emphasize variety, maximize suspense, and exaggerate conflict. This has meant less focus on the official proceedings and more on other activities. In 1984 the three major networks devoted only 40 percent of their coverage to what went on at the podium. It was the anchormen and the correspondents, not the party celebrities, who received the most attention. On the night of his nomination, Walter Mondale got less air time on CBS than did its own anchorman, Dan Rather![8]

As an action medium, television is constantly scanning the convention for dramatic events and human interest stories. Delegates are pictured talking, eating, sleeping, parading, even watching the convention on television. Interviews with prominent individuals, rank-and-file delegates, and family and friends of the prospective nominee are conducted. To provide a balanced presentation, supporters and opponents are frequently juxtaposed. To maintain the audience's attention, the interviews are kept short, usually focusing on reactions to actual or potential political problems.[9] This creates the impression of division, often making the convention seem more fractured to the viewer than to the participant.[10]

A variety of factors heightens this discordant effect: the simultaneous picturing of multiple events, the compactness of the interviews, the crowd of delegates pressed together or milling around the hall. When compared with the calm of the anchor booth, the floor appears to be a sea of confusion.[11]

Presidential nominees and their organizations try to moderate the negative effect of this coverage in a variety of ways. They make top campaign officials and members of the candidate's family available for interviews. They create photo opportunities for the press. They release personal information about the candidate and private polls designed to present his chances in the most favorable light.

Where there is little discord, they may even try to create tension as a device to hold the audience. The most frequent unresolved question is, Who will be the vice presidential nominee? Unless an incumbent President and Vice President are seeking renomination, the vice presidential recommendation of the presidential nominee is usually not revealed until the morning of the final day. Lyndon Johnson went so far as to ask the two most likely candidates to join him in Washington during the convention, to heighten the drama.

For a variety of reasons, including the desire for suspense, presidential candidates have not made in-depth inquiries about their running mates. This had serious repercussions in 1972, when Thomas Eagleton, the Democratic vice presidential nominee, was forced to leave the ticket after his history of mental depression became known. George McGovern had not been aware of Eagleton's past illness when he picked him. The Democrats were also hurt in 1984, when allegations of previous campaign irregularities and incomplete financial disclosures by Geraldine Ferraro were made at the start of the general election campaign.

In 1980 the vice presidential charade reached new heights. Throughout the first three days of the Republican convention, network correspondents speculated on who Reagan's running mate would be. On the second day of the convention, unbeknownst to the public, officials of the Reagan organization approached former President Ford, who expressed interest in the nomination. As private talks were being conducted, Ford indicated his willingness to consider the Vice Presidency during a television interview. This immediately fueled public speculation and turned the media focus from the convention to the Reagan-Ford negotiations. When these negotiations failed, Reagan ended the speculation himself by coming to the convention to generate support for his second choice, George Bush.

The media tend to play up various other contests, such as credentials and platform disputes. While some of these have had a major impact on convention decisions, others have not. Despite the publicity given to the challenges to the regular Democratic delegation from Mississippi in 1964 and the South Carolina delegation in 1972, neither had a tangible effect on the outcome of the convention, although both had symbolic significance. Similarly, the tight control exercised over the 1964 Republican convention by Goldwater supporters and over the 1968 Democratic convention by those sympathetic to Hubert Humphrey gave the platform debates of those years the character of media events.

Even more controversial than television coverage *in* recent conventions has been the networks' coverage *outside* the conventions. Television's reporting of the 1968 Chicago demonstrations in particular generated considerable public and party criticism. Not only were the networks charged with overemphasizing the disruptions to the detriment of their convention coverage, they were seen as helping to incite the demonstrators by the mere presence of their live cameras in the streets.

Claiming that the events were newsworthy and certainly not of their own creation, the networks responded by denying that the demonstrations received disproportionate coverage. CBS News reported that it had devoted only thirty-two minutes to these events out of more than thirty-eight hours of total convention coverage.[12] Nonetheless, the combination of outside disturbances and inside conflict led to the association of turmoil and division with the Democratic party in the public mind in 1968.

The Democrats also feared that demonstrations by gay-rights groups in 1984 would have a harmful effect on the party. The networks, however, devoted little attention to these events, or to the even smaller demonstrations that occurred outside the Republican convention of that year in Dallas.

RULES, CREDENTIALS, AND PLATFORMS

Adopting the Rules

Obviously there can be a real basis for controversy at national conventions. Since recent presidential nominations have usually not been in doubt, the rules, credentials, and/or platform have become the subjects for debate and often of division. All three can have a major impact on what the convention decides and how it appears to the public.

Rules govern the manner in which the convention is conducted. They are interpreted by the chair of the convention, with the convention itself having ultimate authority. The rules committee can propose changes, but these changes must be approved by the delegates.

In formulating the rules, there is a natural tension between the desire of the minority for extended debate and easy floor challenges and the interest of the majority, especially the leadership, for an efficiently run convention that has a cohesive effect on party members and presents a unifying image to the electorate. A humorous incident at the 1956 Republican convention illustrates this tension. In the nomination for Vice President, Richard Nixon was expected to be the unanimous choice. A movement to dump him from the ticket, led by perennial candidate Harold Stassen, had failed. When the roll of states was called for nominations, a delegate from Nebraska grabbed the microphone and said he had a nomination to make. "Who?" said a surprised Joseph Martin, chairman of the convention. "Joe Smith," the delegate replied. Martin did not permit the name of Joe Smith to be placed in nomination, although the Democrats were later to argue that any Joe Smith would have been better than Nixon.

For the most part, convention rules have not caused much wrangling. Those that have generated the most controversy have concerned voting for the party's nominees. Until 1936 the Democrats operated under a rule that required a two-thirds vote for winning the nomination. James K. Polk's selection in 1844 was a consequence of Martin Van Buren's failure to obtain the support of two-thirds of the convention, although Van Buren had a majority. The two-thirds rule in effect permitted a minority of the delegates to veto a person they opposed.

The Democratic party also enforced the unit rule, a requirement that some states adopted to maximize their voting strength. The rule obligated all members of a delegation to vote for the delegation majority's person or position regardless of their own views. Beginning in 1968, the Democratic convention refused to enforce unit voting any longer. The elimination of this majority-take-all principle obviously reduced the probability that state delegations would vote as units, and ultimately weakened the power of the state party leaders. The Republicans never sanctioned or prohibited unit voting. When the Mississippi delegation decided to vote as a unit at the 1976 convention to enhance its influence and perhaps tip the balance to Ford, there was little Reagan could do or party officials would do.

Among the recent rules controversies that have divided the Republican party, two stand out. In 1952, Eisenhower supporters challenged the credentials of a sizable number of Taft delegates from southern states. Before deciding on the challenges, however, the convention adopted a "fair play" amendment that prohibited contested delegates from voting on any question, including their own credentials. This rule, which effectively prevented many Taft delegates from voting, swung the challenges and eventually the nomination to Eisenhower.

The other recent dispute that became a precursor of the presidential vote occurred during the 1976 Republican convention, when the Reagan organization proposed a rules change that would have required Ford to indicate his choice for Vice President before the vote for President, as Reagan had done. Ford's supporters strongly opposed and subsequently beat this amendment. As a consequence, there was no way for Reagan to shake the remaining delegates loose from Ford's coalition. Ford won the presidential vote 1,187 to 1,070—a margin almost identical to that of his rules victory.

An even more acrimonious division over party rules occurred in 1980 at the Democratic convention. At issue was a proposed requirement that delegates vote for the candidate to whom they were publicly pledged at the time they were chosen to attend the convention. Trailing Carter by about 600 delegates, Kennedy, who had previously supported the requirement, urged an open convention in which delegates could vote their consciences rather than merely exercise their commitments. This would have required rejection of the pledged delegate rule. Naturally, the Carter organization favored the rule and lobbied strenuously and successfully for it. By a 600-vote margin the convention accepted the binding rule, thereby assuring President Carter's renomination.[13] The Democrats have subsequently repealed this rule, requiring instead that delegates reflect in good conscience the sentiments of those who elected them.[14]

Challenging Credentials

Disputes over credentials have been more frequent and, in general, have had greater impact on conventions than those that have involved rules. Approximately 7 percent of all Republican delegates and 3.5 percent of all Democratic delegates were challenged between 1872 and 1956.[15] In 1912, and again in 1952, these challenges affected the outcome of the Republican convention. William Howard Taft's victory over Theodore Roosevelt in 1912 and Dwight Eisenhower's over Robert Taft in 1952 resulted from convention decisions to seat certain delegates and reject others.

In both cases, grass roots challenges to old-line party leaders generated competing delegate claims. The convention in 1912 rejected these challenges and seated the regular party delegates, producing a walkout by Roosevelt's supporters and giving the nomination to Taft. In 1952 the delegates denied the nomination to Taft's son. By deciding to prevent challenged delegates from voting until their credentials were accepted, the convention neutralized Taft's advantage and eventually tilted the vote toward Eisenhower.

Recent Democratic conventions have also witnessed credentials fights. In 1964 the all-white Mississippi delegation was challenged by a biracial group known as the Mississippi Freedom Democratic party, on the grounds that the regular Democratic party excluded blacks. Although the regular delegation was seated, two delegates from the insurgent group were also given delegate status, symbolically indicating the party's desire for greater racial equality. In 1968 and again in 1972, challenges were based on allegations that certain party members had been excluded from participating in caucuses and conventions, that certain delegations did not possess sufficient minority representation, and that some were chosen in a manner that did not conform to party rules.

The California challenge at the 1972 Democratic convention illustrates the last of these complaints. McGovern had won the primary and, according to California law at the time, was entitled to all the delegates. The credentials committee, however, decided that the state's delegates should be divided in proportion to the popular vote because the commission that had revised the Democratic rules for 1972, a commission that McGovern initially headed, had affirmed the principle of proportional voting, although it did not require states to change their law to conform to this principle until 1976. McGovern challenged the ruling and won on the convention floor, thereby making his nomination all but certain. There have been no serious delegate challenges at either convention since 1972.

Drafting the Platform

Traditionally, the platform has been the focus of much public attention during the convention. In recent years, it has been the subject of considerable controversy. The Democrats, in particular, have found themselves divided over a variety of policy proposals. Far from unifying the party, Democratic platform debates in 1968 and 1972 have exacerbated the divisions within the party.

Two often conflicting aims lie at the heart of the platform-drafting process. One has to do with winning the election and the other with pleasing the party's coalition. In order to maximize the vote, platforms should not alienate. They must permit people to see what they want to see. This is accomplished by increasing the level of vagueness and ambiguity on the most controversial and emotionally charged issues. When appealing to the party's coalition, on the other hand, traditional images must be evoked and "bread and butter" positions stressed. A laundry list of promises is frequently presented, with something for everyone.

The tension resulting from "the electoral incentives to fudge and the coalition incentives to deliver"[16] has caused real problems for platform drafters and has resulted in documents that contain rhetoric, self-praise, and unrealistic goals. This, in turn, has led to the criticism that platforms are substantially meaningless and politically unimportant, that they bind and guide no one. There may be some truth to this criticism, but it also overstates the case.

Promises and Performance. While platforms contain rhetoric and self-praise, they also consist of goals and proposals that differentiate them from one another. In an examination of the Democratic and Republican plat-

Table 5–4   SIMILARITY AND CONFLICT IN PLATFORM PLEDGES*

	(N)	One-Party Pledge Only	Bipartisan Pledges	Conflicting Pledges
Election Year				
1944	(102)	70%	28%	2%
1948	(124)	51	42	7
1952	(205)	52	29	19
1956	(302)	61	34	5
1960	(464)	51	39	10
1964	(202)	70	19	11
1968	(457)	77	16	7
1972	(698)	83	13	5
1976	(640)	76	17	7
Policy Topic				
Foreign	(509)	60	34	6
Defense	(166)	74	22	4
Economics	(397)	76	15	9
Labor	(180)	65	17	18
Agriculture	(243)	66	27	7
Resources	(338)	69	22	9
Welfare	(696)	71	19	10
Government	(441)	78	18	4
Civil rights	(225)	63	35	2
All pledges	(3,194)	69%	23%	8%
N Total	3,194	2,218	731	245

Source: Gerald Pomper, with Susan S. Lederman, *Elections in America,* 2nd ed. (New York: Longman, 1980), p. 169. Copyright © 1980 by Longman, Inc. All rights reserved.
*Rows add up horizontally to 100 percent for the three columns.

forms between 1944 and 1976, Gerald Pomper found that most of the differences were evident in the planks incorporated by one party but not by the other.[17] (See Table 5–4.) Over these years the Republicans emphasized defense and general governmental matters, while the Democrats stressed economic issues, particularly those of labor and social welfare.

Party platforms are directed to broad constituencies. As the minority party, the Republicans have sought to extend their electoral base by appealing to independents and Democrats on the basis of national issues, which tend to affect the society as a whole. In contrast, the Democrats have designed their platforms to appeal to many of the groups that make up their coalition. They have tended to emphasize domestic issues, such as those that involve social and economic policies.

The 1984 platforms reflected many of these differences. The Republicans naturally lauded the accomplishments of the Reagan administration, particularly in the areas of defense and foreign policy. Strength was the dominant image the platform wished to convey. In calling for the continuation of increased defense spending and decreased domestic spending, the platform proclaimed, "the prospect for peace is excellent because America is strong again."[18]

In contrast, the Democratic platform criticized the administration's confrontational foreign policy, contending that the United States had not become more secure. The Democrats also raised fears about the nation's future and questions about the fairness of the Reagan administration's domestic programs, urging a more equitable tax system, more government involvement in the protection of individual and civil rights, and fewer cuts in social and economic programs.

Platform differences are important. Despite the conventional wisdom that platforms are forgotten once the convention is over and the campaign concluded, elected officials of both parties have a relatively good record of meeting their pledges. While approximately three-quarters of party platforms are rhetoric, about one-fourth contains fairly specific promises. Of these, Pomper found that almost 75 percent have been kept.[19]

One reason that so many of the convention promises have been acted upon is that elected officials participate in the drafting of platforms; in fact, they hold many of the key committee positions. For the party in power the incumbent President usually takes the lead, exercising the most influence when seeking reelection. For the party out of power, members of Congress, mainly the leadership, tend to exercise the greatest influence.[20]

Accommodations and Disagreements. The platform drafting process has traditionally been designed to accommodate outside interests, but to do so in a way that maximizes the leadership's control over the final document. In the first stage the party holds public meetings and invites individuals and group representatives to present their ideas and make their claims. On the basis of these hearings, the new proposals are advanced and the traditional positions of the party are retained or refined, as are the stands that the candidates, especially the front-runner, have taken during the nominating campaign. An initial draft is then written by the staff and presented to the platform committee when it convenes, approximately one week before the convention begins.

To some extent the committee repeats this exercise. Subcommittees, organized on the basis of policy areas, hold hearings, revise the staff draft, and present it to the full committee, which, in turn, reviews its subcommittees' reports. After the committee has adopted a completed platform, it reports it to the convention for its approval.

Between 1944 and 1960, conventions made few significant changes in their platform committees' reports. The exception during this period was in 1948. A major dispute arose that year over the civil rights section of the Democratic platform. Delegates from the southern states offered three amendments designed to promote a "states' rights" position. The convention rejected them and instead adopted a proposal that further strengthen the party's commitment to civil rights. This led to a walkout of delegates from several southern states.

Beginning in 1964 and continuing through recent conventions, the acquiescence that had greeted earlier party platforms has been replaced by acrimonious debate. While the majority has continued to carry the day, minority proposals now receive attention on the floor (and in the media). These proposals often reveal deep cleavages within the parties.

In 1964, Republicans Nelson Rockefeller and George Romney proposed platform amendments that condemned extremism and urged a stronger civil rights position. Goldwater partisans soundly defeated these challenges. The 1968 Democratic convention witnessed an emotional, four-hour debate on United States policy in Vietnam. While the convention voted to sustain the majority position, which had the approval of President Johnson, the discussion reinforced the image of a divided party to millions of home viewers. In 1980 a major debate over economic and social issues again divided the Democrats.

A variety of factors have contributed to the increasing number of platform disputes in recent years. The development of caucus groups within the party, such as women, blacks, and Hispanics, has generated additional demands on the platform and pressures to politicize the process. These groups have become better organized and more adept at bargaining.

Changes in the selection process seem to have produced more issue-oriented delegates who are less dependent on and loyal to party leadership. These issue activists tend to gravitate to the platform committee and, specifically, to the subcommittee considering "their" issues. This has tended to exaggerate rather than minimize the policy differences among the delegates.

Finally, television has also magnified the problem (at least from the perspective of the party) by providing publicity for platform challenges. Even if groups cannot get their goals adopted and incorporated into the platform, they can attract attention by just stating their positions and making demands. The publicity enables them to gain new members, retain old ones, and take in more contributions. It also provides public "proof" that the leadership is working for its membership.

Although the platform-drafting process has become more open and more divisive in recent years, it has not affected the parties equally. The Republicans have suffered less than the Democrats. As the more homogeneous and smaller of the two parties, it has been subjected to fewer and less intense pressures from organized interest groups. The Democrats, on the other hand, have had to contend with larger and more cohesive caucus groups. Their disputes have tended to be more numerous, more prolonged, and more likely to be decided on the convention floor than those involving the Republicans.[21]

PRESIDENTIAL AND VICE PRESIDENTIAL SELECTION

Strategies and Tactics

There are a number of prizes at nominating conventions. The platform contains some of them. Credentials, rules, and procedures can also be important, but the big prize is the presidential nomination. When that is in doubt, all the efforts of the leading contenders must be directed at obtaining the required number of votes. When it is not in doubt, the leading contenders can concentrate on uniting the party and converting the convention into a huge campaign rally for themselves. In 1976 the Reagan organization focused its attention on winning the nomination; in

1980 it sought to present a united front; in 1984 it orchestrated a corona-tion ceremony. In recent Democratic conventions the front-runners have tried to heal the wounds of the nomination contest by appealing to disaffected delegates to join them and the party for the fall campaign.

The key to success, regardless of the objective, is organization. Re-cent conventions have seen the operation of highly structured and effi-cient candidate organizations. Designed to maximize the flow of information and extend political influence, these organizations usually have elaborate communications systems connecting floor supporters to a command center outside the convention hall. Key staff members at the command center monitor reports, articulate positions, and make strategic decisions.

Floor organizations can make a difference. In 1976, Ford's conven-tion operation was far superior to Reagan's. It enabled Ford to shore up his small delegate lead and prevent defection. Here's how political scien-tist F. Christopher Arterton described it:

> The Convention floor was divided into zones each coordinated by a floor leader wearing a red hat for easy visual identification. In communicating upward, each floor leader had phones tied to the Ford trailer. The chain reached downward into the delegations through assistants responsible for the states in their zone. These assistants could communicate either with the Ford leader in their states or with designated coordinators ("whips") of four to eight delegates. Thus, wavering delegates might be contacted by one of three separate means: by the operatives from the primary floor structure of zones, by a designated Ford "delegation monitor," coordinated by phone on the old geographical desk system, or, by a backup system of eight "floaters" roving the floor, wearing yellow hats, and using walkie-talkies to connect them with the trailer. The Ford committee went so far in their preparations as to have repairmen standing by to replace sabotaged phone lines.[22]

In contrast, the Reagan organization of that year had designated only a few individuals to speak for the candidate. They depended on the geographic leaders of the campaign to pass on the word on the floor. This proved to be insufficient. When the need for mobile and rapid decision making occurred, such as when the Mississippi delegation caucused on the floor before a crucial vote, Arterton reports that Reagan's key coordinators had to fight their way through crowded aisles to get to the delegation, only to find that it was too late.[23]

Reagan learned his lesson. In 1980 and 1984 his convention organization was smooth and efficient, controlling activities on the floor and coordinating those at the podium with media coverage.

In addition to having an effective organization, candidates need a general strategy, the contours of which are shaped by the aspirant's status at the time of the convention. The object for leading candidates is to maintain the momentum, win on the first ballot, and prepare for the general election. For those who are behind, the goal is to challenge the certainty of the initial balloting, despite public predictions to the contrary, and to demonstrate the ability to win the nomination and the election. Thus, Gary Hart in 1984 continued to maintain the possibility of his receiving the Democratic nomination until the actual balloting put Walter Mondale over the top.

Front-runners must avoid taking unnecessary risks. Ford followed this strategy in 1976, as Carter did in 1980 and Mondale in 1984. They compromised on key platform planks but held their ground on rules challenges that could have jeopardized their nomination.

Sometimes it is necessary for front-runners to show their strength. They must be careful not to flaunt it, however, and thus accentuate divisions created by the primaries and caucuses. Once the nomination is assured, the object of front-runners is to unify the faithful and present a united front for the general election. To do this requires reaching out to disaffected members of the party. Reagan's behavior at the 1980 Republican convention is illustrative. He met with women unhappy with the party's stance on the ERA, appeased moderates by his selection of George Bush as his running mate, and appealed to Democrats and independents by references to Franklin Roosevelt and to nonpartisan themes in his acceptance speech.

For the non–front-runner there are two immediate needs: to indicate the vulnerability of the front-runner and to emphasize his own capacity to win the nomination. Two tactics have been employed by challengers to accomplish these ends. One is to release polls showing the strength of the non–front-runner and the weakness of the convention leader in the general election. The objective here is to play on the delegates' desire to nominate a winner. The Rockefeller campaign planned such a move for the 1968 Republican convention. By not entering the primaries, Rockefeller hoped to demonstrate his popularity by pointing to public opinion polls that showed him to be a stronger candidate than Nixon. His stratagem failed when the final Gallup Poll showed Nixon to be the more popular Republican.

Gary Hart also toyed with the possibility of utilizing the polls as a vehicle for wresting the Democratic nomination from Mondale. A nation-wide survey conducted after the final primary showed him running ten points ahead of Mondale in a hypothetical election against President Reagan. In the end, Hart was unable to sway Mondale delegates and had to settle instead for a prime-time convention speech, platform amendments, and the promise of rules changes for 1988, in return for his support of the Democratic ticket in 1984.

A second tactic, one that has been used in recent conventions, is to create an issue before the presidential balloting and win on it. If the issue affects rules that affect the vote—so much the better. Reagan in 1976 and Kennedy in 1980 tried this ploy without success. Their defeats on key votes confirmed their status as also-rans but did not end their campaigns. They then concentrated on the platform. Each had a variety of motives: to influence the party and its nominee, to save face, to position themselves for the next battle in four years. For the most part, the front-runners did not accept these platform challenges, choosing instead to concede policy positions in order to obtain their opponents' backing in the forthcoming campaign.

The Presidential Consensus

The voting for President is usually anticlimactic. Since 1924, when the Democrats took 103 ballots to nominate John W. Davis, there have only been four conventions (two Democratic and two Republican) in which more than one ballot has been needed. (See Tables 5–5 and 5–6.) In 1932 the Democrats held four roll calls before the required two-thirds agreed on Franklin Roosevelt. After the Democrats had abolished their two-thirds rule, they needed more than one ballot only once—in 1952, when three were required to nominate Adlai Stevenson. In 1940, Republican Wendell Willkie was selected on the eighth ballot, breaking a deadlock among Thomas Dewey, Arthur Vandenberg, and himself. Eight years later, Dewey was nominated on the third ballot.

What explains the one-ballot phenomenon? For one thing, the desire to support the winner helps generate a bandwagon effect. The bandwagon attracts candidate-oriented delegates who are more likely to submerge their ideological and issue preferences in order to be on the victorious side. They estimate who will win and then vote accordingly.[24]

Unsuccessful candidates can usually read the handwriting on the wall. They tend to withdraw before the balloting begins. This enhances the prospects for a first-round decision and makes the tally not necessarily indicative of the actual competition for the nomination. Not only does the level of competition decrease as the convention nears but most nomination processes have not been all that competitive.

Two political scientists, William R. Keech and Donald R. Matthews, have categorized presidential nominations as consensual, semiconsensual, and nonconsensual.[25] Consensual nominations have occurred in ten of the last twenty-six conventions. The successful nominee, in five cases an incumbent President, has faced little or no opposition within his party. He was the party's most popular nominee in the preprimary and postprimary periods. Examples include Johnson in 1964, Nixon in 1972, and Reagan in 1984. Each was the overwhelming choice of his party's rank and file. The delegates simply ratified their selection. Their convention took on the aura of a coronation.

In semiconsensual nominations, there is a provisional leader, supported by most factions of the party, who survives the preconvention process to win the nomination. Adlai Stevenson (1956), John Kennedy (1960), Richard Nixon (1968), and Walter Mondale (1984) are examples of semiconsensual candidates. In cases of a semiconsensus, the delegates unite behind the nominee. The convention is a family reunion.

The absence of a preconvention leader characterizes nonconsensual nominations. A number of candidates actively compete to be their party's standard-bearer. The winner is the person who gains a majority of the delegates. Barry Goldwater (1964), Hubert Humphrey (1968), George McGovern (1972), Gerald Ford (1976), and Jimmy Carter (1980) are recent examples. The convention never really coalesces. It is like a large town meeting. Some delegates leave happy, others grumble. The nominee usually loses the election.

Jimmy Carter's nomination in 1976 does not exactly fit this pattern. No consensus was present at the beginning of that nomination process, but one did emerge by the end. This suggests that primaries can *build* as well as destroy party unity, that they can create a consensus when none exists.[26]

Characteristics of the Nominee

The nomination of a one-term southern governor by the Democrats in 1976 and the nomination of a former movie actor and ex–California governor by the Republicans in 1980 also indicate that changes in the preconvention process may have affected the kind of people chosen by their parties. In theory, many are qualified. The Constitution prescribes

Table 5–5   DEMOCRATIC PARTY CONVENTIONS AND NOMINEES, 1832–1988

Year	City	Dates	Presidential Nominee	Vice Presidential Nominee	No. of Pres. Ballots
1832	Baltimore	May 21–23	Andrew Jackson	Martin Van Buren	1
1835	Baltimore	May 20–22	Martin Van Buren	Richard M. Johnson	1
1840	Baltimore	May 5–6	Martin Van Buren	*	1
1844	Baltimore	May 27–29	James K. Polk	George M. Dallas	9
1848	Baltimore	May 22–25	Lewis Cass	William O. Butler	4
1852	Baltimore	June 1–5	Franklin Pierce	William R. King	49
1856	Cincinnati	June 2–6	James Buchanan	John C. Breckinridge	17
1860	Charleston	April 23–May 3	Deadlocked		57
1860	Baltimore	June 18–23	Stephen A. Douglas	Benjamin Fitzpatrick Herschel V. Johnson†	2
1864	Chicago	August 29–31	George B. McClellan	George H. Pendleton	1
1868	New York	July 4–9	Horatio Seymour	Francis P. Blair	22
1872	Baltimore	July 9–10	Horace Greeley	Benjamin G. Brown	1
1876	St. Louis	June 27–29	Samuel J. Tilden	Thomas A. Hendricks	2
1880	Cincinnati	June 22–24	Winfield S. Hancock	William H. English	2
1884	Chicago	July 8–11	Grover Cleveland	Thomas A. Hendricks	2
1888	St. Louis	June 5–7	Grover Cleveland	Allen G. Thurman	1
1892	Chicago	June 21–23	Grover Cleveland	Adlai E. Stevenson	1
1896	Chicago	July 7–11	William J. Bryan	Arthur Sewall	5
1900	Kansas City	July 4–6	William J. Bryan	Adlai E. Stevenson	1
1904	St. Louis	July 6–9	Alton B. Parker	Henry G. Davis	1
1908	Denver	July 7–10	William J. Bryan	John W. Kern	1
1912	Baltimore	June 25–July 2	Woodrow Wilson	Thomas R. Marshall	46

Year	City	Presidential nominee	Vice Presidential nominee	
1916	St. Louis	Woodrow Wilson	Thomas R. Marshall	1
1920	San Francisco	James M. Cox	Franklin D. Roosevelt	43
1924	New York	John W. Davis	Charles W. Bryan	103
1928	Houston	Alfred E. Smith	Joseph T. Robinson	1
1932	Chicago	Franklin D. Roosevelt	John N. Garner	4
1936	Philadelphia	Franklin D. Roosevelt	John N. Garner	Acclamation
1940	Chicago	Franklin D. Roosevelt	Henry A. Wallace	1
1944	Chicago	Franklin D. Roosevelt	Harry S. Truman	1
1948	Philadelphia	Harry S. Truman	Alben W. Barkley	1
1952	Chicago	Adlai E. Stevenson	John J. Sparkman	3
1956	Chicago	Adlai E. Stevenson	Estes Kefauver	1
1960	Los Angeles	John F. Kennedy	Lyndon B. Johnson	1
1964	Atlantic City	Lyndon B. Johnson	Hubert H. Humphrey	Acclamation
1968	Chicago	Hubert H. Humphrey	Edmund S. Muskie	1
1972	Miami Beach	George McGovern	Thomas F. Eagleton‡	1
			R. Sargent Shriver‡	
1976	New York	Jimmy Carter	Walter F. Mondale	1
1980	New York	Jimmy Carter	Walter F. Mondale	1
1984	San Francisco	Walter Mondale	Geraldine Ferraro	1
1988	Atlanta			

Source: Updated from *National Party Conventions, 1831–72* (Washington, D.C.: Congressional Quarterly, 1976), pp. 8–9. Copyrighted material reprinted with permission of Congressional Quarterly Inc.

*The 1840 Democratic convention did not nominate a candidate for Vice President.

†The 1860 Democratic convention nominated Benjamin Fitzpatrick, who declined shortly after the convention adjourned. On June 25 the Democratic National Committee selected Herschel V. Johnson as the party's candidate for Vice President.

‡The 1972 Democratic convention nominated Thomas F. Eagleton, who withdrew from the ticket on July 31. On August 8 the Democratic National Committee selected R. Sargent Shriver as the party's candidate for Vice President.

Table 5-6   REPUBLICAN PARTY CONVENTIONS AND NOMINEES, 1856–1988

Year	City	Dates	Presidential Nominee	Vice Presidential Nominee	No. of Pres. Ballots
1856	Philadelphia	June 17–19	John C. Fremont	William L. Dayton	2
1860	Chicago	May 16–18	Abraham Lincoln	Hannibal Hamlin	3
1864	Baltimore	June 7–8	Abraham Lincoln	Andrew Johnson	1
1868	Chicago	May 20–21	Ulysses S. Grant	Schuyler Colfax	1
1872	Philadelphia	June 5–6	Ulysses S. Grant	Henry Wilson	1
1876	Cincinnati	June 14–16	Rutherford B. Hayes	William A. Wheeler	7
1880	Chicago	June 2–8	James A. Garfield	Chester A. Arthur	36
1884	Chicago	June 3–6	James G. Blaine	John A. Logan	4
1888	Chicago	June 19–25	Benjamin Harrison	Levi P. Morton	8
1892	Minneapolis	June 7–10	Benjamin Harrison	Whitelaw Reid	1
1896	St. Louis	June 16–18	William McKinley	Garret A. Hobart	1
1900	Philadelphia	June 19–21	William McKinley	Theodore Roosevelt	1
1904	Chicago	June 21–23	Theodore Roosevelt	Charles W. Fairbanks	1
1908	Chicago	June 16–19	William H. Taft	James S. Sherman	1
1912	Chicago	June 18–22	William H. Taft	James S. Sherman Nicholas Murray Butler*	1

1916	Chicago	June 7–10	Charles E. Hughes	Charles W. Fairbanks	3
1920	Chicago	June 8–12	Warren G. Harding	Calvin Coolidge	10
1924	Cleveland	June 10–12	Calvin Coolidge	Charles G. Dawes	1
1928	Kansas City	June 12–15	Herbert Hoover	Charles Curtis	1
1932	Chicago	June 14–16	Herbert Hoover	Charles Curtis	1
1936	Cleveland	June 9–12	Alfred M. Landon	Frank Knox	1
1940	Philadelphia	June 24–28	Wendell L. Willkie	Charles L. McNary	6
1944	Chicago	June 26–28	Thomas E. Dewey	John W. Bricker	1
1948	Philadelphia	June 21–25	Thomas E. Dewey	Earl Warren	3
1952	Chicago	July 7–11	Dwight D. Eisenhower	Richard M. Nixon	1
1956	San Francisco	August 20–23	Dwight D. Eisenhower	Richard M. Nixon	1
1960	Chicago	July 25–28	Richard M. Nixon	Henry Cabot Lodge	1
1964	San Francisco	July 13–16	Barry Goldwater	William E. Miller	1
1968	Miami Beach	August 5–8	Richard M. Nixon	Spiro T. Agnew	1
1972	Miami Beach	August 21–23	Richard M. Nixon	Spiro T. Agnew	1
1976	Kansas City	August 16–19	Gerald R. Ford	Robert J. Dole	1
1980	Detroit	July 14–18	Ronald Reagan	George Bush	1
1984	Dallas	August 20–23	Ronald Reagan	George Bush	1
1988	New Orleans	August 15–18	George Bush		1

Source: Updated from *National Party Conventions, 1831–72* (Washington, D.C.: Congressional Quarterly, 1976), pp. 8–9. Copyrighted material reprinted with permission of Congressional Quarterly Inc.

*The 1912 Republican convention nominated James S. Sherman, who died on October 30. The Republican National Committee subsequently selected Nicholas Murray Butler to receive the Republican electoral votes for Vice President.

only three formal criteria for the Presidency: a minimum age of thirty-five, a fourteen-year residence in the United States, and native-born status. Naturalized citizens are not eligible for the office.

In practice, a number of informal qualifications limit the pool of potential nominees. Successful candidates have usually been well known before the delegate selection process. Most have had promising political careers and have held high government positions. Of all the positions from which to seek the presidential nomination, the Presidency is clearly the best. Only five incumbent Presidents (three of whom were Vice Presidents who succeeded to the office) failed in their quest for the nomination. It should be noted, however, that several others were persuaded to retire rather than face tough challenges. An incumbent President's influence over his party, especially before 1972, his record as President (which his party cannot easily disavow), and the prominence of his office all contribute to his renomination potential.

Over the years, there have been a variety of other paths to the White House. When the congressional caucus system was in operation, the position of secretary of state within the administration was regarded as a stepping stone to the nomination if the incumbent chose not to seek another term. When national conventions replaced the congressional caucus, the Senate became the incubator for most successful presidential candidates. After the Civil War, governors emerged as the most likely contenders, particularly for the party that did not control the White House. Governors of large states in particular possessed a political base, a prestigious executive position, and leverage by virtue of their control over their delegations.

The position of governors as potential candidates weakened with the development of national television networks in the 1950s. With most statehouses not located in major population centers, governors did not get as much exposure as Washington-based officials. Lacking national media coverage in an age of television, and national political experience at the time the role of government in Washington was expanding, most governors also did not possess the staffing resources that the White House and Senate provided. It is no wonder that between 1960 and 1972 all party nominees came from the upper legislative chamber or the White House.[27] The nominations of Carter and Reagan have broken this trend. While the rules changes and finance legislation have once again increased the opportunities for governors, they have not reduced the advantage a national reputation and Washington experience can provide as an apprenticeship for the Presidency.

There are other informal criteria, although they have less to do with qualifications for office than with public prejudices. Only white males have ever been nominated by either of the major parties. Until 1960, no Catholic had been elected, although Governor Al Smith of New York was nominated by the Democrats in 1928. Nor has there been a candidate without a northern European heritage, a surprising commentary on a country that has regarded itself as a melting pot.

Personal matters, such as health and family life, can also be factors. After George Wallace was crippled by a would-be assassin's bullet, even his own supporters began to question his ability to withstand the rigors of the office. Senator Thomas Eagleton was forced to withdraw as the Democratic vice presidential nominee in 1972 when his past psychological illness became public. Today, presidential and vice presidential candidates are expected to release detailed medical reports on themselves.

Family ties have also affected nominations and elections. There have been only two bachelors elected President, James Buchanan and Grover Cleveland.[28] During the 1884 campaign, Cleveland was accused of fathering an illegitimate child. He was taunted by his opponents: "Ma, Ma, Where's my Pa?/Gone to the White House/Ha! Ha! Ha!" Cleveland admitted responsibility for the child, even though he was not certain he was the father.

Until 1980 no person who was divorced had ever been elected. However, Andrew Jackson married a divorced woman, or at least a woman he thought was divorced. As it turned out, she had not been granted the final court papers legally dissolving her previous marriage. When this information was revealed during the 1828 campaign, Jackson's opponents asked rhetorically, "Do we want a whore in the White House?"[29] Jackson and Cleveland both won.

In more recent times, candidates have been hurt by marital problems and allegations of sexual misconduct. The dissolution of Nelson Rockefeller's marriage and his subsequent remarriage seriously damaged his presidential aspirations in 1964. During the critical California primary against Barry Goldwater, Rockefeller's second wife gave birth, thereby calling attention to the remarriage and prompting much anti-Rockefeller feeling. "We need a leader, not a lover" was the slogan of Goldwater partisans in California. That Adlai Stevenson was divorced also did not improve his chances, particularly after his ex-wife spoke out against him. Senator Edward Kennedy's marital problems and the Chappaquiddick incident were serious detriments to his presidential candidacy in 1980 while Gary Hart's alleged "womanizing" forced his withdrawal in 1988.

Reagan's election in 1980, however, suggests that at least one former taboo, being divorced, is no longer a relevant factor, at least for those who have been happily remarried for some time.

Finally, the most recent presidential nominees have tended to be wealthy. Dwight Eisenhower, Gerald Ford, Walter Mondale, and, to a lesser extent, Richard Nixon were exceptions. While government subsidies have somewhat lessened the impact of personal wealth on electability, they have not eliminated it entirely. Having a secure financial base contributes to one's ability to seek and win the nomination, and is particularly important in the years before the nomination.

These characteristics of the presidential nominee have in general been matched by those of the vice presidential candidate as well. However, the nomination of a woman by the Democrats in 1984 may remove or reduce sex as a barrier and make it easier for candidates from minority groups to be nominated as well.

The vice presidential search has also been affected by the perceived need for geographic and ideological balance. Presidential aspirants have tended to choose vice presidential candidates primarily as running mates and only secondarily as governing mates. Despite statements to the contrary, most attention is given to how the prospective nominee would help the ticket.

Mondale chose Geraldine Ferraro for precisely this reason. Winning the nomination after a long, grueling, and divisive campaign, facing an uphill battle within the Electoral College, trailing Reagan badly in the preelection polls, Mondale needed a running mate who could unify the party, enliven the campaign, and excite the electorate. The Ferraro candidacy offered this possibility. It provided a demographic balance by having a Catholic woman of Italian heritage running with a Protestant man of Scandinavian background. The ticket, however, did not provide geographic or ideological balance. In the end its overwhelming defeat raised the question whether such a demographic balance was important to achieve.

SUMMARY

Presidential nominating conventions have existed since the 1830s. Picking the party's nominees, determining its platform, and unifying the party remain the principal tasks. There have been changes, however. Caused in part by the mass media and electoral reforms, these changes have resulted in greater emphasis on the public aspects of conventions and less on internal party matters.

Nominating conventions have become more visible and more open as a consequence of television. They have also become more theatrical. Television covers them as news events. It does so by emphasizing activity and stressing conflict, thereby producing the impression of a divided convention. Party leaders have tried to counter this impression by streamlining and staging their convention to present the image of a unified group of delegates. To the extent that they have been successful, the convention has become more an orchestrated political extravaganza and less a participatory town meeting.

The big prize is the presidential nomination. It comes at the end of the convention, but early maneuvering can camouflage the continuous quest for delegate votes. Disputes on rules or credentials are usually fought by candidate organizations, and can forecast the presidential ballot. Platform issues, on the other hand, tend to reflect infighting within the party's electoral coalition. The increasing institutionalization of organized groups has enhanced their desire for recognition, publicity, and policy goals. This has affected the content of party platforms and the process of drafting them. The demands of these groups have also produced more platform challenges.

The tension between the needs of groups and the goals of the party has increased the tasks that leaders face at the nominating conventions. In the past, state party officials made the principal demands. In most cases, their object was to extend their political influence, rather than to achieve substantive policy goals. Today, the reforms have weakened the influence of the leadership, strengthened candidate organizations, and led to the selection of fewer party professionals as delegates—a trend that the Democrats have now reversed with their superdelegates. These changes have in general made compromise more difficult, although they have also tended to make politicians of amateurs and purists. The hope of winning the nomination is still the most compelling reason for giving in—witness Ford's acquiescence on foreign-policy planks in 1976 and Carter's on economic issues in 1980.

When the nomination is no longer in doubt, accommodation and conciliation are the order of the day. For the would-be standard-bearer the aim is to win in November, and the immediate need is for a united party, as indicated by a supportive, nondivisive convention. Naturally, if the nomination is still in doubt, a more pressing goal is to amass or hold on to a majority of the delegates. A tight organization, geographically based, with a communications system that reaches into every state delegation, is an essential instrument. Promises made to different factions within the party may also be necessary. Creating a bandwagon or maintaining a lead requires that the candidate be poised and have a good working organization.

Since the object of the game is to win, projecting the image of a winner is essential. Public prominence contributes to this. To party professionals especially, the best evidence of future success is past success. Factors which might detract from such success, whether political, ideological, or personal, lessen the odds of getting the nomination. This is the reason many presidential nominees possess very similar social and political attributes. In politics, the norm is often considered the ideal.

The changes in the delegate selection process, however, have enlarged the selection zone for potential nominees. It is unlikely that a Democratic convention before 1972 would have chosen a McGovern or even a Carter, or that a Reagan would have come as close as he did to defeating an incumbent President in 1976. Moreover, the selection of a woman by the Democrats in 1984 indicates that sex may no longer be a major consideration—at least for second place on the ticket. It remains to be seen how quickly other barriers such as those of race and religion will be eliminated as well.

NOTES

1. Perhaps the most famous of all keynote addresses was William Jennings Bryan's. A relatively unknown political figure, Bryan at the age of thirty-six electrified the Democratic convention of 1896 with his famous "Cross of Gold" speech. His remarks generated so much enthusiasm that the delegates turned to him to lead them as standard-bearer. He did, and lost.

2. In 1988, Democratic committees will be apportioned by the same formula used to determine the number of delegates for each state. Democratic rules also specify that state representation on the committees should be as evenly divided as possible between men and women. The composition of the Republican committees in 1988 will be similar to previous conventions—one man and one woman chosen by each state delegation.

3. In 1964, aides to presidential aspirant William Scranton, Republican from Pennsylvania, bused students from the University of California at Berkeley to the Republican convention to demonstrate on Scranton's behalf. Armed with signs supplied by the Scranton organization, they marched around the floor when Scranton's name was placed in nomination. Goldwater partisans were furious at this invasion of outsiders. After Goldwater received the nomination, some of his California supporters persuaded officials at the university's Berkeley campus to impose a rule preventing political solicitation on

campus. Berkeley students protested this denial of their freedom of speech. Their protest, known as the Free Speech Movement, marked the first of the demonstrations on college campuses that rocked the 1960s.

4. Malcom Moos and Stephen Hess, *Hats in the Ring* (New York: Random House, 1960), pp. 157–158.

5. Walter Mondale, Address before the Democratic convention, San Francisco, California, July 19, 1984.

6. Thomas E. Patterson, *The Mass Media Election* (New York: Praeger Publishers, 1980), pp. 72–74.

7. Ibid., p. 103.

8. Dan Nimmo, "Unconventional Coverage," *Campaigns and Elections* (May/June 1986), p. 53.

9. William C. Adams has written that this focus has led to networks ignoring significant stories. In 1984, for example, the media missed the defection of moderates and conservatives from the Democratic party and the changing public image of the Republican party on economic issues—two important factors which Adams argues affected the 1984 presidential election. William C. Adams, "Convention Coverage," *Public Opinion*, 7 (Dec./Jan. 1985), 43–48.

10. David L. Paletz and Martha Elson, "Television Coverage of Presidential Conventions," *Political Science Quarterly*, 91 (1976), 124–127.

11. Ibid.

12. "Republicans Orchestrate a Three-Night TV Special," *Broadcasting*, August 28, 1972, p. 12.

13. Carter's renomination was assured because only a small percentage of the delegates were uncommitted and thus able to vote their consciences after the binding rule was accepted.

14. This requirement means in essence that the convention will not force pledged delegates to exercise their pledges. However, presidential aspirants still have the right to approve delegates identified with their candidacies. Once the delegates have been approved, however, they cannot be removed if they threaten to vote against the candidate to whom they were committed.

15. Paul T. David, Ralph M. Goldman, and Richard C. Bain, *The Politics of National Party Conventions* (Washington, D.C.: Brookings Institution, 1960), p. 263.

16. This marvelously descriptive phrase comes from Jeff Fishel, "Agenda-Building in Presidential Campaigns: The Case of Jimmy Carter" (paper presented at the annual meeting of the American Political Science Association, Washington, D.C., September 1–4, 1977), p. 20.

17. Gerald M. Pomper, "Control and Influence in American Politics," *American Behavioral Scientist*, 13 (1969), 223–228; Gerald M. Pomper with Susan S. Lederman, *Elections in America* (New York: Longman, 1980), p. 161.

18. Quoted from the Republican party platform adopted by the Republican National Convention at Dallas, August 21, 1984.

19. Naturally, the party controlling the White House has an advantage in accomplishing its goals. According to Pomper, between 1944 and 1968 the party in office achieved about four-fifths of its program, but even the losers gained some of their objectives. During the Nixon administration, the Democrats actually fulfilled more of their pledges than did the Republicans. Pomper with Lederman, *Elections in America*, p. 161.

20. The head of the platform committee is appointed by the chairman of the national committee usually with the concurrence of the leading candidates. That head, in turn, chooses the staff, invites the testimony of witnesses, negotiates disputes, and generally oversees the process. The committee members, chosen by the state delegations, reflect sentiment within the convention. At least a plurality of the committee tend to support the winning nominee.

21. In 1984 the Democrats strove to avoid or at least moderate their internal conflict. Interest groups were accommodated by specific planks that addressed their needs and concerns. Platform language was carefully drafted so as to be acceptable to three principal candidates. The Mondale faction, which controlled the platform committee, acceded to most of Hart's proposals for change so as to avoid divisive floor fights. Only one Hart plank and four of Jackson's were contested before the full convention, and even here, the Mondale and Jackson organizations reached an accord on the working of an affirmative-action amendment that permitted it to be approved by acclamation of the delegates.

In examining recent promises and performances, Jeff Fishel has noted that Ronald Reagan made fewer campaign promises than any of his predecessors (except Johnson) and has redeemed fewer as well. For the first four years of his administration, Fishel found that Reagan had fulfilled 35 percent completely and 18 percent partially. Fishel, *Presidents and Promises: From Campaign Pledge to Presidential Performance* (Washington, D.C.: Congressional Quarterly, 1985), p. 39.

22. F. Christopher Arterton, "Strategies and Tactics of Candidate Organizations," *Political Science Quarterly*, 92 (1977–1978), 664–665.

23. Ibid., p. 664.

24. Estimates may be based on hunches, on inside information, or, increasingly, on public polls of how the delegates will vote. Three political scientists have even gone so far as to devise a formula for predicting the convention winner based on these surveys. It works like this: Take the candidate's support in the most recent poll or convention ballot (S_1), subtract the support from the next-to-last poll or convention ballot (S_2), and divide that figure $(S_1–S_2)$ by the minimum proportion of the vote needed to win the nomination (Q) minus the support the candidate began with (S_1). The result is what they call a Gain-Deficit ratio (R). Thus,

$$R = \frac{(S_1 - S_2)}{(Q - S_1)}.$$

If R exceeds .360, then the candidate who has attained this critical value should win.

When tested, this formula was successful in predicting the outcome of nine of eleven majority-rule conventions before 1952 and all of them after 1952. Moreover, these predictions could be made even before all the delegates were chosen. The authors found that when 80 percent were selected, the outcome of the convention was predictable. Donald S. Collat, Stanley Kelley, Jr., and Ronald Rogowski, "The End Game in Presidential Nominations," *American Political Science Review*, 75 (1981), 428.

25. William R. Keech and Donald R. Matthews, *The Party's Choice* (Washington, D.C.: Brookings Institution, 1976), pp. 160–167. The discussion of these three types of nominations is based on their description.

26. One testimony to the presence of such a consensus by the end of the nomina-

tion period is that the successful candidate has become the party's most popular leader. The candidate who was leading in the final public opinion poll won the nomination in twenty-two of the last twenty-three conventions. The lone exception was Estes Kefauver in 1952.

27. The House of Representatives has not been a primary source. Only one sitting member of the House, James A. Garfield, has ever been elected President, and he was chosen on the thirty-fifth ballot. In recent nomination contests however, a number of representatives have sought their party's nomination. Representative Morris Udall finished second to Jimmy Carter in 1976; Representative John Anderson competed for the Republican nomination in 1980 before running as an independent candidate in the general election. In 1988 Representatives Jack Kemp (Republican) and Richard Gephardt (Democrat) were candidates for the nomination.

28. Historian Thomas A. Bailey reports that in his quest for the Presidency, Buchanan was greeted by a banner carried by a group of women reading, "Opposition to Old Bachelors." Thomas A. Bailey, *Presidential Greatness* (New York: Appleton-Century-Crofts, 1966), p. 74.

29. Ibid.

Selected Readings

Davis, James W. *National Conventions in an Age of Party Reform.* Westport, Conn.: Greenwood Press, 1983.

Keech, William R., and Donald R. Matthews. *The Party's Choice.* Washington, D.C.: Brookings Institution, 1976.

Malbin, Michael J. "The Conventions, Platforms, and Issue Activists," in Austin Ranney (ed.), *The American Elections of 1980.* Washington, D.C.: American Enterprise Institute, 1981, pp. 99–141.

Paletz, David L., and Martha Elson. "Television Coverage of Presidential Conventions," *Political Science Quarterly,* 91 (1976), 109–131.

Parris, Judith. *The Convention Problem.* Washington, D.C.: Brookings Institution, 1972.

Pomper, Gerald. *Nominating the President: The Politics of Convention Choice.* New York: Norton, 1966.

Roback, Thomas. "Amateurs and Professionals: Delegates to the 1972 Republican National Convention," *Journal of Politics,* 37 (1975), 436–468.

Sullivan, Denis, Robert T. Nakamura, Martha Wagner Weinberg, F. Christopher Arterton, and Jeffrey L. Pressman. "Exploring the 1976 Republican Convention," *Political Science Quarterly,* 92 (1977–1978), 633–682.

Sullivan, Denis, Jeffrey Pressman, and F. Christopher Arterton, *Exploration in Convention Decision Making.* San Francisco: Freeman, 1976.

PART III

THE CAMPAIGN

Chapter 6

ORGANIZATION, STRATEGY, AND TACTICS

Introduction

Elections have been held since 1788, but campaigning by presidential candidates is a more recent phenomenon. For much of American history, major party nominees did not themselves run for office. Personal solicitation was viewed as demeaning and unbecoming of the dignity and status of the Presidency.

This tradition of nonparticipation by the nominees was broken in 1860. Senator Stephen A. Douglas, Democratic candidate for President, spoke out on the slavery issue, in an attempt to heal the split that had developed within his party. However, he also denied his own ambitions while doing so. "I did not come here to solicit your votes," he told a Raleigh, North Carolina, audience. "I have nothing to say for myself or my claims personally. I am one of those who think it would not be a favor to me to be made President at this time."[1] Abraham Lincoln, Douglas's Republican opponent, refused to reply, even though he had debated him two years earlier in their contest for the Senate seat from Illinois, a contest Douglas won. Lincoln even felt that it was not proper to vote for himself. He cut his own name from the Republican ballot before he cast it for other officials in the election.[2]

Douglas did not set an immediate precedent. Presidential candidates remained on the sidelines, with party supporters making appeals on their behalf, for the next eight elections. It was not until 1896 that another divisive national issue, this time free silver, galvanized the country and elicited a public discussion by a presidential candidate.[3] Again, it was the Democratic nominee who took to the stump. William Jennings Bryan, who had received the nomination following his famous "Cross of Gold" speech,[4] pleaded his case for free silver to groups around the country. By his own account, he traveled more than 18,000 miles and made more than 600 speeches, and, according to press estimates, he spoke to almost five million people.[5]

Bryan's opponent that year, William McKinley, was the first Republican candidate to campaign, albeit from his own front porch. Anxious not to degrade the office to which he aspired, yet desirous of replying to Bryan's speeches, McKinley spoke to the throngs who came to his Canton, Ohio, home. The Republican party ensured that there would be large and responsive audiences by recruiting and in some cases transporting many of the 750,000 who came to hear their candidate speak.[6]

In 1912, Theodore Roosevelt campaigned actively on the Progressive, or "Bull Moose," ticket. Republican candidates, however, did little more than front-porch campaigning until the 1930s. Democrats were more active. Woodrow Wilson and Al Smith took their campaigns to the public in 1912 and 1928, respectively. Wilson, a former university professor and president, spoke on a variety of subjects, while Smith, governor of New York and the first Roman Catholic to run for President, tried to defuse the religious issue by addressing it directly.

Radio was first used in a presidential campaign in 1928. Smith's heavy New York accent and rasping voice were faithfully captured on the airwaves, probably to his detriment; the thunderous applause he received in a famous speech given in Oklahoma City on the subject of his religion was not nearly as clear. The applause and shouts sounded like a disturbance. Listeners could not tell whether Smith was being cheered or jeered.[7]

Franklin Roosevelt was a master of radio, and employed it effectively in all his presidential campaigns. He also utilized the "whistle-stop" campaign train, which stopped at stations along the route to allow the candidate to address the crowds who came to see and hear him. In 1932, Roosevelt traveled to thirty-six states—some 13,000 miles. His extensive travels, undertaken in part to dispel a whispering campaign about his health, forced President Herbert Hoover onto the campaign trail.[8]

Instead of giving the small number of speeches he had originally planned, Hoover logged over 10,000 miles, traveling across much of the country. He was the first incumbent President to campaign actively for reelection. Thereafter, with the exception of Franklin Roosevelt during World War II, personal campaigning became standard for incumbents and nonincumbents alike.

Harry Truman took incumbent campaigning a step further. Perceived as the underdog in the 1948 election, Truman whistle-stopped the length and breadth of the United States, traveling 32,000 miles and averaging ten speeches a day. In eight weeks, he spoke to an estimated six million people.[9] While Truman was rousing the faithful by his down-home comments and hard-hitting criticisms of the Republican-controlled Congress, his opponent, Thomas Dewey, was promising new leadership but providing few particulars. His sonorous speeches contrasted sharply and unfavorably with Truman's straightforward attacks.

Unlike the Roosevelt years, when voter reactions to the President were known long before the campaign began, Dewey's unexpected loss suggested that campaigns could affect election outcomes. The results of the election illustrated not only the need for incumbents to campaign but also the advantage of incumbency in campaigning, a lesson that was not lost on future Presidents.

The end of an era in presidential campaigning occurred in 1948. Within the next four years television came into its own as a communications medium. By 1952 the number of sets and viewers had grown sufficiently to justify, in the minds of campaign planners, a major television effort. The Eisenhower organization budgeted almost $2 million for television, while the Democrats promised to use both radio and television "in an exciting, dramatic way."[10]

Television made a mass appeal easier, but it also created new obstacles for the nominees. Physical appearance became more important. Styles of oratory changed. Instead of just rousing a crowd, presidential aspirants had to make a more personal appeal to television viewers. Attention began to focus on the images candidates projected, in addition to the positions they presented.

The use of public-relations techniques influenced how campaigns were planned and who planned them, what messages could be conveyed, and when and by what means. Large, complex organizations developed. Carefully calculated strategies and tactics based on fundamentals of market research were employed by candidates of both parties.

The participants were also affected. Public-relations experts were called on to apply the new techniques. Pollsters and media consultants regularly supplemented savvy politicians in designing and executing presidential campaigns. Even the candidates seemed a little different. With the possible exception of Johnson and Ford, who succeeded to the Presidency through the death or resignation of their predecessors, incumbents and challengers alike reflected in their appearances the grooming and schooling of the age of television. And where they didn't, as in the case of Walter Mondale, they fared poorly.

This chapter and the one that follows discuss these aspects of modern presidential campaigns. Organization, strategy, and tactics serve as the principal focal points of this chapter, while image creation, projection, and impact are addressed in the next one.

The following section describes the structures of modern presidential campaigns and the functions they perform. It examines attempts to create hierarchical campaign organizations, but also notes the decentralizing pressures. The tensions between candidate organizations and the regular party structure are discussed as well.

The basic objectives that every strategy must address are explored next. These include designing a basic appeal, highlighting relevant themes, and building a winning coalition. The last section of the chapter deals with tactics. It begins by describing the techniques for communicating the message, then turns to the targeting and timing of appeals during the campaign, and finally considers turning out the voters on election day. Examples from past contests are used to illustrate some of these tactics of presidential campaigning.

ORGANIZATION

Running a campaign is a complex, time-consuming, nerve-racking venture. It involves coordinating a variety of functions and activities. These include advance work, scheduling, press arrangements, issue research, speech writing, polling, media advertising, finances, and party and interest-group activities. To accomplish these varied tasks, a large, specialized campaign organization is necessary.

All recent presidential campaigns have had such organizations. The organizations have similar features. There is a director who orchestrates the effort and acts as a liaison between the candidate and the party; a manager charged with supervising day-to-day activities; usually an administrative head of the national headquarters; division chiefs for special operations; and a geographic hierarchy that reaches to the state and local levels.

Within this basic structure, organizations have varied somewhat in style and operation. Some have been very centralized, with a few individuals making most of the major strategic and tactical decisions; others have been more decentralized. Some have worked through or in conjunction with national and state party organizations; others have disregarded these groups and created their own field organizations. Some have operated from a comprehensive game plan; others have adopted a more incremental approach.

The Goldwater organization in 1964, the Nixon operation in 1972, and the Reagan effort of 1984 exemplify the tight, hierarchical structure in which a few individuals control decision making and access to the candidate. In Goldwater's case, his chief advisers were suspicious of top party regulars, most of whom did not support the senator's candidacy. They opted for an organization of believers, one that would be run in an efficient military fashion.[11] This produced tension between the regular Republican organization and the citizen groups that had helped Goldwater win the nomination.

There are tensions in every campaign between the candidate's organization and the party's, between the national headquarters and the field staff, and between the research and operational units. Some of these tensions are the inevitable consequence of ambitious people operating under severe time constraints and pressures. Some are the result of the need to coordinate a large, decentralized party system for a national campaign. Some result from limited resources and the struggle over who gets how much. In Goldwater's case, however, the tensions were aggravated by his circumvention of party regulars, by his concentration of decision making in the hands of a few, and by his attempt to operate with two separate campaign organizations in many states.

The same desire for control and for circumventing the party was evident in Richard Nixon's reelection campaign in 1972. Nixon's organization, larger than Goldwater's, had a staff of 337 paid workers and thousands of volunteers. Completely separated from the national party, even in title, the Nixon committee raised its own money, conducted its own public relations (including polling and campaign advertising), scheduled its own events, and even had its own security division, which planned and executed the dirty tricks and the Watergate burglary. The excesses of this division illustrate both the difficulty of overseeing all the aspects of a large campaign organization and the risk of placing nonprofessionals in key positions of responsibility. Had the more experienced Republican National Committee exercised more of an influence over the Nixon campaign, there might have been less deviation from accepted standards of behavior.

The Reagan effort in 1984 operated more closely with state Republican party organizations than had either Goldwater's or Nixon's. Directed by a separate campaign manager, but linked to the White House, the organization aimed to achieve and impose centralized decision making on a decentralized campaign. Field operations were coordinated by six regional directors, who dealt directly with the Reagan-Bush and Republican party organizations within the states. At the national headquarters functional responsibilities and lines of authority were more clearly designated than in 1980, when a group of senior advisers had tried to oversee the entire operation.

Democratic campaign organizations have tended to be looser in structure and more decentralized in operation than Republican organizations. For many years the Democrats had stronger state parties and a weaker national financial base. As a consequence, their presidential candidates relied more heavily on state party organizations. This is no longer the case.

In recent years Democratic candidates, like their Republican counterparts, have established separate organizations to run their presidential campaigns. They have used out-of-state coordinators to oversee activities within the state, creating some tension with party regulars in the process.[12] Moreover, there has been little coordination with the national committee or with congressional campaign committees. Major decisions have been made by the presidential candidate and his inner circle of advisers.

In 1984 the Mondale organization had difficulty carrying out a coordinated campaign effort. The problems were partially structural. In theory a small group of longtime associates held principal positions in his organization and were responsible for making key recommendations on resource allocation, press relations, policy positions, and media imagery, as well as day-to-day tactical decisions. In practice, however, Mondale consulted with a wide range of experts and supporters, often changing directions and reversing decisions in midstream. His organization and campaign in the presidential election were not nearly so well structured nor nearly so efficient in operation as during the nomination period.[13]

The tendency to circumvent the national party in the planning and conduct of presidential campaigns has serious implications for the party. Put simply, it makes the President less dependent on and less sensitive to the institutional needs of the party. He has less incentive to build a strong national organization and more incentive to convert it into a personal one, responsive to his needs, particularly reelection. Frequently, key party leaders are replaced by loyal supporters of the successful nominee.[14] However, when that nominee leaves office, these supporters lose their patron and ultimately their position. When the party loses a presidential campaign, the candidate's organization disintegrates and the party, blamed in part for the defeat, must try to rebuild itself.

Not only does this situation contribute to frequent turnover among national party leaders, but it weakens the party's influence on a White House held by its own nominee. It also weakens the President's ability to mobilize partisan support for his policy objectives.

STRATEGIC OBJECTIVES

All campaigns must have strategies. Most are articulated before the race begins; others develop during the election itself. In 1984, Reagan strategists designed an elaborate plan well before the Republican conventions. In contrast, Humphrey's 1968 strategy emerged after his nomination.

Certain decisions cannot be avoided when developing an electoral strategy. These decisions stem from the rules of the system, the costs of the campaign, and the character of the electorate. Each of them involves identifying objectives, allocating resources, and monitoring and adjusting that allocation over the course of the campaign. This is what a strategy is all about. It is a plan for developing, targeting, and tracking campaign resources.

Designing a Basic Appeal

In constructing a campaign strategy, it is important at the outset to design a basic appeal. The appeal is presented as the reason for voting for a particular candidate and cited as the explanation of that vote. It has two primary components: one consists of the emphasis placed on partisan affiliation and partisan issues; the other is the personal leadership dimension.

Partisanship. The partisan disposition of the electorate has been considered important in designing an appeal. All things being equal, Democratic candidates would seem to have an advantage. With a larger number of potential supporters within the population, Democrats can maximize their votes by linking themselves to their party. Since the 1930s all Democratic presidential candidates have done so, urging Democrats to remain faithful to their political allegiances and vote for their party's candidates.

Republicans cannot depend on partisanship to win. In fact, in the past, they tended to avoid it. Ford's official campaign poster contained only his picture. His partisan affiliation was not even included. Nixon went so far as to separate his entire presidential campaign from his party's efforts for other Republicans. In contrast, Ronald Reagan did not hide his party label in 1980 or 1984. Rather, he proclaimed it, urging voters to support other Republican candidates. With their partisan disadvantage declining in recent years, Republican presidential nominees today have less reason to run as if they were independents.

Normally the candidates of the minority party have tended to emphasize the issues of the day and their own leadership qualities. For the most part, they have not focused on ideology. Before Reagan, only Senator Barry Goldwater had stressed his conservatism.

Identifying or not identifying with the party is only one way in which to activate and reinforce the partisan orientations of the electorate. Recalling the popular images of the party is another. For the Democrats, common economic interests are still the most compelling link uniting the party's electoral coalition. Perceived as the party of common folks, the party that got the country out of the Great Depression, the party of labor and minority groups, Democrats have tended to do better when economic issues are salient. This is why their candidates for President underscore the "bread and butter" issues: low unemployment, high minimum wage, maximum social security benefits, and tax cuts for low- and middle-income families. Democratic candidates also emphasize the ties between the Republicans, Republican candidates, and big business.

For the GOP, the task used to be to downplay economic issues. However, the increasing size of the upper middle class and its concern with high taxes and particularly with inflation, and the prosperity that has occurred during the Reagan years indicate that the Republicans may no longer be disadvantaged by pocketbook issues. In 1980 Reagan pointed to the economic failures of the Carter administration, promising new policies and new leadership. In 1984 he contrasted the results of those policies and his leadership with the performance of the previous administration. His messages received a favorable hearing, even among traditional Democratic voting groups (see Table 6–1).

Table 6–1   REAGAN'S TARGETED VOTE, 1984

	Reagan Vote 1980 (%)	Reagan Vote 1984 (%)	Target to Win (%)	Over or (Under) Target (%)	Difference 1980–1984 (%)
Total	51	58	52	6	7
Female	48	54	47	7	6
Male	55	62	56	6	7
18–24	46	66	53	13	20
25–34	48	62	53	9	14
35–44	54	55	56	(1)	1
45–54	55	59	54	5	4
55–64	53	57	52	5	4
65+	49	53	48	5	4
Base GOP	87	93	90	3	6
Independent	53	64	56	8	11
Base Democrat	25	19	17	2	(6)
Farm Belt	56	61	55	6	5
Great Lakes	52	53	48	5	1
New England	45	65	50	15	20
Mid Atlantic	48	54	45	9	6
Mountain	63	61	60	1	(2)
Pacific	51	53	52	1	2
Outer South	50	63	56	7	13
Deep South	51	65	51	14	14
Blue collar	45	56	45	11	11
Professional	51	61	58	3	10
Other white collar	56	66	62	4	10
Retired	51	53	48	5	2
Other	40	54	32	22	14
Hispanic	25	46	30	16	21
White	55	62	58	4	7
Black	12	12	10	2	0
Other	49	54	50	4	5
Catholic	49	57	47	10	8
Baptist	42	58	45	13	16
Other Protestant	57	64	58	6	7
Jewish	43	33	30	3	(10)
Strong GOP	91	98	95	3	7
Not-so-strong GOP	83	90	82	8	7
Independent/Lean GOP	79	95	87	8	16
Independent	52	63	56	7	11
Independent/Lean Democrat	22	19	25	(6)	(3)
Not-so-strong Democrat	35	38	35	3	3
Strong Democrat	15	6	10	(4)	(9)

Source: Richard Wirthlin, as reprinted in Peter Goldman and Tony Fuller, *The Quest for the Presidency, 1984* (Toronto: Bantam, 1985), p. 456.

Although the Republicans have gone a long way toward shedding their negative economic image, they have not been so successful in altering the perception that they are the party of the rich. Thus, future Republican nominees are likely to target their general economic message to the growing middle class rather than to lower-income voters. Democrats, in contrast, will continue to refer to the unfairness of the government's revenue and expenditure policies in appealing to the concerns of those in the lower socioeconomic strata and to the social consciousness of more affluent sectors of the electorate.

When foreign and national-security issues have been salient, Republican candidates have traditionally done better. By emphasizing their competence to deal with national-security matters, Republican nominees rekindle the more favorable perception their party has enjoyed in the foreign-policy area. In the process they also negate their partisan disadvantage to some extent, since international issues have traditionally not engendered the same degree of partisanship that domestic issues have.

Dwight Eisenhower and Richard Nixon stressed their competence in foreign affairs. In 1952 Eisenhower campaigned on the theme "Communism, Corruption, and Korea," projecting himself as the most qualified candidate to end the war. Nixon did a similar thing in 1968, linking Humphrey to the Johnson administration and the war in Vietnam. Four years later, Nixon varied this tactic, painting McGovern as the "peace at any price" candidate and himself as the experienced leader who could achieve peace with honor. Gerald Ford, though, was not nearly so successful in conveying his abilities in foreign affairs, in part because of the acknowledged expertise and statesmanship of his secretary of state and national security adviser, Henry Kissinger. Reagan pointed to the Russian invasion of Afghanistan and to the Iranian hostage situation to criticize the foreign policy of the Carter administration and to urge greater expenditures for defense. When seeking reelection in 1984, he pointed to the increased defense capacity of the United States and to its success in containing the expansion of Communism.

The perception that the Democrats are weaker in foreign and military affairs has prompted recent standard-bearers of that party to talk even tougher than their opponents. In his 1976 campaign Carter vowed that an Arab oil embargo would be seen by his administration as an economic declaration of war. In 1984 Walter Mondale supported the buildup of American defenses, including Reagan's Strategic Defense Initiative. He even criticized the President for proposing to give this new technology to the Russians. In 1980, however, Carter had taken the opposite tack. He contrasted his moderate, reasoned leadership style in foreign affairs with what might be anticipated from his ideological, "shoot-from-the-hip" opponent. Carter's failure underlines the primacy of personal evaluation in assessing the merits of a candidate's issue appeal.

Leadership. Regardless of their partisan affiliation, ideological orientation, and issue emphases, candidates for the Presidency must stress their own abilities. They must project an image of leadership. In the past, this was more difficult and important for the Republicans, given their partisan disadvantage within the electorate. Today, it may be more difficult and important for the Democrats, given the heterogeneous nature of their party and recent Electoral College voting patterns (see Table 6–2).

The increasing number of independent and weak party identifiers, the declining number of issues that differentiate the parties or emphasize their past distinctions, and the growing importance of television, which focuses more on personality than on policy, all point to leadership as the critical component of any campaign appeal.

Candidates must appear presidential. In an election between an incumbent and a challenger, the tasks of projecting such an image are obviously not equal. The incumbent has an advantage. The best testimony to the power of incumbency is the success of incumbent Presidents who have sought election or reelection. In the twentieth century, fifteen incumbent Presidents have run for election, and eleven of them have won. Franklin Roosevelt was reelected three times.

Three Republican Presidents, William Howard Taft, Herbert Hoover, and Gerald Ford, and one Democratic incumbent, Jimmy Carter, lost in the twentieth century. Extraordinary circumstances help explain the Republicans' defeats. The Bull Moose candidacy of Theodore Roosevelt in 1912 divided the larger Republican vote between Roosevelt (4.1 million) and Taft (3.5 million). Woodrow Wilson's 6.3 million was thus sufficient to win. The growing Depression of the 1930s and the seeming incapacity of the Hoover administration to cope with it swung Republican and independent votes to Franklin Roosevelt. The worst political scandal in the nation's history and the worst economic recession in forty years adversely affected Ford's chances, as did his pardon of the person who had nominated him for the Vice Presidency, Richard Nixon. Nonetheless, Ford almost won.

Having a record in office helps to generate an image of leadership. Clearly, this tends to benefit incumbents. But a record, or especially a lack of achievement, can be harmful as well. Carter's inability to obtain the

THE INCUMBENCY ADVANTAGE

The advantage of incumbency stems from the visibility of the office, the esteem it engenders, and the influence it provides. Being President guarantees recognition. The President is almost always well known. A portion of the population usually has difficulty at the outset in identifying his opponent, although the primaries have contributed to the name recognition of the challenger.

Another benefit of incumbency is the credibility and respect that the office usually engenders. Naturally, this rubs off on the President. In the election, the incumbent's strategy is obvious: run as President. Create the impression that it is the President against some lesser-known and less qualified individual. In the words of Peter Dailey, Nixon's chief media adviser in 1972:

> Our basic effort was to stay with the President and not diffuse the issue. We thought that the issue was clearly defined, that there were two choices—the President (and I mean that distinction—not Richard Nixon, but the President) and the challenger, the candidate George McGovern. We wanted to keep the issue clearly defined that way.[15]

The ability of a President to make news, to affect events, and to dispense the "spoils" of government can also magnify the disparity between an incumbent and a challenger. Presidents are in the limelight and can maneuver to remain there. The media focus is always on the President. In the spring of 1984 the media extensively covered President Reagan's travels to Europe and Asia. These visits allowed Reagan to dominate the news on his own terms, and made it unnecessary to purchase commercial time to run his own advertisements. He benefited enormously from the contrast of the dignified head of state representing all citizens of the country with the bickering Democratic candidates battling for their party's nomination.

Presidents have another advantage. Presumably, their actions can influence events. Economic recoveries are usually geared to election years. In 1984 the economy's performance peaked as election day neared. Foreign-policy decisions can also be timed to maximize or minimize their electoral impact. In October 1984 President Reagan held a White House meeting with Soviet Foreign Minister Andrei Gromyko, thereby blunting Mondale's charge that Reagan was not interested in pursuing an arms-control agreement with the Russians.

Incumbents are generally perceived as more experienced and knowledgeable, as leaders who have stood the tests of the office in the office. From the public's perspective, this creates a climate of expectations that works to the incumbent's benefit most of the time. Since security is one of the major psychological needs that the Presidency serves, the certainty of four more years with a known quantity is likely to be more appealing than the uncertainty of the next four years with an unknown one—provided the past four years are viewed as acceptable.

Translated into strategic terms, this requires that the incumbent play on public fears of the future. His campaign normally highlights his opponent's lack of experience and contrasts it with his own experience and record in office. Johnson in 1964, Nixon in 1972, and Ford in 1976 all adopted this approach. Carter used a variation of it in 1980. He emphasized the arduousness of the job in order to contrast his energy, knowledge, and intelligence with Reagan's.

In 1984, however, the situation was reversed. High public approval of Reagan's performance in office forced Democratic challenger Mondale to play on the voters' fears of the future. Mondale claimed that rising budget deficits and an imprudent foreign policy threatened the nation's future. Reagan sought to reassure voters that his policies would make the country safer in the years ahead.

Finally, being President provides an incumbent with the capacity to benefit certain individuals, groups, and areas of the country. The timing of grants, the making of appointments, the supporting of legislation have political impact. White House staff and cabinet officials, acting as surrogates for the President, can be used effectively to promote the President's programs and policies around the country. While these activities occur throughout an administration, they are more newsworthy and potentially more influential during a campaign. A President can damage his reputation, however, if his actions appear to be solely or primarily for political purposes, as did Ford's pardon of Nixon in 1974 and Carter's announcement of grants during his 1980 reelection campaign.

release of the Iranian hostages illustrates how inaction can adversely affect a President's image. Moreover, bad times can hurt an incumbent. Rightly or wrongly, the public places responsibility for economic conditions, social relations, and foreign affairs on the President. That he may actually exercise little control over some of these external factors seems less relevant to the electorate than do their perception of the conditions, their desire that they be improved, and their expectation that the President should do something about them.

Incumbency is a two-edged sword. It can strengthen or weaken a claim to leadership. That is why incumbents point to their accomplishments, note the work that remains, and sound a "let us continue," "stay the course" theme. Challengers, in contrast, will argue that it is time for a change and that they can do better, while at the same time alluding to their own presidential qualities. In the end the advantage seems to be with the incumbent if conditions are generally favorable, and if a sufficient number of grievances have not accumulated.

What implications does the advantage of incumbency have for governance? It promotes continuities in presidential policy and in executive personnel. It maximizes the benefits that personal relations and political and policy expertise can bring to presidential decision making and consensus building. It provides a stabilizing element that fosters international cooperation and serves to reinforce the desire for predictability in leadership.

The disadvantages are twofold. First, the new ideas and leadership potential of the challenger may never be realized. Second, after reelection, an incumbent frequently finds himself in a weakened position, less able to provide the kind of leadership he did his first term. Ineligible for reelection (a lame duck), facing a more independent and frequently more hostile Congress, and "heading" a party that will become more divided and over which he is likely to exercise less influence as his administration progresses, the President finds himself with fewer allies, growing opposition, and, obviously, more difficulty in achieving his objectives. On the other hand, expectations of his performance remain high, enlarged in part by his first term successes. This is the problem Reagan faced at the beginning of his second term.

Whereas incumbent Presidents have an advantage seeking reelection, incumbent Vice Presidents seeking election as President do not. The benefits of being Vice President stem from the recognition and status it provides and the organizational and financial support it usually engenders. The limitations result primarily from being number two, a loyal follower but not an independent leader. The Vice President is free neither to dissent from unpopular, unwise, or unsuccessful administration policies nor to take credit for popular, wise, and successful ones. Thus, he has the worst of two worlds: he is unlikely to receive support from those who dislike the administration, nor will he necessarily inherit the votes of those who do. Perhaps this helps explain why the last incumbent Vice President to be elected directly to the Presidency was Martin Van Buren, in 1836!

The difficulties that sitting Vice Presidents have in getting elected have the opposite effect that the incumbency advantage has on governance. They contribute to discontinuities in policy and turnover in personnel.

Highlighting Relevant Themes

In articulating themes, candidates must know what is on the voters' minds. They must know how the electorate perceives them and their opposition. Armed with this knowledge, they try to reinforce the positive and alter or downplay the negative.

Pollsters are critical to this task. They provide the benchmark from which the appeal is generated, and suggest the targets to which it should be directed. Over the course of the campaign they track its effectiveness on the voters.

The 1984 campaign illustrates the use of these positive and negative themes. For the Reagan reelection effort, Republican adviser Stuart Spencer compiled a list of issues that elicited negative perceptions of the President's candidacy. They included:

1. Fairness—the perception that Republican policies favor the wealthy over working people and defense spending over domestic priorities;
2. Social Security—the perception that Reagan wants to reduce benefits for the elderly;
3. Nervousness—the perception that the Administration is more likely to use force in a world crisis than would a Democratic President;
4. Disengagement—the perception that Reagan is not on top of the job; and
5. The Deficit and Interest Rates—the perception that the economy will falter in the years ahead.[16]

To change these perceptions, Spencer argued for a strong positive thrust in the campaign. "We must maintain that our program has helped the entire country and that everyone has shared and will continue to share in our economic successes, not just particular constituencies," he wrote in a memo to Reagan campaign officials.[17]

The President sought to make the 1984 election a referendum on his record, emphasizing his administration's first-term successes (economic recovery, strengthened defenses, and a renewed feeling of national pride), rather than articulating a detailed agenda for a possible second term. Four years earlier, then Governor Reagan had also sought a referendum on the Carter administration. But then, he had emphasized the nation's problems and the weakness of Carter's presidential leadership.[18]

There was a negative thrust to Reagan's 1984 campaign as well. It too was designed to exploit his opponent's weaknesses: his affiliation with Carter, his liberal positions, and his lack of leadership. Mondale was portrayed as a captive of special interests—a charge his Democratic opponents had levied before his nomination. His party was described as one of negativism and stagnation.

Naturally, Mondale's appeal was designed to enhance his image. After several decades of government service, he had considerable name recognition, but little was known about him personally. Thus, the initial phase of his campaign was designed to provide the electorate with more information about the candidate. Mondale's experience, compassion, knowledge, and strength were emphasized. He was presented as a Democrat in the tradition of Franklin Roosevelt, Harry Truman, and John Kennedy, but not of Lyndon Johnson or Jimmy Carter.

The negative themes used in the Mondale campaign came later. Their principal objective was to raise questions and tap fears about the country's future. Reagan's competence, his intelligence, and, indirectly, his age (his energy level), were cited as possible reasons for concern, as were the long-term implications of his economic and foreign policies. The focus was on the danger of keeping Reagan in office for a second term, rather than on the President's record during his first term.

Building a Winning Coalition

Once a general appeal is designed and specific themes are articulated, a winning coalition must be assembled. Geography is of critical importance since the election is decided by the Electoral College. The primary objective must always be to win a majority of the College, not necessarily of the popular vote.

The Electoral College strategies almost always require that the candidates concentrate much of their resources in the large industrial states with the most electoral votes. Failure to win a majority of these states makes it extremely difficult to put together a victorious coalition. The basic strategic consideration is, how much of a candidate's resources should be devoted to these states? The answer is, a lot. In fact, it has been calculated as greater than the proportional share of the vote these states have in the Electoral College.[19] This large-scale allocation of resources makes candidates, particularly Democrats, sensitive to the policy issues and political needs of the big industrial states. This sensitivity frequently extends to presidential decision making as well.

In building their electoral majorities, candidates begin from positions of geographic strength, move to states in which they have some support, and compete in most of the large states regardless of the odds. Since the establishment of their current coalition in the 1930s, the Democrats have focused on the northeastern and midwestern states. New York, Pennsylvania, Ohio, Michigan, and Missouri form the core of the party's political base. With many of their support groups concentrated in these large states, the Democrats have traditionally needed to win fewer states than the Republicans to gain an Electoral College victory.

A shift in population since World War II to southern and western states has made it more difficult for the Democrats to win a majority of the Electoral College.[20] The number of electoral votes of the traditional Democratic states in the Northeast and Midwest has declined, while those of the states in the more Republican Sunbelt have increased. Table 6–2 shows each party's electoral base. Twenty-three states, totaling 202 electoral votes, have voted for the Republican candidate in each of the last five presidential elections. During the same period only the District of Columbia, with 3 votes, has shown the same loyalty to the Democrats. Thus, other things being equal, the Republican candidate begins the campaign with a considerably larger base of support than does his Democratic opponent.

The Republican base has not always been so imposing. In 1964, Goldwater was ready to concede the East and concentrate his efforts on the rest of the country. His basic strategy was to go for the states Nixon had won in 1960 plus several others in the South and Midwest. As one of Goldwater's aides put it:

> It was a regional strategy based on the notion that little campaigning would be needed to win votes in the South, no amount of campaigning could win electoral votes in New England and on the East Coast, but that votes could be won in the Midwest and on the West Coast. As the Senator said, "Go hunting where the ducks are."[21]

In 1968, Nixon strategists set their sights on ten battleground states—the big seven plus New Jersey, Wisconsin, and Missouri—where Humphrey provided the main opposition, and on five peripheral southern

Table 6–2 VOTING BLOCS IN THE ELECTORAL COLLEGE, 1968–1984

Number of Elections	States Voting Republican Since 1968			States Voting Democratic Since 1968		
	Five	Four	Three	Three	Four	Five
	Alaska 3	Arkansas 6	Alabama 9	Hawaii 4	Minnesota* 10	District of Columbia 3
	Arizona 7	Connecticut 8	Louisiana 10	Maryland 10		
	California 47	Delaware 3	Mississippi 7	Massachusetts 13		
	Colorado 8	Florida 21	New York 36	Rhode Island 4		
	Idaho 4	Kentucky 9	Pennsylvania 25	West Virginia 6		
	Illinois 24	Maine 4	Texas 29	Total votes 37		
	Indiana 12	Michigan 20	Total votes 116			
	Iowa 8	Missouri 11				
	Kansas 7	North Carolina 13				
	Montana 4	Ohio 23				
	Nebraska 5	South Carolina 8				
	Nevada 4	Tennessee 11				
	New Hampshire 4	Washington 10				
	New Jersey 16	Wisconsin 11				
	New Mexico 5	Total votes 158				
	North Dakota 3					
	Oklahoma 8					
	Oregon 7					
	South Dakota 3					
	Utah 5					
	Vermont 3					
	Virginia 12					
	Wyoming 3					
	Total votes 202					

*Each time Minnesota voted Democratic, one of the Democratic candidates was from Minnesota. Georgia voted twice for Republican candidates, twice for Democratic candidates, and once for the American Independent Party candidates (George Wallace and Curtis E. LeMay).

A majority of the Electoral College needed to elect a President is 270.

states where George Wallace was the principal foe. Together, these states had 298 electoral votes. Nixon needed to win at least 153 of them to combine with his almost certain 117 electoral votes from other states. He actually won 190.

Nixon's strategy of targeting the industrial states contrasted sharply with that of his previous presidential campaign. In 1960, he had promised to visit all fifty states, a promise he was to regret. On the day before the vote, he had to fly to Alaska to keep his campaign pledge, while Kennedy visited five East Coast states and ended with a torchlight parade in Boston.

In 1976, Ford found himself in a situation that required a broad-gauged national effort. Because of the nomination of a southerner by the Democrats, he could not count on the South or on as many other states as the Republicans had had in previous years. In fact, his strategists saw only 83 electoral votes from fifteen states as solidly Republican at the beginning of the campaign. Assuming these states to be theirs, and conceding ten states and the District of Columbia (87 electoral votes) to Carter, Ford's planners proposed a nationwide media effort to win the necessary 187 votes from the remaining twenty-five states.

In contrast, Carter's strategy in 1976 was to retain the traditional Democratic states and regain the South. His goal was to win at least 71 votes from the large industrial states. He achieved each of these objectives, but only in the South was his performance really impressive. Not since 1960 had a majority of states from this region gone Democratic.

In 1980, Carter attempted to hold his 1976 coalition together. His Electoral College strategy was to secure the South, focus on the larger industrial states, and campaign in smaller states in which there appeared a reasonable chance of victory. As the campaign progressed, Carter all but conceded the West to Reagan, mounting effective campaigns only in four Pacific states: Washington, Oregon, California, and Hawaii.

The Reagan plan in that election, the result of elaborate calculations, was to build a base in the West, target several states on the outer southern rim (Texas, Florida, and Virginia), and battle for the industrial heartland, specifically, Michigan, Illinois, and Ohio.[22] Other states, including most of those in the South, were added during the campaign when polls showed them to be within the range of victory.

Reagan's strategy in 1984 was to use the primary season to secure his western base and to solidify his support in the South. Assured by polling data that the Sunbelt, with its 266 electoral votes, was firmly in tow, the campaign then shifted to selected northern industrial states, primarily Ohio and Michigan. As election day neared and a fifty-state sweep appeared within his grasp, Reagan intensified his campaigning in the Northeast and Midwest. Only Minnesota and the District of Columbia fell outside the reach of the Reagan landslide.

Mondale had hoped to reassert Democratic strength in northeastern and midwestern states and to capitalize on rising black registration to win several southern states. The choice of Geraldine Ferraro as the Democratic vice presidential candidate was intended to solidify the support of traditionally Democratic ethnic voters in the key industrial states. However, when the Democratic ticket of two northern, liberal candidates received an unsympathetic hearing in Sunbelt states, Mondale had no choice but to concentrate on the Frostbelt. It was this concentration that prompted the Reagan-Bush campaign to saturate Ohio and Michigan with money, media, and appearances by the candidates and well-known supporters. If Mondale were denied these two critical industrial states, Reagan advisers believed, there was no way the Democratic ticket could win a majority in the Electoral College. For all intents and purposes, the election would be over.

The Reagan strategies in 1980 and 1984 are likely to provide the operational model that the Republican nominees will follow in 1988. The Democrats, on the other hand, are likely to look to a variation of Carter's 1976 approach, emphasizing the South and/or West in addition to the large industrial states. It is clear that the costs of writing off an area of the country are too high for either party to accept.

TACTICAL CONSIDERATIONS

Whereas the basic objectives set the contours of the campaign strategy, tactical considerations influence day-to-day decisions. Tactics are the specific ways by which the ends are achieved. They involve techniques to communicate the message and the targets and timing of that message: how appeals will be made, to whom, and when. Unlike strategy, which can be planned well in advance, tactics change with the environment and events. The circumstances, in short, dictate different tactical responses.

Communicating Techniques

There are a variety of ways to convey a political message. They include door-to-door canvassing, direct mail, and media advertisements. At the local level especially, door-to-door campaigning may be a viable

THE REAGAN STRATEGY IN 1984

Basic Objectives

"Our primary goal is to expand our current lead and inhibit Mondale's ability to draw Democratic-leaners back to the ticket. This can be accomplished by dominating the issues and depriving Mondale of the opportunity to establish his campaign agenda. Our mode must be offensive rather than defensive, as we work to solidify our lead.

We need to establish the overarching themes required in a national election. . . . There needs to be a central message to our campaign. This election will be decided on the major issues of the economy, peace, and the President's personal qualities, particularly his leadership and competence.

The umbrella theme will be leadership. The President has fundamentally changed the direction of the country, particularly the economy, in a manner that has produced good results and will continue to do so."

Source: Stuart Spencer, Campaign Memorandum, August, 1984 as reprinted in Peter Goldman and Tony Fuller, *The Quest for the Presidency, 1984* (Toronto: Bantam, 1985), p. 416.

"Strategic Themes
1. Negative/Substantive. Paint Mondale as:
   a. "Carter-Mondale," responsible for the failed policies of the past;
   b. "special-interest liberal," not yet aware that the failed policies of the '70s have been replaced by new approaches for the '80s—ones that work.
2. Negative/Personality. Paint Mondale as:
   a. weak
   b. a creature of special interests
   c. old-style
   d. unprincipled
   e. soft in his defense of freedom, patriotic values, American interests
   f. in short, Carter II
      (NOTE: Insofar as possible, sharp negative material should not be in the President's voice. Much can be done by implication and through Democratic voices.)
3. Positive/Substantive. Associate RR with:
   a. "America is Back—Prouder, Stronger, Better"
      • economic progress
      • peace through strength
      • traditional values renewed
      • Pioneering spirit re-invigorated

   b. "America's Best Is Still to Come"
     • no more "malaise"; RR has program for America's future that is
       consistent with the best of America's past. . . .
   4. Positive/General Image. Paint RR as the personification of all that is
      right with, or heroized by, America. Leave Mondale in a position
      where an attack on Reagan is tantamount to an attack on America's
      idealized image of itself—where a vote against Reagan is, in some
      subliminal sense, a vote against a mythic 'AMERICA.' "

Source: Richard Darman, Campaign Memorandum, June, 1984. Ibid.

Geographic Coalition
   "The West is very strong Republican territory indeed. Of the 13
states in the region, 12 are solidly in our corner. We can count on *107* of
the West's 111 electoral votes; this is almost 40% of the 270 electoral votes
required to win the Presidency.
   To this Western stronghold, Ronald Reagan can add the
South. . . . To secure the South, we should take the following steps:
   1. Target campaign voter registration drives in the South. . . .
   2. Openly welcome disgruntled Southern Democrats into the Reagan-
      Bush/Republican fold. . . .
   3. Continue to stress traditional American values. . . .
   4. Add populist/anti-Establishment twists to our rhetoric. . . .
   5. Wherever possible, drive a wedge between the liberal Democrats who
      run the national party and traditional Southern Democrats. . . .
   6. Allow the Democrats to tear themselves apart with no interference
      from our side. . . .
   The payoff: *155* electoral votes from the South, to add to our *107*
solid votes from the West. . . . With a Southern and Western base, we enter
the 1984 contest with *262* secure electoral votes, just 8 shy of a majority."

Source: Lee Atwater, Campaign Memorandum, November 5, 1983, made available to the
author.

Group Appeal
   "Our base of support from 1980 is still available to us. We can expect
to improve our support from two groups, younger voters between the ages
of 18 and 24 and suburban ticket-splitters. Our key constituency, however,
remains middle-income working people. Farmers, middle-income people,
and small business owners should be the focus of our efforts throughout the
campaign."

Source: Stuart Spencer, Campaign Memorandum, August 1984, as reprinted in Goldman and
Fuller, *The Quest For The Presidency, 1984*, p. 417.

option. Obviously, presidential candidates and their national staffs cannot directly engage in this kind of activity in the general election, even though they may have in some of the primaries. They can, however, encourage these efforts by others.

The Kennedy organization in 1960 was one of the first to mount such a campaign on the local level. Using the canvass as a device to identify supporters and solicit workers, Kennedy's aides built precinct organizations out of the newly recruited volunteers. The volunteers, in turn, distributed literature, turned out the voters, and monitored the polls on election day. They were instrumental in Kennedy's narrow victory in several states.

Personal contact is generally considered to have a greater impact on voters than any other kind of campaign activity. It is most effective in stimulating voting. To a lesser extent, it may also influence the decision on how to vote. The problem with personal contact is that it is time-consuming, volunteer intensive, and, with limited funds available, not cost-effective at the presidential level. Increasingly, presidential campaigns have depended on state and local parties to perform these activities for them.

Direct mailings, frequently utilized in fund-raising, have also been employed to distribute information about the candidate and the party. Letters can be targeted to specific groups. They can be made to look personal. Modern computers can even include the addressee's name in different parts of the letter. For conveying a substantive message to a specific audience, direct mail can be efficiently used, although its effectiveness varies with level of education and, to some extent, geographic area. It tends to have greater impact on those who are less educated, particularly those who do not receive a lot of other mail.

Another option is television. Although costly and impersonal, it has many benefits. Television can reach large numbers of people. It is less taxing on the candidate than extensive personal campaigning. It facilitates control over the political environment. While messages cannot be tailored as precisely as they can in individualized letters, they can be designed to create and project favorable images and can be aimed at well-defined groups of voters. That is why an increasing proportion of expenditures by the presidential campaigns are on media. In 1976 media spending accounted for approximately half the campaign budget; in 1984 it was almost two-thirds. Reagan pumped an estimated $25 million into media and Mondale around $22 million.

But no matter how extensive a candidate's use of television may be, a certain amount of personal campaigning has always been necessary.

Appearances by presidential hopefuls create news, often becoming media events themselves. They promote a sense of unity in the party, make the candidates seem real to the voters, and testify to their concern for the people. No area or group likes to be taken for granted.

The problem with personal appearances is that they are personally wearing, have limited impact, cost a lost of money, and can be dangerous. Making arrangements is itself a complex, time-consuming venture. It requires the work of experts to make certain that everything goes smoothly from scheduling to physical arrangements to the rally itself. Jerry Bruno, who "advanced" Democratic presidential campaigns in the 1960s, described his task in the following manner:

> It's my job in a campaign to decide where a rally should be held, how a candidate can best use his time getting from an airport to that rally, who should sit next to him and chat with him quietly in his hotel room before or after a political speech, and who should be kept as far away from him as possible.
>
> It's also my job to make sure that a public appearance goes well—a big crowd, an enthusiastic crowd, with bands and signs, a motorcade that is mobbed by enthusiastic supporters, a day in which a candidate sees and is seen by as many people as possible—and at the same time have it all properly recorded by the press and their cameras.[23]

Bruno did not work alone. Numerous people are employed on advance staffs.

Even with all the advance preparations, the public appearance may have a limited impact—or, even worse, a negative one. If the crowds are thin, if the candidate is heckled, if a prominent public figure refuses to be on the platform with the candidate or if a controversial one does appear, or if the candidate makes a verbal slip, then the appearance may do more harm than good. Mondale got off to an embarrassing start in 1984 when an early-hour Labor Day parade in which he was to appear drew relatively few onlookers. The news was the absence of spectators. Television cameras pictured Mondale walking down near-empty streets in New York City.

The arduous and exhausting schedules of modern campaigns have also contributed to displays of emotion by candidates that have embarrassed them and damaged their public image. One of the most highly publicized of these incidents occurred during the 1972 New Hampshire primary. Senator Edmund Muskie, the Democratic front-runner, seemed to break into tears when defending his wife from the attacks of William Loeb, publisher of the *Manchester* (New Hampshire) *Union Leader*. In the minds of some, the incident made Muskie look weaker and less presidential. It raised the question, could he withstand the pressures of the Presidency? George McGovern, who benefited from the Muskie episode, expressed his own frustration toward the end of his presidential campaign. When passing a vociferous heckler at an airport reception, McGovern told his critic, "Kiss my ass!" The press dutifully reported the senator's comment.[24]

In more recent campaigns each of the major-party candidates made questionable statements that were highlighted by the media. In the midst of the Democratic primaries in 1976, Carter stated that he saw nothing wrong with people trying to maintain the "ethnic purity" of their neighborhoods. After some people interpreted his remarks as racist, Carter indicated that he had made an error in his choice of words, promptly retracted them, and apologized.[25] During his second debate with Carter, President Ford asserted that the Soviet Union did not dominate Eastern Europe. His comment, picked up and repeated by the media, led critics to wonder whether he really understood the complexities of international politics, much less appreciated the Soviet Union's influence in Eastern Europe. Ronald Reagan's much-quoted reference to trees as being a primary source of pollution brought him considerable ridicule during his 1980 campaign, although the remark was made before it. Some of President Reagan's one-liners have worked to his advantage, however, such as his dismissal of the age issue in his second debate with Mondale—"I will not make age an issue of this campaign, I am not going to exploit for political purposes my opponent's youth and inexperience."

Targeting Messages

Candidates are normally very careful about their public utterances. Knowing that the press focuses on inconsistencies and highlights controversies, presidential candidates tend to stick to their articulated public positions. Moreover, they try to control the thematic content of the campaign.

The plan of the Reagan organization in 1984 was to introduce a new theme every ten days to two weeks. All presidential speeches and appearances were to be keyed to this theme. Situations that might have distracted public attention or confused it were carefully controlled.

Speeches are frequently tailored for specific groups. The general practice is to tell the audience what they want to hear. Naturally, this creates a favorable response which, in turn, helps to project a positive image when covered by the media.

Occasionally, however, candidates will use the opposite tactic. In order to exhibit their courage and candor, they will announce a policy to an unsympathetic audience. Carter did this in 1976 when he told an American Legion convention of his intention, if elected, to issue a blanket pardon to Vietnam draft dodgers. Barry Goldwater took a similar approach in 1964: In order to emphasize the purity of his conservative convictions, Goldwater made a speech in Appalachia criticizing the War on Poverty as phony, and in Tennessee he suggested the possibility of private ownership of the Tennessee Valley Authority. While the Senator did not win many converts, he did succeed in maintaining his image as a no-nonsense conservative.

A third approach when discussing issues is simply to be vague. This allows potential supporters to see what they want to see in a candidate's position. Dwight Eisenhower succeeded with this approach in 1956, as did Reagan in 1984, but Thomas Dewey, eight years before Eisenhower, did not. Dewey lacked the popularity and credibility that Eisenhower and Reagan were both to enjoy after their first four years in office.

Candidates often use a variation of this approach, conveying a plan of action without encumbering it with a myriad of details. Reagan was able to pull this off in 1980. Bernard Aronson, a speechwriter for Jimmy Carter and adviser to Walter Mondale, indicated in a memo to Mondale why he though Reagan had been so successful.

> Reagan may have sounded corny and hokey to us. But he moved and impressed the American people. He gave damn good speeches and beat the pants off Carter—not because he was more narrowly correct on each issue—Carter clearly was the A student who had read all his books three times and underlined them twice.
>
> But Reagan projected an image of himself and of America that was larger than life. He unabashedly summoned up America's idealism. He invoked his image of a City on a Hill. And while I would not suggest that you ape Reagan in any particular way, his evocation of universal themes of hope and activism is the basic winning model for presidential candidates from Roosevelt to Kennedy.[26]

In 1984 Reagan again expressed optimism, exuded confidence, and displayed his leadership capabilities without offering a specific agenda for the future, while Mondale seemed to get bogged down in detail without articulating a philosophy or generating confidence in how or where he would lead the country as President.

Timing Appeals

In addition to the problem of whom to appeal to and what to say, it is also important to decide when to make the appeal. Candidates naturally desire to build momentum as their campaigns progress. This usually dictates a phased effort, especially for the underdog.

Goldwater's campaign of 1964 illustrates the plight of the challenger. Having won the Republican nomination after heated primary contests with Nelson Rockefeller, the senator initially had to reunite the party. The first month of his campaign was directed toward this goal. Endorsements were obtained; the party was reorganized; traditional Republican positions were articulated. Phase two was designed to broaden Goldwater's electoral support. Appeals to conservative Democratic and independent voters were made on the basis of ideology. The third phase was the attack. Goldwater severely criticized President Johnson, his Great Society program, and his liberal Democratic policies. In phase four, the Republican candidate enunciated his own hopes, goals, and programs for America's future. Finally, at the end of the campaign, perceiving that he had lost, Goldwater became increasingly uncompromising in presenting his conservative beliefs.

In 1976, Gerald Ford also faced the problem of unifying the Republican party after a divisive selection process. The first stage of his campaign was directed to this goal as well as to broadening his popular appeal. Cutting Carter down to size was the focus of stage two. Like Goldwater, Ford also trailed his Democratic rival in the polls. Unlike Goldwater, he was able to close the gap by pointing to Carter's personal and political vulnerabilities. In the third part of his campaign, Ford sought to accentuate the positive. His speeches and advertisements stressed the achievements of his administration and his goals for the future. The theme of his ads, "feeling good about America," was designed to generate a positive feeling and build momentum in the final days of the campaign. It was aimed at the more independent voters who tend to be less involved, less informed, and more likely to make their decision closer to election day.

Turning Out Voters

When all is said and done, it is the electorate that makes the final judgment. Who comes out to vote can be the critical factor in determining the winner in a close election. Although turnout is influenced by a number of variables, including the demographic characteristics and political attitudes of the population, registration laws and procedures, the kind of election and its competitiveness, and even the weather, it can also be affected by the campaign itself.

On balance, lower turnout tends to hurt the Democrats more than the Republicans, because a larger proportion of their party identifiers are less likely to vote.[27] Thus, a key element in the strategy of most Democratic candidates since Franklin Roosevelt has been to maximize the number of voters by organizing large registration drives.

Traditionally it is party organizations, not the candidate's central headquarters, that mount the drive. A party divided at the time of its convention can seriously damage its chances in the general election. A case in point was the Humphrey campaign of 1968. Humphrey received the nomination of a party that took until late October to coalesce behind his candidacy. This was too late to register a large number of voters. Had it not been for organized labor's efforts in registering approximately 4.6 million voters, Humphrey probably would not have come as close as he did.

Whereas Humphrey's loss in 1968 can be attributed in part to a weak voter registration drive, Carter's victory in 1976 resulted in part from a successful one. The Democratic National Committee coordinated and financed the drive. With the support of organized labor, Democrats outregistered Republicans. Labor's efforts in Ohio and Texas contributed to Carter's narrow victory in both states. A successful program to attract black voters also helped increase Carter's margin of victory. In 1980, Carter's lukewarm support from labor and his party's weak financial position adversely affected Democratic registration efforts.

One of the most sophisticated registration efforts by either party occurred in 1984. The Reagan-Bush organization used the prenomination period to identify potential unregistered supporters. Lists of people, grouped precinct by precinct, were supplied to state and local Republican committees for the purposes of enlarging the potential Republican vote. In contrast, the Democrats lacked the organizational mechanism and financial support to match the Republican effort. They fell far short of their goal of registering five to six million new voters.

SUMMARY

Campaigning by presidential nominees is a relatively recent phenomenon. Throughout most of the nineteenth century, presidential campaigns were fairly simple in organization and operation and rather limited in scope. With the exception of William Jennings Bryan, there was little active involvement by the candidates themselves.

Changes began to occur in the twentieth century. They were largely the consequence of developments in transportation and communications that permitted more extensive travel and broader public appeals. First the railroad and then the airplane encouraged campaigning across the country; first radio and then television enabled the candidates to reach millions of voters directly. These developments made campaigning more complex, more expensive, and more sophisticated. They required more activity by the candidates and their staffs. Campaign strategy and tactics became more highly geared to the mass media.

Campaign organizations have increased in size and expertise. Supplementing the traditional cadre of party professionals are the professionals of the new technology: pollsters, media consultants, direct mailers, lawyers, accountants, and a host of other specialists. Their inclusion in the candidate's organization has had two major effects: it has made the coordination of centralized decision making more difficult and more necessary, and it has accelerated the division between the national party and its nominee. Two separate organizations, one very loosely coordinated by the national committee and the other more tightly controlled by the candidates and their senior aides, now function in presidential elections.

The job of campaign organizations is to produce a unified and coordinated campaign effort. Most follow a general strategy prepared in advance to accomplish this primary objective. In designing such a strategy, planners must consider the attitudes and perceptions of the electorate, the reputations and images of the nominees, and the geography of the Electoral College.

In designing a basic appeal, Democratic candidates emphasize their link to the party and those bread-and-butter economic issues that have held their majority coalition together since the 1930s. Republican candidates, on the other hand, often focus on foreign policy and on national-security matters. Increasingly, they have also stressed such issues as employment and inflation. The economic successes of the Reagan administration have clouded or reversed public perceptions of the Democrats as the party more likely to bring prosperity to the country.

Nominees of both parties must also try to project images of leadership, trumpeting their own strengths and exploiting their opponent's weaknesses. Generally speaking, incumbents have an advantage in conveying their capacity to lead. Being President, making critical decisions, exercising the powers of the office, is evidence of the leadership that presidential candidates have to demonstrate. Psychologically, the electorate generally finds it safer to keep a known commodity in office than gamble with an unknown one unless times are bad, a national problem persists, or personal factors about the candidates dictate a change.

The third strategic component is assembling a winning coalition. The geography of the Electoral College is a critical factor here. In recent years Democratic candidates have found themselves at a disadvantage in obtaining an electoral majority. With the South and the West more heavily Republican at the presidential level, the Democrats can afford to lose fewer of the large industrial states in which both parties concentrate the bulk of their resources.

While strategy is more long-term in conception and even in execution, tactics have a greater effect on day-to-day events. Key tactical decisions include what techniques will be utilized, when, and by whom. They also include what appeals will be made, how, and when.

Other than that flexibility is essential, it is difficult to generalize about tactics. Much depends on the basic strategic plan, the momentum of the campaign, and the development of events. In the end, the methods that mobilize the electorate by getting people excited about a candidate are likely to be of the greatest benefit in turning out and influencing this vote. Image creation, production, and projection lie at the heart of this process. The next chapter explores this aspect of campaigning.

NOTES

1. Stephen A. Douglas, quoted in Marvin R. Weisbord, *Campaigning for President* (New York: Washington Square Press, 1966), p. 45.

2. Ibid., p. 5.

3. In 1893 the country suffered a financial panic and slid into a depression. Particularly hard hit were the farmers and silver miners of the West. Angered at the repeal of the Sherman Silver Purchase Act, which had required the government to buy a certain amount of silver and convert it into paper money, farmers, miners, and other western interests wanted new legislation to force the government to buy and coin an unlimited amount of silver. Eastern financial interests opposed the free coinage of silver, as did President Cleveland. Their opposition split the Democratic party at its convention of 1896 and in the general election of that year.

4. The speech was made during the platform debate. Bryan, arguing in favor of the free and unlimited coinage of silver, accused eastern bankers and financiers of trying to protect their own parochial interests by imposing a gold standard. "You shall not press down upon the brow of labor this crown of thorns, you shall not crucify mankind upon a cross of gold," he shouted at the end of his remarks. Bryan's speech moved the convention. Not only did the free-silver interests win the platform fight, but Bryan himself won the presidential nomination on the fifth ballot.

5. William Jennings Bryan, *The First Battle* (Port Washington, N.Y.: Kennikat Press, 1971), p. 618.

6. Keith Melder, "The Whistlestop: Origins of the Personal Campaign," *Campaigns and Elections* (May–June 1968), p. 49.

7. Weisbord, *Campaigning for President*, p. 116.

8. Roosevelt had been crippled by polio in 1921. He wore heavy leg braces and could stand only with difficulty. Nonetheless, he made a remarkable physical and political recovery. In his campaign, he went to great lengths to hide the fact that he could not walk and could barely stand.

9. Cabell Phillips, *The Truman Presidency* (New York: Macmillan, 1966), p. 237.

10. Stanley Kelley, *Professional Public Relations and Political Power* (Baltimore: Johns Hopkins Press, 1956), pp. 161–162.

11. Karl A. Lamb and Paul A. Smith, *Campaign Decision-Making: The Presidential Election of 1964* (Belmont, Calif.: Wadsworth, 1968), pp. 59–63.

12. Carter chose to keep his campaign headquarters in Atlanta, Georgia, rather than move it to Washington, D.C., in 1976, for symbolic as well as practical reasons. An Atlanta address underscored the outsider image Carter desired to project, and made it more difficult for Washington-based Democrats to interfere with the conduct of his campaign.

13. Diane Granat, "Mondale's Campaign Team: Can It Do the Job?" *Congressional Quarterly* (September 22, 1984), pp. 2307–2312.

14. The presidential nominee generally gets to choose or approve the chairman of the national committee. In 1984 Walter Mondale sought to exercise this prerogative by announcing his intent to replace Democratic chairman Charles T. Manatt with Bert Lance, a former head of the Office of Management and Budget who had had to resign his position in 1977 after improprieties concerning his behavior as a banker were alleged. Not only did Mondale choose a controversial individual for chairman, but he chose a controversial time, one week before the Democratic convention, to make his announcement. Considerable criticism followed, and Mondale was forced to abandon his planned change.

15. Peter Dailey, quoted in Ernest R. May and Janet Fraser (eds.), *Campaign '72* (Cambridge, Mass.: Harvard University Press, 1973), p. 244.

16. Stuart Spencer, Campaign Memorandum, August 1984, as reprinted in Peter Goldman and Tony Fuller, *Quest for the Presidency* (Toronto: Bantam, 1985), p. 417.

17. Ibid, p. 416.

18. Richard Wirthlin, Republican pollster, summarized these weaknesses as follows:

"1. an ineffective and error-prone leader;
2. incapable of implementing policies;
3. mean-spirited and unpresidential;
4. too willing to use his presidential power politically;
5. vacillating in foreign policy, creating a climate of crisis."

Richard Wirthlin, Vincent Breglio, and Richard Beal, "Campaign Chronicle," *Public Opinion*, 4 (Feb./Mar. 1981), 44.

19. A political scientist, Steven J. Brams, and a mathematician, Morton D. Davis,

have devised a formula for the most rational way to allocate campaign resources. They calculated that resources should be spent in proportion to the 3/2's power of the electoral votes of each state. To calculate the 3/2's power, take the square root of the number of electoral votes and cube the result. Brams offers the following example: "If one state has 4 electoral votes and another state has 16 electoral votes, even though they differ in size only by a factor of four, the candidates should allocate eight times as much in resources to the larger state."

	Electoral Votes	Square Root	Cube	Result
State A	16	4	64	
State B	4	2	8	=8

In examining actual patterns of allocation between 1960 and 1972, they found that campaigns generally conformed to this rule. Steven J. Brams and Morton D. Davis, "The 3/2's Rule in Presidential Campaigning," *American Political Science Review*, 68 (1974), 113.

20. Under the current aggregation of electoral votes, John F. Kennedy would have won 282, 19 fewer than he actually received in 1960. Rhodes Cook, "Democrats Target Frost Belt in Quest for Electoral Majority," *Congressional Quarterly* (July 7, 1984), p. 1741.

21. Lamb and Smith, *Campaign Decision-Making*, p. 95.

22. In devising an Electoral College strategy, Reagan's strategists first calculated the odds of winning each state. To do this they utilized historical and current survey data. Information from polls was added as the campaign progressed. Those states in which the probability of winning was less than 70 percent but more than 30 percent were then ranked in order of population size and geographic area. Priority targets were then identified among the large, middle, and small states. The initial calculations were made in March 1980. The targets were revised in June and over the course of the campaign. Wirthlin, Breglio, and Beal, "Campaign Chronicle," p. 46.

23. Jerry Bruno and Jeff Greenfield, *The Advance Man* (New York: Morrow, 1971), p. 299.

24. George Bush made a similar off-color remark when addressing a group of supporters following his 1984 debate with Geraldine Ferraro. He stated that he had intended "to kick ass" during the debate. The comment, obviously designed to show Bush's forcefulness as a candidate, was greeted with enthusiasm by his supporters.

Another well-reported incident, this one involving Vice President Nelson A. Rockefeller, occurred in 1976. It too was precipitated by heckling. The Republican vice presidential candidate of that year, Senator Robert Dole, accompanied by Rockefeller, was trying to address a rally in Binghamton, New York. Constantly interrupted by the hecklers, Dole and then Rockefeller tried to restore order by addressing their critics directly. When this failed, Rockefeller grinned and made an obscene gesture, extending the middle fingers of his hands to the group. The Vice President's response was captured in a picture that appeared in newspapers and national magazines across the country, much to the embarrassment of the Republican ticket.

25. In 1976 Carter damaged his image by comments he made during an interview with *Playboy* magazine. In articulating his religious views, Carter quoted Christ as saying,

"Anyone who looks on a woman with lust has in his heart already committed adultery." He went on to add, "I've looked on a lot of women with lust. I've committed adultery in my heart many times." Jimmy Carter, Interview, *Playboy* (November 1976), p. 86.

26. Bernard Aronson, Memorandum, December 1981, as reprinted in Goldman and Fuller, *The Quest for the Presidency*, p. 388.

27. The conventional wisdom that high voter turnout helps the dominant party is not universally accepted. For a critique of this view see James DeNardo, "Turnout and the Vote: The Joke's on the Democrats," *American Political Science Review*, 74 (1980), 406–418. For a critique and defense of the DeNardo thesis see Harvey J. Tucker, Arnold Vedlitz, and James DeNardo, "Does Heavy Turnout Help Democrats in Presidential Elections?" *American Political Science Review*, 80 (1986), 1291–1304.

Selected Readings

Caddell, Patrick H. "The Democratic Strategy and Its Electoral Consequences," in Seymour Martin Lipset (ed.), *Party Coalitions in the 1980s*. San Francisco: Institute for Contemporary Studies, 1981, pp. 267–303.

Goldman, Peter, and Tony Fuller. *The Quest for the Presidency, 1984.* Toronto: Bantam, 1985.

Light, Paul C., and Celinda Lake. "The Election: Candidates, Strategies, and Decisions," in Michael Nelson (ed.), *The Elections of 1984*. Washington, D.C.: The Congressional Quarterly, 1985, pp. 83–110.

"Moving Right Along? Campaign '84's Lessons for 1988: An Interview with Peter Hart and Richard Wirthlin," *Public Opinion*, 7 (Dec./Jan. 1985), 8–11.

Schram, Martin. *Running for President 1976: The Carter Campaign.* New York: Stein & Day, 1977.

White, Theodore H. *The Making of the President 1960*. New York: Pocket Books, 1962.

———. *The Making of the President 1964.* New York: Atheneum, 1965.

———. *The Making of the President 1968.* New York: Atheneum, 1969.

———. *The Making of the President 1972.* New York: Atheneum, 1973.

———. *America in Search of Itself: The Making of the President, 1956–1980.* New York: Harper and Row, 1982.

Wirthlin, Richard B. "The Republican Strategy and Its Electoral Consequences," in Seymour Martin Lipset (ed.), *Party Coalitions in the 1980s*. San Francisco: Institute for Contemporary Studies, pp. 235–266.

Wirthlin, Richard, Vincent Breglio, and Richard Beal. "Campaign Chronicle," *Public Opinion*, 4 (Feb./Mar. 1981), 43–49.

Chapter 7

IMAGE-BUILDING AND THE MEDIA

Introduction

Images are mental pictures that people rely on to make the world around them understandable. These pictures are stimulated and shaped by the environment as well as by personal attitudes and feelings. What is projected affects what is seen. However, different people also see the same thing differently. This suggests that their attitudes color their perceptions. To some extent, beauty is in the eye of the beholder; to some extent, it is in the object seen.

The electorate forms different images of the parties, candidates, and issues. These perceptions help make and reinforce judgments on election day. The images of the party affect how the candidates and the issues are perceived. Strong party identifiers tend to see "their" candidate in a more favorable light than the opposition and perceive his or her position on the issues as closer to their own. Independents also use their beliefs and feelings to shape their perceptions of the candidates and the issues, although they are less likely to be encumbered by preconceived partisan perspectives in making their evaluations.

This is not to imply, however, that what candidates say and do or how they appear is irrelevant. On the contrary, even strong party supporters can be influenced by what they see, read, and hear. George McGovern's poor showing among Democrats in 1972 and Walter Mondale's in

1984 dramatically illustrate how a candidate's image can adversely affect his partisan support. McGovern was perceived as incompetent and Mondale as ineffectual by much of the electorate.

Candidate images are short-term factors that are more variable than party images. In addition to being affected by partisan attitudes, they are also conditioned by the situation and the environment. It is difficult to separate a candidate's image from the events of the real world. Incumbents, especially, tend to be evaluated on the basis of their performance in office. Richard Nixon's image improved between the elections of 1968 to 1972, as did Ronald Reagan's from 1980 to 1984, but Jimmy Carter's declined from 1976 to 1980. The changes were a consequence of the public's perception of their performance as President.

Personal qualities are also important. Perceived strength, moral integrity, seriousness of purpose, candor, empathy, and style all contribute to the impression people have of public figures. In fact, these personal characteristics are frequently cited as the reason for voting for or against a particular person.

In view of the weakening of party loyalties and the media's emphasis on personality politics, this is not surprising. For many, the images of the candidates provide a cognitive handle for interpreting the campaign and making a qualitative judgment. Candidates who enjoy a higher assessment have an advantage. They can use it to offset unpopular partisan, ideological, or issue positions.

The task for presidential candidates is to project as beneficial an image as possible. Normally, just being a presidential candidate helps. The public's inclination to look up to the President usually extends to his opponent. Recent elections have provided exceptions to this rule, however. Carter and Reagan were perceived negatively by a majority of the electorate in 1980, and so was Mondale four years later.

A favorable image, of course, cannot be taken for granted. It has to be built, or at least polished. To do this, it is necessary to know what qualities the electorate looks for in its presidential candidates and how to project those qualities. The first section of this chapter discusses those traits that the public considers most desirable for the Presidency. Illustrations from recent campaigns are used as examples. In the succeeding sections, the presentation and projection of presidential images in the media are explored. The increasing use of political advertisements, the attempts to shape campaign coverage, and the actual impact of that coverage on the electorate are assessed.

PRESIDENTIAL TRAITS

The American electorate has traditionally valued certain traits in its presidential candidates.[1] These reflect the public's psychological needs and its expectations of those in office. These traits also provide a model of an ideal President, one that is used to evaluate an incumbent and to rate a challenger.

Surveys of public opinion indicate that certain qualities are absolutely essential. The contemporary President is expected to be strong, assertive, dominant—a father figure to millions of Americans. He is expected to be skillful, knowledgeable, and analytic—a problem solver in an age of technology. He is also expected to be a person who can bring significant political, organizational, and managerial skills to bear on making the system work—the head of an effective government. Finally, the President should be able to empathize with the people as well as to embody their most redeeming qualities. He must be understanding and inspiring, honest and honorable, reasonable and rational, respected and responsive—a leader and a follower. In presenting themselves to the voters, candidates must naturally try to project these traits and create the image of an ideal President or President-to-be.

Strength, boldness, and decisiveness are intrinsic to the public's image of the office. During times of crisis or periods of social anxiety these leadership characteristics are considered absolutely essential. The strength that Franklin Roosevelt was able to convey by virtue of his successful bout with polio, Eisenhower by his military command in World War II, and Reagan by his tough talk, clear-cut solutions, and consistent policy goals contrasted sharply with the perceptions of Stevenson in 1956, McGovern in 1972, Carter in 1980, and Mondale in 1984 as weak, indecisive, and vacillating.

The Presidency usually implies strength. When Gerald Ford and Jimmy Carter were criticized for their failure to provide strong leadership, their organizations countered by focusing on their presidential activities. For nonincumbents the task of seeming to be assertive, confident, and independent (one's own person) can best be imparted by a no-nonsense approach, a show of optimism, and a conviction that success is attainable. Kennedy's rhetorical emphasis on activity in 1960 and Nixon's tough talk in 1968 about the turmoil and divisiveness of the late 1960s helped to generate a take-charge impression. Kennedy and Nixon were perceived as leaders who knew what had to be done and would do it. Reagan's references to his economic and defense policies, combined with his "Can Do,

America" appeal, were designed to convey a similar impression in 1980 and 1984.

In addition to seeming tough enough to be President, it is also important to appear competent, to exhibit sufficient knowledge and skills for the job. In the public's mind, personal experience testifies to the ability to perform. However, all experience is not equal. Having held an executive or legislative office at the national level is usually considered necessary, since the public does not think of the Presidency as a position that any political novice could easily or adequately handle.

The advantage of incumbency is obvious. Presidents are presumed to be knowledgeable because they have been President. They have met with world leaders, dealt with national and international crises, and coped with everyday problems of running the country. Even if they stumble on the facts, as Reagan did in the 1984 campaign, their incumbency testifies to their competency. Nonincumbents have to demonstrate that they have the capacity to provide such leadership. They have to show their presidential qualities without having been President.

A trip abroad is a first step that many take even before declaring their candidacy. By meeting and conversing with officials of other countries, a candidate hopes to convey the impression of a well-traveled, well-schooled, diplomat who is competent in foreign affairs. Jesse Jackson boosted his reputation significantly in 1984 by traveling to Syria to negotiate successfully the release of a U.S. naval aviator whose plane had been shot down over Lebanon.

Most candidates refer to some direct and relevant personal experience in presenting their qualifications for the office. In 1960, Kennedy pointed to his service in the Senate, particularly on the Foreign Relations Committee, as evidence of his knowledge of foreign affairs; in 1972, McGovern spoke of his years as an Air Force bomber pilot to lend credence to his views on the war in Vietnam and to his patriotism; in 1976, Carter noted his involvement with the Trilateral Commission, a group of prominent individuals interested in the United States' relations with Western Europe and Japan, as an indication of his interest and proficiency in foreign relations; in 1980, Reagan talked about his governorship of California as qualifying him to handle the executive duties of the Presidency, while Mondale referred to his experience as a senator and as Vice President in preparing him for the nation's top job.

Citing figures and facts in a seemingly spontaneous manner is another tactic frequently employed by candidates to exhibit their knowledge and intelligence and problem-solving skills. Nonincumbents in particular have used the forum of the debates to recite, without notes, statistics on the economy, foreign policy, and national-security matters. Their objective is to equalize the information advantage that their opponents are perceived to have by virtue of their positions as Vice President or President. So concerned were Ford's supporters about the public's perception of his intellectual abilities that they released information about his record in college and law school. Reagan was frequently pictured in a library-like setting during his 1980 campaign.

In addition to strength, decisiveness, knowledge, and competency, empathy is also an important attribute for presidential candidates. The public wants a person who can understand feelings and who responds to their emotional needs, one who understands what and how they feel. As the government has become larger, more powerful, and more distant, empathy has become more important. Roosevelt and Eisenhower radiated warmth. By comparison, McGovern and Nixon appeared cold, distant, and impersonal. Carter was particularly effective in 1976 in generating the impression that he cared, creating a vivid contrast with the conception of the imperial Presidency and the stereotypical image of his Republican opponents. In 1980, however, his personal criticism of Ronald Reagan undercut his own attractive qualities of compassion and fair play. His rhetoric made him look mean, nasty, and petty—all very undesirable traits. Reagan appeared and sounded less strident in contrast. He had a *cool* presence, particularly on television. His rhetoric was tough, but his voice was comforting and his manner reassuring.

Candor, integrity, and trust emerge periodically as important attributes in presidential image-building. Most of the time these traits are taken for granted. Occasionally, however, a crisis of confidence, such as Watergate, dictates that political skills be downplayed and these qualities stressed. This happened in 1952 and again in 1976. It may also occur in 1988.

In summary, candidates try to project images of themselves that are consistent with public expectations of the office and its occupant. Traits such as inner strength, decisiveness, competence, and experience are considered essential for the office, and others, such as empathy, sincerity, credibility, and integrity, are viewed as necessary for the individual. Which traits are considered most important varies to some extent with the assessment of the strengths and weaknesses of the incumbent. The negative attributes of the sitting President become the essential traits for the next one. That is why candidates must constantly monitor public opinion to discern which qualities are most salient during a particular period. Candidates who seem to be lacking one of them may have an image problem, but one that can be rectified; candidates who appear to lack more than one, however, are in more serious trouble.

The next section discusses some of the ways in which candidates use media to try to overcome their image problems.

CONTROLLED MEDIA

Candidates are marketed. Their advertisers use "Madison Avenue" techniques to persuade people to support them. Gaining attention, making a pitch, and leaving an impression are all basic objectives. The end, of course, is to get the electorate to do something—vote for specific candidates on election day.

Strategy

To mount a successful advertising campaign a team of experts must be assembled and a plan put into effect. The magnitude of the task and the time constraints imposed normally dictate that outside experts be hired to supplement the regular campaign staff. In 1984 the Reagan-Bush organization recruited forty top advertising executives to coordinate its media efforts. Known as the Tuesday Team for its mission—to reelect Ronald Reagan and George Bush on the Tuesday following the first Monday in November—the group began producing ads as early as the spring of 1984.[2] In all, the team produced forty-nine spots and one half-hour film that were aired, thirty ads that were never shown, and almost one hundred others that were written but never produced, at a total expenditure of $27 million.

Mondale's media campaign was coordinated by Richard Leone and produced by the political advertising firm of David H. Sawyer and Associates, at a cost of $23 million. A number of other Mondale advisers, however, also participated in strategic media decisions. They included pollsters Peter Hart and Patrick Caddell, campaign director Jim Johnson, preconvention media producer Roy Spence, and several other top aides. Disagreement among members of this group impeded a coordinated advertising effort.

At the beginning of the campaign, it is customary to design a media plan. The plan is a strategic blueprint, setting out the assumptions and objectives of the candidates. These include the personality traits that need to be emphasized, the issues that should be raised, and the images that have to be created. The plan, designed with the mood of the country in mind, outlines the form that the advertising should take and the way it should be marketed, targeted, and phased.

The assumptions of the plan relate to the environment and the candidate's position at the beginning of the campaign. The objectives indicate where the candidate would like to be at the end. The goal, of course, is to get there. Take the situation in which Carter found himself in the summer of 1980. He was perceived as a weak, indecisive, inconsistent leader, a President who seemed unable to devise solutions that would revive the nation's economy and reverse setbacks in foreign affairs. The task, as his advisers saw it, was to change significant portions of that image. They developed an advertising plan designed to emphasize Carter's activities as President and to highlight the incumbent-challenger contrast. (See box.)

Technique

The advantage of advertising particularly on television is that there are no intermediaries. Nor is there any interference from the media. Candidates can say and do what they want. The problem, however, is to make it look real. Candidate-sponsored programs are not unbiased, and the public knows it. Generating interest and convincing viewers are more difficult for advertisers than newscasters.

Thus, for advertising to be effective, it must be presented in a believable way. Having a candidate interact with people is one way of doing this. The use of ordinary citizens rather than professional actors increases the sense of authenticity. Joseph Napolitan, Humphrey's media consultant in 1968, recalled an advertisement that was not shown for precisely this reason. It looked stilted.

> One of the storyboard presentations DDB (Doyle Dane Bernbach) made at the convention in Chicago showed a little old lady talking about why she was going to vote for Humphrey, why she couldn't possibly vote Republican. In the drawing, she looked like everybody's grandmother; we thought it would be a good Medicare/senior citizen kind of spot, so we told DDB to go ahead and produce it.

> Most *political* film producers would have gone out and found a real person and filmed her. But DDB, and I suppose this is common procedure in their sphere, hired a model. Instead of the sweet little old lady, we were shown an elegantly coifed, beautifully gowned woman wearing a string of pearls

CARTER'S ADVERTISING PLAN IN 1980

There should be a positive and negative media campaign plan for the Fall. The positive campaign should begin September 4th. The negative campaign should begin in October.

1. The Positive Campaign.

Jimmy Carter should run for re-election on his record. It is a sign of how bad things have become that this suggestion would be ridiculed if made publicly. The public is now convinced that Jimmy Carter is an inept man. He has tried hard but he has failed. He is weak and indecisive—in over his head. We have to change people's minds.

This is a formidable task. If we adopt this approach we will not be doing "responsive chord" type spots—quick and easy re-inforcements of existing perceptions. We will be trying to turn perceptions around; to educate. Not an easy thing to do with television spots.

The message should be this: "We know you think Carter has not done much as President. But give us your attention—and an open mind—for a few minutes and we think you may be surprised by what you learn. . . .

Obviously, the effectiveness of this approach will depend upon the believability of the case we make. The spots will have to be long (probably five minutes) and packed with hard and surprising facts. The presentation can't be dull. We may want to use an actor to present our case. We'll need pictures, shots of the President, some use of the Cabinet, endorsement from world leaders . . . , Governors, Mayors, business leaders, labor leaders, other groups and common people. The over-all should present a *lot* of information presented in an interesting and credible way. . . .

The other positive message that we have to offer is this: CARTER IS SMARTER THAN REAGAN. The President is a man who grasps what is going on. We must show Carter as a man who comprehends the facts. A cornerstone of our positive media campaign will be the town meetings held during the general election. We will film these, then produce 30 minute programs, run them in the key states within a week of the President's visit.

2. The Negative Campaign

CARTER	REAGAN
SAFE/SOUND	UNTESTED
YOUNG	OLD
VIGOROUS	OLD

SMART	DUMB
COMPREHENSIVE MIND	*SIMPLISTIC*
ENGINEER	*ACTOR*
EXPERIENCED PRESIDENT	*NAIVE/INEXPERIENCED*
COMPASSIONATE	*REPUBLICAN*
MODERATE	*RIGHT-WING*

The negative campaign will be similar to the primary media campaign against Kennedy.

In his strategy memo, Pat Caddell wisely suggests the Election Definition as "The Presidency—A Serious Business." This is an excellent definition. We plan to make this the tone of our media campaign. Wrapping Carter—the only President running—in the mantle of the Presidency should give pause to those misguided souls who perceive Reagan as the lesser of two evils.

We are already producing a 15–16 minute convention film which touches on this—talking about Carter's real accomplishments in the context of the qualities that we expect of our Presidents and setting Jimmy Carter in a historic perspective while pointing out WHAT IT TAKES TO BE PRESIDENT.

1. A DEEP UNDERSTANDING of the difficult and complex problems that face our country and our world. . . .

2. EXPERIENCE with a staggering number of procedures and institutions—Congress, the federal bureaucracy, our nation's defense system, state and local governments, foreign policy. . . .

3. A SENSE OF MODERATION to avoid the dangers of ideological excess. . . .

4. COMPASSION for those who need government most—the poorest and the weakest in society as well as for the working person trying to bring the American Dream within his grasp.

5. THE COURAGE to do what is best even when it's not popular and to tell the truth to the American people even when it hurts.

Source: Rafshoon Communications, Excerpts from "The 1980 General Election Media Plan," July 3, 1980.

that looked as though it had just come out of Harry Winston's window, filmed against a brocaded chair in a lavishly appointed setting, acting for all the world as though she had to get through the spot quickly because she was keeping her chauffeur waiting. And I swear to God she spoke with at least a hint of an English accent.[3]

Underlining all television advertising is the need to maintain viewer interest. Frequently, this means action. The ad must move. The Carter campaign in 1976 was particularly skilled in creating this effect. Carter was seen walking on his farm, talking with local citizens, speaking to business and professional groups, and addressing the Democratic convention. His movement gave the impression of agility, of a person who was capable of meeting the heavy and multiple responsibilities of the Presidency. His 1980 ads pictured him as an active President. In contrast, Reagan's advertising of that year was more static. Fearful that a slick presentation would bring attention to his career as an actor, the commercials presented the candidate as a talking head with as few gimmicks and diversions as possible. In 1984 this approach was modified to produce smoother, more subtle advertising. Some of it included only brief appearances of the President.

Political ads take many forms. The most popular ones from the perspective of the advertisers are the short spots of 30 and 60 seconds, which are interspersed with other commercials in regular programming. Longer advertisements that preempt part of the standard fare and full-length productions such as interviews, documentaries, and campaign rallies have also been employed.

The primary benefits of the short spots are that they make a point, are cheaper to produce and air, and are usually viewed by a larger, more captive audience. Longer programs, which may go into greater detail about the candidate's career, qualifications, and beliefs, are generally seen by fewer people and usually the wrong ones—those who have already decided to vote for that candidate. While it may be necessary to energize these true believers and get them to the polls, the principal targets of most campaign advertising are the undecided and the indifferent. For them, the commercial must capture their attention, present a message, shape an image, and work toward motivating them to vote for the candidate.

Political documentaries have the advantage of combining a story with a message in pictorial form. Film biographies are particularly good at image building for lesser-known candidates or for explaining the accomplishments of those who have been in office but whose records have not jelled in the minds of the voters. Even the Ford campaign ran a short biography of the incumbent President to draw attention to parts of his career that were not well known to the general public (perhaps because he had not previously run in a national campaign).

In addition to format, timing is also a critical component of campaign advertising. When commercials are shown affects who will see them. Purchasing time-slots is a specialized art, and campaign organizations hire experts to do it. The object is to have the largest viewing audience, or, in the jargon of the trade, the highest Nielsen rating.[4] In 1984 it was a Mondale ad that had the best rating and a Reagan one that had the worst.[5]

For the candidate who appears to be ahead, the advertising should be scheduled at a steady rate over the course of the campaign in order to maintain the lead. Nixon in 1968 and 1972 and Carter in 1976 followed this practice. Reagan in 1984 did not. Benefiting from the extensive and favorable coverage a President usually receives, and from Reagan's large lead in the preelection polls, the Reagan-Bush organization decided to hold much of its advertising for the final two weeks of the campaign, just in case a problem developed. In contrast, Mondale was forced to run many of his commercials early to try to improve his image and his standing in the polls.

If a candidate needs to catch up, however—provided he is not too far behind—a concentrated series of ads that builds toward the end of the campaign is more desirable. Humphrey in 1968 and Ford in 1976 adopted this approach. Humphrey had no choice. With no postnomination campaign plan in place, no usable television commercials on file, and no money to purchase time on television, his organization had to create, purchase, and package the advertising and then buy slots when money became available. Independent candidate John Anderson in 1980 was in a similar financial bind, and was forced to run all of his ads in the final ten days.

Most campaign advertising must be sequenced as well. At the outset it is necessary to identify the candidate with information about his or her family, experience, and qualifications for the office. Once the personal dimension is established, the position of the candidate can be articulated in the second stage. This is the argumentative phase in which themes are presented and policy positions noted. In the third stage, the candidate frequently goes on the offensive. His campaign runs a series of negative ads in which the reasons not to vote for the opponent are stressed. Known as confrontational ads, they usually generate the most controversy, often leading to spirited defenses and counterattacks. Candidates like to end their campaign on a positive note. In the final phase, "feel good" commercials are shown. Replete with catchy and upbeat jingles, smiling faces, and much Americana, they strive to make voters feel good about supporting the candidate.[6]

Although most campaign advertising goes through these four stages, the periods frequently overlap. Different types of commercials are shown at the same time. In the 1986 congressional elections, negative advertising was used frequently at the beginning of some campaigns to increase the public awareness of an opponent's principal weaknesses. In general, negative advertising is needed more by challengers than incumbents, to give the public a reason for voting against the person in office.

In addition to television advertising on the major networks, candidates usually supplement their appeals on radio, cable television, and in newspapers and magazines. Cheaper in cost, these communication vehicles normally reach a smaller but more clearly defined audience. As a consequence, advertisements on these media can be more effectively targeted to readers or listeners than can television commercials on the major networks. Computerized direct mail can be the most specific of all. It facilitates different people receiving different messages.

Content

The name of the game is image-making. With the emphasis on leadership, it is essential to demonstrate those traits the public associates with the position. For a President seeking reelection, use of the White House as a backdrop is standard. The incumbent's advertising pictures the President as President—meeting with the leaders of other governments, with members of Congress, and with his own top aides, presiding over official ceremonies, greeting visiting dignitaries, and working late and often alone in the Oval Office.

One of Jimmy Carter's most effective 1980 commercials showed him in a whirl of presidential activities ending as darkness fell over the White House. A voice intoned, "The responsibility never ends. Even at the end of a long working day there is usually another cable addressed to the Chief of State from the other side of the world where the sun is shining and something is happening." As a light came on in the President's living quarters, the voice concluded, "And he's not finished yet."

While all candidates must demonstrate their presidential abilities, they also need to distinguish themselves from their opponents. Carter did this in 1976 by emphasizing his atypical leadership qualities. He was portrayed as a fresh, independent, people-oriented candidate who would provide new leadership. His slogan, "A leader, for a change," his less formal appearance, even the deep green color of his literature, conveyed how different he was from the old-style Washington politician and the two previous Republican Presidents.

In 1980 Reagan stressed his new solutions to the nation's old and persistent policy problems. In 1984 his commercials recounted his success: his strong leadership, defense buildup, and his no-nonsense attitude toward the Soviet Union. How to do this without provoking fears of a nuclear confrontation was the task his advertisers faced. Their artful solution was the "bear" commercial.

The commercial begins with a menacing grizzly bear moving through the woods. As the bear prowls, a drum is heard beating, beating, beating like a heart. It is an ominous sound. Suddenly the bear senses another predator, stops, and sees a man with a rifle slung over his shoulder. The bear takes a step backward. The announcer provides a closing refrain: "President Reagan, Prepared For Peace."

One of Mondale's difficulties in 1984 was that he could not claim to be new and different (as Carter could in 1976 and Reagan in 1980) nor could he match his opponent's perceived strong leadership and clear policy goals. Given the high performance ratings for the President, Mondale was forced to focus on the future, contrasting his energy and flexibility with the 74-year-old Reagan's dogmatism and steadfastness. One of Mondale's most effective ads pictured a roller coaster speeding up and down a track. On the down cycle an announcer says, "1982, Reaganomics sinks our country into the deepest recession and unemployment in fifty years." As the roller coaster goes rapidly down again, the ad ends with the announcer proclaiming, "If you're thinking of voting for Ronald Reagan in 1984, think of what will happen in 1985."

Mondale's ad is an example of negative advertising. Instead of playing to a candidate's strength, negative advertising exploits the opposition's weaknesses. Perhaps the most famous (or infamous) negative political commercial was created by advertising executive Tony Schwartz in 1964 for use against Barry Goldwater. It was designed to reinforce the impression that Goldwater was a trigger-happy zealot who would not hesitate to use nuclear weapons against a Communist foe.

Pictured first was a little girl in a meadow plucking petals from a daisy. She counted to herself softly. When she reached nine, the picture froze on her face, her voice faded, and a stern-sounding male voice counted down from ten. When he got to zero there was an explosion, the little girl disappeared, and a mushroom-shaped cloud covered the screen. Lyndon Johnson's voice was heard: "These are the stakes—to make a world in which all of God's children can live, or go into the dark. We must either love each other, or we must die." The ad ended with an announcer saying, "Vote for President Johnson on November 3. The stakes are too high for you to stay home."

The commercial was run only once. Goldwater supporters were outraged, and protested vigorously. Their protest kept the issue alive. In fact, the ad itself became a news item, and parts of it were shown on television newscasts. Schwartz had made the point stick.

In 1972 and 1976 the Republican candidates ran a series of very effective negative commercials. The anti-McGovern ads were sponsored by Democrats for Nixon and introduced by John Connally, former Democratic governor of Texas, but were paid for by Nixon's Committee to Re-Elect the President. One showed a profile of McGovern, with an announcer stating a position that McGovern had taken and later changed. When the change in position was explained, another profile of McGovern, but one looking in the opposite direction, was flashed on the screen. This tactic of position change and profile rotation was repeated several times. Finally, when the announcer asked, "What about next year?" McGovern's face spun rapidly before viewers. A similar negative ad was directed against Carter in 1980.

In 1976, Ford's media advertisers created a very effective negative ad referred to as the man-in-the-street commercial. It began with interviews with a number of people in different areas of the country who indicated their preference for Ford. The focus then gradually changed. Some people were uncertain; others voiced reservations about Carter. Most convincing were the Georgia critics. "He didn't do anything," stated one man from Atlanta. "I've tried, and all my friends have tried, to remember exactly what Carter did as governor, and nobody really knows." The commercial concluded with an attractive woman, also from Georgia, saying, in a thick southern accent, "It would be nice to have a President from Georgia—but not Carter." She smiled. The ad ended.

The "man-in-the-street" commercials showed a contrast. They not only suggested that President Ford enjoyed broad support but also served to reinforce doubts about Carter, even among Georgians. Moreover, the fact that the people interviewed were not actors gave the ads more credibility. They seemed like news stories, and that was not coincidental. They were so effective, in fact, that most candidates now employ similar types of commercials in their primary and general election campaigns.

Negative advertising has been used against vice presidential candidates as well. One of the most clever of these ads appeared in 1968. It was a twenty-second spot that began with the words "Agnew for Vice

President" on the screen. The audio consisted almost entirely of a man laughing. As the laughter began to fade away, a solemn-sounding announcer stated, "This would be funny if it weren't so serious."

Effectiveness

Most advertisements are evaluated by campaign officials and a sample of the general public before being aired. The candidate will frequently see them as well. The commercials are also shown to focus groups around the country. Members of these groups, who are usually preselected by the candidate's pollster, are asked to discuss their reaction to the ads with campaign officials. A favorable response normally clears the way for the commercials to be shown, but the evaluation process continues. In the days following the airing of a spot, in-depth interviews are conducted by telephone with randomly selected people. Their recall and reaction are ascertained, and the impact of the ad is calculated.

In 1984 one of the most extensively tested spots was the Reagan bear commercial. Before airing, it was shown to one hundred focus groups, and after airing extensive interviews were conducted. The response suggested its impact: more than 60 percent of those interviewed remembered seeing the ad; 30 percent understood its message of peace through strength: A vigilant, strong United States is necessary to stop the Soviet bear.[7]

UNCONTROLLED MEDIA

From the perspective of image-building, political advertising gives the campaign the most control over what the voters see. The environment can be predetermined, the words and pictures can be created and coordinated, and the candidate can be rehearsed to produce the desired effect. Moreover, the message can be targeted.

News events are more difficult to influence. A candidate's media advisers do not control the environment, nor do they produce the product. In some cases, the message is partially mediated by the structure of the event. Interviews and debates provide a format that shapes but does not always direct the discussion. In other cases, the message and the image are directly affected by the media's orientation. Remarks are edited for the sake of the story. A candidate can be interrupted, his comments interpreted, and his policies evaluated. Major statements can even be ignored—if, for example, hecklers are present, or if the candidate makes some goof, such as slipping or even bumping his head. Under these circumstances, aspirants for the Presidency exercise much less leverage. They are not powerless, however.

Debates

Candidates have viewed presidential debates as a way to improve their image and damage their opponent's. The first series of televised debates occurred in 1960. Kennedy wanted to counter the impression that he was too young and inexperienced. Nixon, on the other hand, sought to maintain his stature as Eisenhower's knowledgeable and competent Vice President and the obvious person to succeed his "boss" in office.

In the three elections that followed, Johnson and then Nixon, ahead in the polls, saw no advantage in debating their opponents, and refused to do so. Ford, however, trailed Carter in 1976. He saw debates as an opportunity to appear presidential and to chip away at his Democratic rival's "soft" backing. The Carter camp, on the other hand, saw them as a means of shoring up their own support. In the words of pollster Patrick Caddell, "Debates would give him (Carter) exposure in depth, would demonstrate his competence in the same arena with an incumbent President, would retain his solid vote—and keep reinforcing it."[8] In 1980 the rationale was similar. From Reagan's perspective, it was a way to reassure voters about himself and his qualifications for office. For Carter, it was another chance to emphasize the differences between himself and Reagan, between their parties, and between their issue and ideological positions.

By 1984 presidential debates had become a recognized institution that even incumbents could not avoid without making their avoidance an issue. Thus, Ronald Reagan was forced by the pressures of public opinion to debate Walter Mondale, even though he stood to gain little, and could have lost much, from their face-to-face encounter.

One reason that debates have become such an integral part of the presidential electoral process is that they regularly attract great interest and many viewers, more than any other single event of the entire campaign. It is estimated that more than half the adult population of the United States watched all the Kennedy-Nixon debates and that almost 90 percent saw one of them.[9] The first Ford-Carter debate in 1976 attracted an estimated 90 million to 100 million viewers, while the Carter-Reagan debate and Reagan-Mondale debates had audiences approaching 120 million.

While presidential debates are here to stay, their number, scheduling, and format are still subject to considerable negotiation between the principal contenders and their staffs. In these negotiations incumbents have had the advantage. Carter refused to debate Anderson in 1980; Reagan set the parameters for the debates with Mondale in 1984.[10]

Despite the appearance of spontaneity, debates are highly scripted. Careful preparation is now a must. Representatives of the candidates study the locations, try to anticipate the questions, and prepare written answers for their candidates. Mock studios are built and the debate environment simulated. The opponent's speeches and interviews are carefully studied for content, style, and other nuances. They are then used in dress rehersals by stand-ins who imitate the opponent when debating their own candidate.[11]

In 1980 this elaborate preparation took a bizarre twist. The Reagan campaign obtained one of Carter's three briefing books. The book contained key lines, Reagan quotes, and pat answers. Knowing the quotes Carter would use, the questions he anticipated, and the answers he was advised to give helped Reagan's strategists prepare their responses to use in rebuttal. In general, all debate participants with the exception of Nixon, in his first debate with Kennedy, have been well prepared.[12]

Much calculation goes into debate strategy. Candidates need to decide what issues to stress and how to stress them; how to catch their opponents off guard or goad them into an error; whether and how to respond to a personal attack and to criticism of their policy positions.

Lewis Kaden, a labor lawyer, served as Mondale's principal coach for his 1984 debates with Reagan. Kaden prepared an issue book with a two page memo on each of forty-five issues. He also developed a debate strategy, articulating the objectives, themes, approaches, and tactics he believed Mondale should pursue. (See box.)

Patrick Caddell also advised Mondale on strategy. He advocated a strategy of surprise in the first debate:

> Ronald Reagan will be heavily "scripted." His side will prepare him to deal with the "Fighting Fritz" Mondale that they and all expect. . . . AND THAT'S OUR OPENING—HIT REAGAN WITH A DIFFERENT MONDALE, UPSET EXPECTATIONS, RENDER HIS SCRIPTED RESPONSES IRRELEVANT.[13]

Caddell also urged Mondale to physically dominate the debate by occasionally turning toward Reagan, taking a step in his direction, and then returning to the lectern to address the American people. Throughout, he

MONDALE'S DEBATE STRATEGY

Mondale Objectives

1. Demonstrate your sense of fairness and contrast it with Reagan's. Show you are more likely to be worried about everyone, not just the few.
2. Focus on the importance of this election to the future of our country. This election is not just a rerun of 1980, and it's not just about 1984. We've learned from our experiences. This election is about 1985 and the rest of this century; that's why it's so important.
3. Show strength in a positive way. Show that you're decisive, interested, steady, and believe strongly in what you're fighting for.
4. Do the above positively, granting Reagan his sincerely held beliefs and persuasive abilities. Instead, emphasize contrasting visions of, and plans for, the future.

Mondale Positive Themes

1. You are concerned about the average family; you have a strong sense of fairness.
2. You are facing reality and are ready to make tough choices to build the future.
3. You have plans/visions for the future of America. You're ready to pick up the challenge to make America greater.

Mondale Negative Themes

1. Reagan is not concerned about the average family; the evidence is that his policies are unfair—they favor the rich and big corporations. That is the historic difference between Democrats and Republicans; that's why his proper heroes are Coolidge, Hoover, and Nixon. The current Republican platform proves it.
2. He is out of touch and doesn't understand. That is why there is such a gap between what he says (good intentions; sounds good) and his policies.

Notes on Approach and Tactics

1. Grant Reagan his optimism, his good intentions, and his beliefs in equality, God, etc.
2. Once his beliefs are granted, use an indirect approach to lead into the contrast of visions and plans. Examples:
   • "I don't think President Reagan understands that . . ."
   • "Perhaps President Reagan hasn't focused on the important details . . ."

- "I don't think President Reagan is aware of the fact that . . ."
- "I don't doubt that President Reagan is sincere, but let me point out that . . ."
- "I grant that that may once have been true, but . . ."
- "I'm sure that's what you want, but your people haven't been going in that direction . . ."

3. Don't attack his record as a matter of course. Reserve the attacks for the most egregious examples of unfairness—Social Security, Medicare, unfair tax breaks, and handicapped children.
4. When you attack his record, link it to the choices we face in the future. Example: "Given our records on Social Security, do you think I would cut it to reduce the debt? Would President Reagan be inclined to do so?"
5. An attack is more effective on television when rhetorical questions are used.
6. Halfway to two-thirds of the way through the debate, you may wish to turn to him and attack his motives on one subject. The best topic: Social Security or Medicare. . . .
7. A story is almost always appropriate as an answer and will be remembered. . . .
8. To continue picking up weak Democrats, portray both yourself and Mr. Reagan as party leaders and emphasize the parties' contrasting visions of the future.
9. When you go first, preempt his answer. When you go second, comment on how President Reagan answered or didn't answer the question.

Source: Lewis Kaden, Memorandum, (October 1984) as appears in Peter Goldman and Tony Fuller, *The Quest for the Presidency, 1984* (Toronto: Bantam Books, 1985), pp. 430–432.

wanted Mondale to appear calm and cool. Mondale followed Caddell's stylistic advice with considerable success.[14]

Using style to achieve effect has been apparent in other debates as well. Kennedy and Carter talked faster than their opponents, to create an action-oriented psychology in the minds of the viewers. Both tried to demonstrate their knowledge by citing many facts and statistics in their answers. Ford and Reagan spoke in more general terms, expressing particular concern about the size and structure of government. They reiterated their basic themes. Reagan's wit and anecdotes in 1980 conveyed a warm, human dimension, in contrast to Carter's all-business, machinelike responses.

The reason style is so important is that the public reacts more to the overall performance and style of the candidates than to any of their specific arguments. In the words of Caddell, "Voters don't remember specific issues, they remember the 'feel' of the candidate—his values, his passions, his competence, his persona—and they are most influenced by the continual consistent drumbeat of the larger messages, i.e., themes, by the candidate."[15]

The media contribute to this reaction by their emphasis on controversy and on personal style. In at least one instance, they directly affected the image a candidate was attempting to project. By highlighting Ford's statement during his second debate with Carter that the Soviet Union did not dominate Eastern Europe, network commentators damaged the President's claim to be more capable and knowledgeable in foreign affairs, essential presidential traits.

The media have tended to assess debates in terms of winners and losers. Their evaluation conditions how the public judges the results. Since most people do not follow the content very closely and do not put much faith in their own evaluation, media commentary can have a considerable impact on public opinion. It can modify the immediate impressions people have, moving it in the direction of an acknowledged winner. This happened in 1976 and again in 1980.

It is difficult to pinpoint precisely the impact of the debates on voting. Perceptions of the candidates change over the course of the campaign. Debates may contribute to these altered perceptions, but other factors do as well. It is easier to assess the short-run impact of debates on public opinion by conducting before-and-after surveys.

There seems to be a two-stage reaction. In stage one, which occurs immediately following the debates, opinions are influenced primarily by partisan orientations and previously held perceptions. The tendency is to see one's own candidate in the more favorable light. In stage two, which occurs a few days after the debate, the media's evaluation, combined with fading memories, can reinforce or alter the public's initial judgment. Ford's second debate with Carter is an excellent illustration of this second-stage effect. Surveys taken within the first twelve hours following the debate indicated that viewers, by almost two to one, believed Ford had won. Few mentioned his remarks on Eastern Europe. Polls taken two to three days after the debate, however, presented a very different picture. By more than two to one, Carter was perceived the winner. In 1980 the percentage of people believing Reagan to be the victor almost doubled within four days following the debate.

With so many people watching, the shaping of perceptions about the candidates' personal attributes and their policy positions can influence the outcome of a close election. The effect the debate has, however, tends to vary with the attitudes and opinions of those watching it. For partisans, the debate tends to solidify support. Those who are more involved are more likely to watch them; those who are more knowledgeable are more likely to learn from them; those who are most partisan are more apt to be convinced by them. The debate confirms their perceptions. It makes them more likely to vote for their party's nominee.

For weaker partisans and independents, the debates can increase interest and can clarify, color, or even change perceptions. Before debating, Kennedy was thought by many to be less knowledgeable and less experienced than Nixon; Carter was seen as an enigma, as fuzzier than Ford; Reagan was perceived to be more doctrinaire and less informed than his Democratic opponent. The debates enabled each of these candidates to overcome these negative perceptions. In the end this proved to be important to the success of their candidacies.

Kennedy and Carter might not have won without the debates. Reagan probably would not have won by as much in 1980. In 1984 the debates did not affect Reagan's support in any appreciable way, although they did create the "age" issue, which might have become a factor had Reagan faltered during the second debate.

Despite Reagan's weak performance in the first debate, public opinion polls showed little decline in the President's support. On the other hand, Mondale increased his as a result of the first debate. Democrats saw him as a more acceptable candidate.

The experiences of Kennedy in 1960, Carter in 1976, and Reagan in 1980 suggest why debates tend to help challengers more than incumbents. Being less well known, challengers have more questions raised about them, their competence, and their capacity to be President. The debates provide them with an opportunity to satisfy some of these doubts in a believable setting and on a comparative basis. By appearing to be at least the equal of their incumbent opponents, the challenger's image as a potential president is enhanced.

News Coverage

News coverage is not likely to benefit a candidate in the same manner as debates or interviews do. The *modus operandi* of news reporting is to inform and interest the public. Rather than improve an image, news coverage can distort or destroy it.

Knowing how the media cover the campaign is critical to understanding how campaign organizations can affect the media. Most people follow presidential campaigns on television. It is the prime source of news for approximately 60 percent of the population.[16] Newspapers are a distant second, with only 20 percent listing them as their principal source. Radio and magazines trail far behind.

News on television seems more believable. People can see what is happening. Being an action-oriented, visual medium, television reports the drama and excitement of the campaign. It does so by emphasizing the contest. Who is ahead? How are the candidates doing? Is the leader slipping? It is this horse-race aspect of the campaign that provides the principal focus for television, as well as for the print media.

The focus serves two primary purposes. It heightens viewers' interests; this, in turn, increases the audience and the profits, since advertising revenue is based on the number of people watching a particular program. Second, it gives the media an aura of objectivity. Rather than presenting subjective reports of the campaign, they can provide more objective data on the public's reaction to the campaign. One evidence of this is the increasing involvement of the major news organizations in the business of polling. One-third of the *New York Times* coverage in the last week of the 1984 election was devoted to stories about public opinion, namely, how do people feel about the candidates and issues, who is going to win, and why.[17]

This trend is not new. In 1976 Thomas Patterson found about 60 percent of television election coverage and 55 percent of newspaper coverage devoted to the campaign as a contest.[18] Michael J. Robinson and Margaret Sheehan's analysis of "CBS Evening News" during the 1980 election revealed that five out of six stories emphasized the competition.[19]

Additionally, media concentrate on candidate-related issues. Have the nominees behaved in a proper manner? Do they have the information and knowledge necessary to make good policy judgments? Do they have the will and capability to exercise strong leadership? In 1984 Clancey and Robinson found that 40 percent of the coverage dealt with these kinds of concerns.[20]

In contrast, policy issues have been relatively neglected. There is little in-depth analysis of the substantive policy questions. Nor is there much discussion of what difference it would make for the country who wins. The study of the "CBS Evening News" in 1980 revealed an average of only 90 seconds per program spent on issues of policy, approximately 20 to 25 percent of the total election coverage.[21] In 1984 no policy question received the attention that Ferraro's finances or Reagan's age did.[22]

This has serious implications for the electoral system. It encourages the candidates *not* to be spontaneous, *not* to be candid, *not* to be specific about what they will do if elected. It gives the voter a lot of information about trivial issues and much less information about substantive policy questions. It practically forces the electorate to make a decision on the basis of personality if they are not going to make a decision on the basis of party.

Not only do the media focus primarily on the candidates, they focus primarily on the *major* party candidates. As aspirants for the nomination, candidates receive coverage roughly in proportion to their popular standing, with the front-runners receiving the most. After the conventions are over, it becomes a two-person contest. Minority party and independent candidates receive little, if any, attention. The exception was John Anderson. In 1980, he obtained one-fourth of the coverage given to Reagan and Carter.[23]

Once the general election campaign begins, both major party candidates get approximately the same amount of coverage. Contrary to popular belief, incumbents seeking reelection do not dominate the news.[24] However, incumbents do tend to receive more critical coverage than their challengers. In 1980 Jimmy Carter was treated more harshly than Ronald Reagan, and in 1984 Reagan was treated more harshly than Walter Mondale. Vice President Bush fared the worst of all. Clancey and Robinson's study of the evening news on the three major networks found no favorable story on Bush during the entire 1984 campaign![25]

Notwithstanding the criticism of the incumbent, the vast majority of coverage tends to be neutral. The media, particularly television, do not evidence an *ideological bias*[26] Conservatives are treated neither better nor worse than liberals. According to Clancey and Robinson, three out of four campaign stories in 1984 had no favorable or unfavorable "spin" at all.[27]

The media do, however, have a *journalistic bias,* one that results in more negative coverage for the front-runner in the primaries and for the incumbent in the general election. It is a bias to make the campaign more exciting, to generate and maintain as high a level of public interest as possible. This is why the contest tends to dominate the coverage.

What is new and unexpected is newsworthy. What is old and predictable is not. A fresh face winning and an experienced candidate losing is news; an experienced one winning and a new one losing is not. Similarly, stump speeches and canned answers are not reported as frequently as are verbal slips, inconsistent statements, and mistakes.

To infuse politics with a sense of drama, to tap the human dimension, to simplify and explain complex statements, issues, and events, the media provide a framework for interpretation. As with the debates, this framework is couched in terms of winners and losers: how the candidates stand in the polls, how they interact with the voters, how they differ from each other on a few major issues. Another reason policy questions do not generate the amount of coverage that candidate issues do is that they are not easily cast within such a framework.

Candidates and their advisers understand this media orientation. They know they must take it into account when trying to affect the quantity and quality of coverage they receive. That is why they play the expectations game, why they speak in careful, calculated language, why they promise to solve the nation's problems but do so without detailing their solutions.

The tactics used to influence the media are many and varied. They include the timing and staging of events, the access given to reporters, and the release of favorable information.

Major announcements are made early enough—usually by 3 P.M.—to get on the evening news. Speeches are timed to maximize the viewing audience. Quiet periods, such as Saturday, are considered a good time to hold a press conference, schedule interviews, or provide a taped radio message. In addition to receiving same-day coverage by television, a Saturday event usually gets prominent treatment in the Sunday paper.

Campaign events are now carefully staged for television. Crowds are compacted.[28] Excitement is generated. Complexity is simplified. Candidates talk in *media bites*, short, pithy statements that sound good and can be presented in the few seconds given to the candidate's remarks by television news. Catchy expressions such as "Where's the Beef?" and "It's Morning in America" are used.

Access is a valuable commodity. So is the careful release of information, not only position papers but items on the personal life of the candidate and his family. To a large extent, those who report the news are dependent on this material. An analysis of news stories in twenty papers in 1968 found that candidates were the principal source of more than half of them.[29] Similar findings were reported in the 1980 campaign by Robinson and Sheehan:

On UPI, just over 40 percent of the Carter news came directly from Carter, his press office, his staff, or his administration. Fewer than 10 percent came via the investigative route. On CBS, it was the same story, so to speak, only more so. A full two-thirds of the "official" news about Carter came via a Carter-controlled news source. Investigative journalism again accounted for less than 10 percent of the reporting.[30]

In short, the candidates can exercise a major influence on the projection of their own images in the news. They cannot control the news, however. They cannot define their coverage completely, divert the media from controversial statements or actions, or prevent or sometimes even counter uncomplimentary evaluations. As Jody Powell said of Jimmy Carter's 1976 candidacy:

There was no way on God's earth we could shake the fuzziness question in the general election, no matter what Carter did or said. He could have spent the whole campaign doing nothing but reading substantive speeches from morning to night and still have had that image in the national press.[31]

In summary, there is both tension and cooperation between the media and the candidate. The tension is compounded by the media's need to highlight controversy and accentuate the negative and the candidate's desire to suppress unfavorable news. The cooperation is generated by the media's need for information and access and the candidate's desire to accentuate the positive. The key questions are: What impact does all this have on the voters? How does media coverage affect image creation during the campaign? The final section of this chapter proposes some answers to these questions.

THE IMPACT OF THE MEDIA

The time, money, and energy spent on image building suggest that it has a major impact on voting behavior. Why else would so many resources be devoted to the media effort? Yet it is difficult to document the precise effect. There is little tangible evidence to support the propositions that television changes people's minds on the candidates and the issues, or that news programs raise their level of knowledge, or that mass appeals affect many voting decisions.

Studies of campaigning in the 1940s indicated that the principal impact of the media was to activate predispositions and reinforce attitudes, rather than to convert voters. Newspapers and magazines provided information, but primarily to those who were most committed. The most committed, in turn, used the information to support their beliefs. Weeding out opposing views, they insulated themselves from unfavorable news and from opinions that conflicted with their own.[32]

With the bulk of campaign information coming from printed matter, voters, particularly partisan voters, tended to minimize cross-pressures and to strengthen their own preexisting judgments. In contrast, the less committed also had less incentive to become informed. They maintained their ignorance by avoiding information about the campaign. The format of newspapers and magazines facilitated this kind of selective perception and retention.

Television might have been expected to change this. It exposes the less committed to more information and the more committed to other points of view. Avoidance is more difficult, since viewers are more captive to the picture than to the printed page.

While the same events get reported, the reports often differ. Robinson and Sheehan found the news on television to be "more mediating, more political, more personal, more critical, [and] more thematic than old-style print."[33] Newspapers describe events. They indicate what candidates say and do. Television presents drama. It provides a visual slice of reality, *not* a compendium of people, places, and things. In this way it mediates between candidates and the public more than newspapers do. It is also more analytic and more negative. Robinson and Sheehan report, "In the end, every major candidate in Campaign '80 got a more critical press on CBS than on UPI, explicitly or implicitly."[34]

The amount of coverage also differs. Television compartmentalizes. The evening news fits a large number of stories into a thirty-minute broadcast (which includes only twenty-three minutes of news). Of necessity, this restricts the time that can be devoted to each item. Campaign stories average ninety seconds on the evening news, the equivalent of only a few paragraphs of a printed account. This helps explain why viewers do not retain much information from television coverage.

Two political scientists, Thomas E. Patterson and Robert D. McClure, who studied how television reported the news during the 1972 campaign, found:

1. Most election issues are mentioned so infrequently that viewers could not possibly learn about them.
2. Most issue references are so fleeting that they could not be expected to leave an impression on viewers.

3. The candidates' issue positions generally were reported in ways guaranteed to make them elusive.[35]

"Television news adds little to the average voter's understanding of election issues," they wrote. "Network news may be fascinating. It may be highly entertaining. But it is simply not informative."[36]

Nonetheless, network news is still important. It, along with the written press, helps set the agenda for the campaign. Its emphasis or lack of emphasis on certain issues affects the content of the debate, the attention that the candidates must give to specific policy questions, and to some extent, the kinds of responses they have to provide. This can be particularly significant for certain types of issues that do not have a direct impact on the voters, such as foreign affairs, space exploration, or even the behavior of public officials. Unlike pocketbook concerns, these issues might not be as salient if they had not been stressed by the media.

The need to emphasize the contest affects which issues are covered when issues *are* covered. The media focus on those issues that provide clear-cut differences between the candidates, those that provoke controversy, and those that can be presented in a simple, straightforward manner. These are not necessarily the issues that the candidates have highlighted during their campaigns. In his research, Patterson has found that

> candidates talk mostly about "diffuse" issues, ones in which the differences between the candidates are either indirect or mostly those of style and emphasis. . . . Such issues in 1976 accounted for about 65 percent of the issue appeals in the candidates' speeches. These issues, however, accounted for only 35 percent of the issue messages in election news.[37]

In addition to its de-emphasis of diffuse issues, news coverage also fails to present background information needed to assess issue stands. While policy positions of the candidates may be reported, these positions are rarely described in detail, much less analyzed. Nor are personal histories or public records of the principal candidates explored in any depth. With the great emphasis on the horserace and hoopla, it is no wonder that people learn so little about their voting choices from the news.

Where, then, do people receive information? One of the most interesting findings of the Patterson and McClure study is that people actually get more information from the advertisements they see on television than from the evening news. The reason seems to be that ads are more repetitive, more compact, and more focused than the news. When placed with other commercials during popular shows, they are difficult to avoid.[38] In fact, studies have shown that television watchers pay about twice as much attention to political advertisements as they do to other kinds of commercials.[39] Special election programs also add to the public's information. Together with advertising, these programs broaden the electorate's information about the candidates and contribute particularly to the perception of their personal attributes.

Do the media affect the election? Do they influence the vote? The answer is yes. They do so by setting the agenda. They do so by providing the criteria by which much of the electorate evaluates the candidates, primarily their potential for leadership. But the influence of the media is limited by the stability of public beliefs and political attitudes, by the compartmentalization of the news and the neutrality of the reporting, and by the lack of attention given to the media by much of the general public.

In general, the effect varies with preexisting beliefs. It tends to reinforce the loyalties of strong partisans rather than challenge those loyalties. The campaign is simply too short, the defenses of these partisans too resilient, and the news too vacuous for large-scale changes of attitude to occur. For those without strong partisan identities, those who are marginally interested in the election but have limited knowledge about the candidates and issues, television in particular may alter perceptions, although it usually does not change opinions or even improve knowledge of substantive policy issues. What happens is that some people begin to see the candidates in a different light. They are persuaded to vote for or against a particular individual.

Media are apt to be more influential during the preconvention period, when less is known about the candidates and when partisan affiliation is not a factor. However, with the decline of strong partisanship in the electorate and the increase in independents, the audience that may be affected in this manner during the general election has become larger for a longer period. That is why campaigns spend so much time and energy on media advertising from the very beginning of the electoral cycle, and why they try to affect news coverage of their candidates throughout the campaign.

SUMMARY

The presentation and projection of images are important to a presidential campaign because the electorate's assessment of the candidates, issues, and parties affects its voting behavior. Influencing that assessment is the goal of the image makers. They work on the assumption that what candidates say affects their image, and that their image, in turn, affects their chances of winning the election.

The increasing dependence on television as a communications medium has forced greater emphasis to be placed on candidate images and less on the party and issues. Candidates try to project images that embody traits people desire in their Presidents. These include the strong, decisive, and intelligent leadership needed by the institution and the personal qualities of empathy, sincerity, candor, and integrity.

Images must be conveyed primarily through the media. Relatively few people come into direct contact with the candidates. The objective of the campaign organizations in communicating information is, of course, very different from that of the media in covering the campaign. Thus, the task from the candidate's perspective is to get the message across as clearly, as frequently, and as cogently as possible.

The easiest (and also the most costly) way to do this is to air an advertisement that sells the candidate much as any product is marketed. Advertising can tap positive or negative dimensions of personality. It can be targeted and timed to maximize its impact. It can even be made to look like news. The more credible the ad, the more likely it will have an effect.

Candidates try to distinguish their message by its thematic content. Presidents Kennedy and Carter stressed activity and decisiveness in the aftermath of conservative Republican years. Johnson and Nixon promised mainstream politics, in contrast to their more reactionary or radical opponents. Ford pointed to his decency and honesty in a not-so-subtle contrast to his Republican predecessor. Reagan articulated traditional values and conservative policies as the best way to cope with the country's economic and military needs. Mondale claimed he had greater energy, flexibility, and competence to deal with future problems.

In addition to political advertising there are other ways of influencing perceptions through the media. Candidates exercise considerable discretion in the words they use and the demeanor they present in interviews, in debates, and even on the news. Despite the appearance of spontaneity, their comments are carefully prepared and well rehearsed. In fact, throughout the entire campaign, public utterances are almost always made and actions taken with the press in mind.

How the media cover campaigns affects how candidates attempt to influence that coverage. The media emphasize the contest. They highlight drama and give controversial statements and events the most attention. There is little a campaign organization can do to affect that focus or divert attention from major blunders and conflicts. There is much, however, it can do to affect the regular reporting of everyday events of the campaign. Its release of information, its timing and staging of activities, and even the access provided the candidate and his senior aides can influence the quantity and quality of coverage and thereby affect the image that is projected to the public.

The overall impact of the media varies with the type of communication. The print media tend to attract a smaller but better-educated, higher-income, more professional audience than do radio and television. Newspapers and magazines require more active involvement of their readers than television does of its viewers, but they also facilitate selective perception to a larger extent. Television, on the other hand, has a more captive and passive audience.

None of the media emphasizes issues. Television news deemphasizes them the most. Instead it focuses on the principal candidates in action, capsuling the major events of their day. Paid media coverage compensates for this focus by providing more substantive information in addition to the favorable or unfavorable profiles it presents. The debates also convey the candidate's general orientation on policy matters.

What effect does all this have on the voters? The literature suggests that newspapers and magazines work primarily to activate and reinforce existing attitudes. For strong party identifiers, television does the same. For weaker partisans and independents, however, television can alter perceptions of the candidates, although it is unlikely to change political attitudes or affect issue positions. How many people are actually influenced is difficult to measure. In a close election, however, even a small number can change the results. Few campaign managers would be willing to discount the impact of the media. This is why candidates are very careful what they say and how they appear whenever cameras and reporters are around.

NOTES

1. An excellent examination of presidential traits appears in Benjamin I. Page, *Choices and Echoes in Presidential Elections* (Chicago: University of Chicago Press, 1978), pp. 232–265. This discussion draws liberally from Page's description and analysis.

2. The object of these first general election ads was to indicate the contrast between the degree of unity of the Republicans and that of the Democrats, between the leadership of the Reagan-Bush and Carter-Mondale administrations, and between the state of the economy in 1980 and 1984.

3. Joseph Napolitan, *The Election Game and How to Win It* (Garden City, N.Y.: Doubleday, 1972), p. 41.

4. The A.C. Nielsen Company rates television programming on the basis of the

size of its viewing audience. These ratings provide a basis for charging advertisers for the time they purchase on television. Needless to add, the higher the rating, the larger the viewing audience.

5. Edwin Diamond and Stephen Bates, "The Ads," *Public Opinion*, 8 (Dec./Jan. 1985), 55.

6. Ibid., 55–57, 64.

7. Although the bear commercial had the highest recall of any Reagan commercial tested, and half of those who recalled it understood it, some people missed its subtlety altogether. According to Reagan officials, the most common misperception was that it was an ad about the environment! Martin Schram, "Reagan Aides Bullish on 'The Bear' Ads," *Washington Post* (November 2, 1984), p. A9.

8. Patrick Caddell, quoted in Stephen Lesher with Patrick Caddell and Gerald Rafshoon, "Did the Debates Help Jimmy Carter?" in Austin Ranney (ed.), *The Past and Future of Presidential Debates* (Washington, D.C.: American Enterprise Institute, 1979), p. 141.

9. Elihu Katz and Jacob J. Feldman, "The Debates in the Light of Research: A Survey of Surveys," in Sidney Kraus (ed.), *The Great Debates* (Bloomington: Indiana University Press, 1962), p. 190.

10. Mondale had wanted six debates on different subjects. His object as challenger was to increase his visibility and demonstrate his superior understanding of the issues. Reagan, as an incumbent with a large lead in the preelection polls, naturally wanted to limit the damage that a poor performance could reap, yet at the same time, wanted to give himself an opportunity to recover if he did poorly, an opportunity that Carter had lacked in 1980. Thus he agreed to two debates between himself and Mondale plus an additional one between Bush and Ferraro.

Mondale wanted to meet Reagan as early as possible to give his campaign a much-needed boost, and also as late as possible to make it difficult for Reagan to overcome any blunders or errors he made. To preclude Mondale's achieving these objectives, Reagan's advisers scheduled two October debates during the second and fourth weeks, with the vice presidential debate sandwiched in between. That way the President's lead could be maintained into the last six weeks, and damage, if any, could be reduced and repaired.

Mondale wanted the two candidates to question each other directly, with little interference from a single moderator. He had done well using this format in New York during the primaries. The Reagan team desired a more structured situation with correspondents from the media, approved by both candidates, asking the questions. Reagan got his way here as well.

The challengers usually need the debates more than the incumbents do. Thus, they take what they can get, conceding points on the details in order to obtain the face-to-face confrontation. The greater the incumbent's lead in the preelection polls, the more easily the incumbent's organization can call the shots.

11. David Stockman, Director of the Office of Management and Budget, played Mondale in the dress rehearsals with Reagan while Michael Sovern, President of Columbia University and an attorney, played Reagan in the rehearsals for Mondale.

12. Nixon had closeted himself alone in a hotel before his first debate with Kennedy. He received only a ten-minute briefing.

13. Patrick Caddell, Memorandum (September 30, 1984) as quoted in Peter Goldman and Tony Fuller, *The Quest for the Presidency, 1984* (Toronto: Bantam Books, 1985), p. 433.

14. This unexpected style seemed to work for Mondale in his first debate. His responses sounded crisp yet firm; his appearance strong yet restrained. In contrast, Reagan seemed confused. His answers were too detailed; themes were lost; his summary wandered. Following the debate, questions were raised about his age and competence. In the second debate, however, Reagan put these questions to rest with a better performance and greater wit.

15. Patrick Caddell (Memorandum, September 30, 1984) in Goldman and Fuller, *Quest,* p. 432.

The public also reacts to physical appearance. In 1960 Nixon's pallid complexion and patronizing manner in his first debate with Kennedy contrasted sharply with his opponent's more polished appearance and aggressive style. The differences were not nearly so noticeable in their subsequent meetings. Height can also be an issue. In 1976 and again in 1980 Jimmy Carter insisted that cameras be positioned so as not to show that his opponents were taller.

16. Robert Agranoff, *The Management of Election Campaigns* (Boston: Holbrook Press, 1976), p. 311.

17. Thomas E. Patterson and Richard Davis, "The Media Campaign: Struggle for the Agenda," in Michael Nelson (ed.), *The Elections of 1984* (Washington, D.C.: Congressional Quarterly, 1985), p. 124.

18. Thomas E. Patterson, "Television and Election Strategy," in Gerald Benjamin (ed.), *The Communications Revolution in Politics* (New York: Academy of Political Science, 1982), p. 30.

19. Michael J. Robinson and Margaret A. Sheehan, *Over the Wire and on TV: CBS and UPI in Campaign '80* (New York: Russell Sage Foundation, 1983), p. 148.

20. Maura Clancey and Michael J. Robinson, "The Media in Campaign '84— General Election Coverage: Part I," *Public Opinion,* 8 (Dec./Jan. 1985), 52.

21. Robinson and Sheehan, *Over the Wire and on TV,* p. 146.

22. Patterson and Davis, "The Media Campaign," p. 119.

23. Robinson and Sheehan, *Over the Wire and on TV,* p. 74.

24. James Glen Stovall, "Incumbency and News Coverage of the 1980 Presidential Election Campaign," *Western Political Quarterly,* 37 (1984), 628.

25. Clancey and Robinson, "General Election Coverage," pp. 49–50.

26. Michael J. Robinson, "The Media in Campaign '84: Part II—Wingless, Toothless, and Hopeless," *Public Opinion,* 8 (Feb./Mar. 1985), 47–48.

27. The authors define spin as "the way the correspondent interprets or embellishes the facts in a story." Spin involves *tone,* the part of the reporting that extends beyond hard news. On October 12, for example, Ronald Reagan's train trip through western Ohio was hard news. But when Dan Rather chose to label the ride "a photo-opportunity train trip, chock full of symbolism and treading on Harry Truman's old turf," Rather added "spin." Clancey and Robinson, "General Election Coverage," p. 50.

28. Ronald Brownstein reported that in Peoria, Illinois, Mondale's advance team decided to close a street to force the 3,500 people who had come to see the candidate to move closer together and create the impression of a very large crowd. It worked. Television pictured a large throng, and one major network correspondent referred to the rally as one of the biggest of the campaign. Ronald Brownstein, "Public Seeing Campaign Through Eye of the TV Cameras," *National Journal* 16 (1984), 1753.

29. Doris A. Graber, "Presidential Images in the 1968 Campaign" (paper delivered

at the annual meeting of the Midwest Political Science Association, Chicago, April 30–May 2, 1970), p. 3.

30. Robinson and Sheehan, *Over the Wire and on TV*, p. 184.

31. Jody Powell, Quoted in F. Christopher Arterton, "The Media Politics of Presidential Campaigns," in James David Barber (ed.), *Race for the Presidency* (Englewood Cliffs, N.J.: Prentice-Hall, 1978), p. 36.

32. Paul Lazarsfeld, Bernard Berelson, and Hazel Goudet, *The People's Choice* (New York: Columbia University Press, 1948); Bernard Berelson, Paul Lazarsfeld, and William McPhee, *Voting: A Study of Opinion Formation in a Presidential Campaign* (Chicago: University of Chicago Press, 1954).

33. Robinson and Sheehan, *Over the Wire and on TV*, p. 9.

34. Ibid., p. 271.

35. Thomas E. Patterson and Robert D. McClure, *The Unseeing Eye* (New York: Putnam, 1976), p. 58.

36. Ibid., p. 54.

37. Thomas Patterson, "The Miscast Institution: The Press in Presidential Politics," *Public Opinion*, 3 (June/July 1980), 47.

38. Patterson and McClure, *The Unseeing Eye*, pp. 109, 122.

39. Patterson, "Television and Election Strategy," p. 32.

Selected Readings

Adams, William C. *Television Coverage of the 1980 Presidential Campaign.* Norwood, N.J.: Ablex, 1983.

Barber, James D., ed. *Race for the Presidency.* Englewood Cliffs, N.J.: Prentice-Hall, 1978.

Bishop, George F., Robert G. Meadow, and Marilyn Jackson-Beeck, eds. *The Presidential Debates.* New York: Praeger, 1980.

Clancey, Maura, and Michael J. Robinson, "The Media in Campaign '84— General Election Coverage: Part I," *Public Opinion*, 8 (Dec./Jan. 1985), 49–54, 59.

Crouse, Timothy. *The Boys on the Bus: Riding with the Campaign Press Corps.* New York: Random House, 1973.

Diamond, Edwin, and Stephen Bates, "The Media in Campaign '84: The Ads," *Public Opinion*, 8 (Dec./Jan. 1985), 55–64.

———. *The Spot.* Cambridge, Mass.: MIT Press, 1984.

Graber, Doris. "Personal Qualities in Presidential Images: The Contribution of the Press," *Midwest Journal of Political Science*, 16 (1972), 46–76.

Joslyn, Richard. *Mass Media and Elections.* New York: Random House, 1984.

McGinnis, Joe. *The Selling of the President, 1968.* New York: Trident Press, 1969.

Page, Benjamin I. *Choices and Echoes in Presidential Elections.* Chicago: University of Chicago Press, 1978.

Patterson, Thomas E., and Richard Davis. "The Media Campaign: Struggle for the Agenda," in Michael Nelson, ed., *The Elections of 1984.* Washington, D.C.: Congressional Quarterly, 1985, pp. 111–127.

Patterson, Thomas E., and Robert D. McClure. *The Unseeing Eye.* New York: Putnam, 1976.

Ranney, Austin, ed. *The Past and Future of Presidential Debates.* Washington, D.C.: American Enterprise Institute, 1979.

Robinson, Michael J. "The Media in Campaign '84: Part II—Wingless, Toothless, and Hopeless," *Public Opinion,* 8 (Feb./March 1985), 43–48.

Robinson, Michael J., and Margaret A. Sheehan. *Over the Wire and on TV: CBS and UPI in Campaign '80.* New York: Russell Sage Foundation, 1983.

PART IV

THE ELECTION

Chapter 8

THE VOTE AND ITS MEANING

Introduction

Predicting the results of an election is a favorite American practice. Politicians do it; the media do it; even the public anticipates the outcome far in advance of the event. It is a form of entertainment—somewhat akin to forecasting the winner of a sporting event.

Presidential elections are particularly prone to such predictions. Public-opinion polls report on the choices of the American public at frequent intervals during the campaign. Television projects a winner long before most of the votes are counted. Election-day surveys of voters exiting from the polls assess the mood of the electorate and present the first systematic analysis of the results. Subsequently, more in-depth studies reveal shifts in opinions and attitudes.

Predictions and analyses of the election are not conducted solely for their entertainment or news value. They provide important information to candidates running for office and to those who have been elected. For the nominees, they indicate the issues that can be effectively raised and those that should be avoided. They also suggest which audience would be most receptive to what policy positions. For the successful candidates, they provide an interpretation of the vote, indicate the range of public attitudes, and signal the amount of support a newly elected President might enjoy.

This chapter will examine the presidential vote from three perspectives. The first section deals with predictions. It discusses national polls, describes their methodology, and evaluates their effect on the conduct of the campaign. The election-eve predictions of the media will also be described.

The next section turns to an examination of the vote itself. After alluding to the election-day surveys, it reports on the findings of studies conducted since 1952 by researchers at the University of Michigan. The major components of the Michigan model are reviewed and the principal conclusions of its evaluation of recent presidential elections are summarized. In this summary, the interplay of partisan, issue, and candidate orientations is emphasized.

The final section of the chapter discusses the relationship between campaigning and governing, between issue debates and public policy-making, between candidate evaluations and presidential style. Do the campaign issues determine the form of agenda building? Does the projected or perceived image of the candidate affect the tone of his Presidency or his actions as President? Can an electoral coalition be converted into a governing party? Does the selection process help or hinder the President in meeting the expectations it creates? These questions will be explored in an effort to determine the impact of the election on the operation of the office, the behavior of the President, and the functioning of the political system.

PREDICTING PRESIDENTIAL ELECTIONS

Public Opinion Polls

The most popular question during a campaign is, who is going to win? The public is naturally interested in the answer, and the media and candidates are obsessed with it, although for different reasons. In focusing on the horse-race aspect of the election, the media feel compelled to report who is ahead and, to a much lesser extent, what the dominant issues are. In forging a winning coalition, candidates and their organizations need to know how the electorate is reacting to their appeals. Both require this information at frequent intervals during the campaign. Waiting until it is all over is obviously too late.

Many of these data can be obtained from surveys of the population. Since 1916 there have been nationwide assessments of public opinion during elections. The largest and most comprehensive of the early surveys were the straw polls conducted by *The Literary Digest*, a popular monthly magazine. The *Digest* mailed millions of ballots and questionnaires to people who appeared on lists of automobile owners and in telephone directories. In 1924, 1928, and 1932, the poll correctly predicted the winner of the presidential election. In 1936, it did not: a huge Landon victory was forecast and a huge Roosevelt victory occurred.

What went wrong? The *Digest* mailed 10 million questionnaires over the course of the campaign, and received 2 million back. As the ballots were returned, they were counted and the results totaled. This procedure tended to cloud, not highlight, trends in the responses.[1] But this was not the major problem. That problem was the sample of people who responded; it was not representative of the total voting population. Automobile owners and telephone subscribers were simply not typical voters in 1936, since most people did not own cars or have telephones. This distinction mattered more in 1936 than it had in previous years, because of the Depression. There was a socioeconomic cleavage within the electorate. The *Literary Digest* sample did not reflect this cleavage; thus, its results were inaccurate.[2]

While the *Digest* was tabulating its 2 million responses and predicting that Landon would be the next President, a number of other pollsters were conducting more scientific surveys and correctly forecasting Roosevelt's reelection.[3] The polls of George Gallup, Elmo Roper, and Archibald Crossley differed from the *Digest's* in two principal respects: They were considerably smaller, and their sample approximated the characteristics of the population as a whole.

The *Digest* went out of business, but Gallup, Roper, and Crossley continued to poll and to improve their sampling techniques. In 1940, Gallup predicted Roosevelt would receive 52 percent of the vote; he actually received 55 percent. In 1944, Gallup forecast a 51.5 percent Roosevelt vote, very close to his actual 53.2 percent. Other pollsters also correctly predicted the results. As a consequence, public confidence in election polling began to grow.

The confidence was short-lived, however. In 1948, all major pollsters forecast a Dewey victory. Their errors resulted from poor sampling techniques, from the premature termination of polling in the middle of the campaign, and from incorrect assumptions about how the undecided would vote.

In attempting to estimate the population in their samples, the pollsters had resorted to filling quotas. They interviewed a certain number of people with different sexual, religious, ethnic, economic, and social characteristics until the percentage of these groups in the sample resembled that in the population as a whole. However, simply because the percentages were approximately equal did not mean that the sample was representative of the population. For example, interviewers avoided certain areas in cities; this biased the results.

Moreover, the interviewing stopped several weeks before the election. In mid-October, the polls showed that Dewey was ahead by a substantial margin. Burns Roper, polling for *Fortune* magazine, saw the lead as sufficiently large to predict a Dewey victory without the need for further surveys. A relatively large number of people, however, were undecided. Three weeks before the election, Gallup concluded that 8 percent of the electorate had still not made up their minds. In estimating the final vote, he and other pollsters assumed that the undecided would divide their votes in much the same manner as the electorate as a whole. This turned out to be an incorrect assumption. Most of those who were wavering in the closing days of the campaign were Democrats. In the end, most voted for Truman or did not vote at all.

The results of the 1948 election once again cast doubt on the accuracy of public-opinion polls. Truman's victory also reemphasized the fact that surveys reflect opinion at the time they are taken, not necessarily two weeks later. Opinion and voter preferences may change.

To better monitor shifts within the electorate, pollsters changed their method of selecting people to be interviewed. They developed more effective means of anticipating who would actually vote. They also extended their surveys to the weekend before the election. Surveyers hired by the candidates began taking continuous polls to identify more precisely and quickly shifts in public sentiment and reactions to campaign events. These changes, plus the continued refinement of the questions, have produced more accurate forecasts.

Between 1936 and 1950, the average error of the final Gallup Poll was 3.6 percent; between 1952 and 1970, it was 1.65 percent; and between 1972 and 1984, it was 1.2 percent. In 1984, the average error was just .2 percent.[4] (See Table 8-1) Very close elections in 1960, 1968, and 1976, however, resulted in several pollsters making wrong predictions. In 1980 the size of Reagan's victory was substantially underestimated in many nationwide polls.

Some of the problems in 1980 were similar to those in 1948. Polling stopped too early. With partisan ties weakening, voting behavior has in recent years become more volatile. The electorate tends to make up its mind later in the campaign and seems more susceptible to influence by

Table 8–1   FINAL PREELECTION POLLS AND RESULTS, 1948–1984

Year	Gallup Poll	Roper Poll	Harris Poll	Actual Results*
1948				
Truman	44.5	37.1		49.6
Dewey	49.5	52.2		45.1
Others	6.0	4.3		5.3
1952				
Eisenhower	51.0			55.1
Stevenson	49.0			44.4
1956				
Eisenhower	59.5	60.0		57.4
Stevenson	40.5	38.0		42.0
1960				
Kennedy	51.0	49.0		49.7
Nixon	49.0	51.0		49.5
1964				
Johnson	64.0		64.0	61.1
Goldwater	36.0		36.0	38.5
1968				
Nixon	43.0		41.0	43.4
Humphrey	42.0		45.0	42.7
Wallace	15.0		14.0	13.5
1972				
Nixon	62.0		61.0	60.7
McGovern	38.0		39.0	37.5
1976				
Carter	48.0	51.0	46.0	50.1
Ford	49.0	47.0	45.0	48.0
Others	3.0	2.0	3.0	1.9
Undecided			6.0	
1980				
Reagan	47.0		46.0	50.7
Carter	44.0		41.0	41.0
Anderson	8.0		10.0	6.6
Others				1.7
Undecided	1.0		3.0	
1984				
Reagan	59.0	52.5	56.0	59.0
Mondale	41.0	42.5	44.0	41.0
Others/Undecided		5.0		

Source: Final Gallup Poll, "Record of Gallup Poll Accuracy," *Gallup Opinion Index,* December 1980, p. 12. Updated with 1984 results.

*Except in 1948, 1976, and 1980 the percentage of voters for minor candidates is not noted in the table.

candidates, issues, and events. In 1980 there were a large number of undecided voters. The CBS News/*New York Times* poll estimated that approximately 20 percent of the electorate made up its mind in the final week of the campaign; many voters did so on the final day. Since most of the public polls were completed by November 1, four days before the election, they did not detect the large surge for Reagan. The candidates' polls, which continued until the eve of the election, did.[5]

In contrast, the 1984 election posed few problems for pollsters. The electorate displayed much less volatility than in the previous election. (See Table 8-2). Many voters decided early that they would support President Reagan for a second term. In fact, nearly one-half of the electorate made its choice before the first primary or caucus was even held.[6]

Television Forecasts

Predictions continue right to the end, until all the votes are tabulated. The final projections are presented by the major television networks during the night of the election. In broadcasting the results the news media have three objectives: to report the vote, to forecast the winners, and to analyze the returns.

To accomplish the first of these objectives, the major networks and news services have pooled their resources. In 1964 they established a consortium known as the News Election Service (NES). Operating on election night to report the results, the NES assigns thousands of reporters to precincts and county election boards around the country. Their job is to telephone the presidential, congressional, and gubernatorial vote to a center, which feeds the returns into a giant computer. Each of the networks (ABC, CBS, and NBC) and news services (Associated Press and United Press International) that participate in the consortium have terminals that indicate how the vote is progressing.[7]

If all the media wished to do were report the results of the vote as rapidly as possible, the NES system would suffice. However, in close elections, the winners and losers might not be obvious for some time. Moreover, the initial reports on who is ahead and likely to win might be misleading. The NES results do not reveal which precincts have reported, whether they tend to be Democratic or Republican, or how their returns compare with those of past elections.

Since the name of the game is accuracy and speed, the networks have developed projection systems to anticipate the results, and exit polls to analyze them. The projections are based on identifying sample pre-

Table 8–2 RICHARD WIRTHLIN'S PREELECTION POLLS, 1984*

September 1984

	4	5	6	7	8	9	10	11	12	13	14	15	16	17	18	19	20	21	22	23	24	25	26	27	28	29	30
Reagan	52	52	51	51	53	53	55	56	56	56	56	57	57	55	55	56	55	56	57	56	56	56	57	56	56	56	56
Mondale	39	39	39	41	39	38	36	34	34	34	34	34	34	36	36	36	37	36	36	37	38	37	36	36	37	37	38

October 1984

	1	2	3	4	5	6	7	8	9	10	11	12	13	14	15	16	17	18	19	20	21	22	23	24	25	26	27	28	29	30	31
Reagan	54	54	54	55	56	56	55	54	52	52	52	52	54	54	54	54	54	55	53	53	52	55	56	57	58	57	55	54	54	55	55
Mondale	38	37	38	37	37	37	37	38	40	40	39	39	38	39	38	36	37	39	40	40	41	38	36	36	36	36	38	39	39	37	37

November 1984

	1	2	3	4	5
Reagan	57	57	56	55	56
Mondale	35	35	37	38	36

Source: Richard Wirthlin as appears in Peter Goldman and Tony Fuller et al. *The Quest for the Presidency 1984* (New York: Bantam Books, 1985), p. 454.
September 4, 1984–October 1984 are nightly tracking samples of 250 interviews per night aggregated over four days for a total sample size of 1,000.
October 5, 1984–October 30, 1984 are nightly tracking samples of 500 interviews per night aggregated over two days for a total sample size of 1,000.
October 31, 1984–November 5, 1984 are nightly tracking samples of 1,000 interviews per night aggregated over two days for a total sample size of 2,000.
The ballot results for the night of November 5 only (N=1000) was 56 Reagan to 37 Mondale.
*Dates begin the day after Labor Day and conclude the day before the election.

CONDUCTING AN ACCURATE SURVEY

The main reason polls have become increasingly accurate is the improvement in sampling procedures. Since the objective of surveying is to generalize from a small number, it is essential that the people interviewed be representative of the population. The odds of the sample's being representative can be estimated when it is randomly selected.

Random selection does not mean haphazard choice. Rather, it means that every element in the population (in this case, the eligible electorate) has an equal chance of being included in the sample, and the choice of any one element would not preclude the choice of any other. The *Literary Digest* sample of 1936 and the quota sample of 1948 were not random. There was no way to determine whether the people interviewed were typical. As it turned out, they were not—at least, not of those who voted on election day.

Random selection is thus the key to sampling. There are several ways of conducting it. Most pollsters employ what is known as a cluster random sample. In such a sample, the population is divided into geographic units and then grouped (stratified) on the basis of the size of communities. Within each stratum, smaller and smaller units are then randomly selected until a block in a city or part of a township is isolated. Then, a number of interviews are conducted according to a carefully prescribed procedure at each of these sampling points. Interviewers have no choice whom they interview or where they conduct the interviews. In 1984, the Gallup organization randomly selected 300 sampling points and held about five interviews at each.

Since sampling is based on probability theory, the likelihood of being right or wrong can be calculated. In a random sample the odds of being right are determined primarily by the size of the sample. The closer the sample approximates the size of the population, the more likely it will be accurate and the more confidence one can place in the results. For national surveys, a sample of approximately 1,100 will yield an error of plus or minus 3 percent in 95 percent of the polls conducted. This means that the results of the sample will not deviate more than 3 percent in either direction from the population as a whole, 95 percent of the time.

The way to improve the accuracy of a sample is to enlarge it. However, enlarging it adds to its cost. At some point a law of diminishing returns sets in. For example, to increase the accuracy of a nationwide sample to plus or minus 2 percent, a total of approximately 2,400 randomly selected respondents would be needed, as opposed to about 9,600 for plus or minus 1 percent and 600 for plus or minus 4 percent.

The accuracy of a poll in measuring public opinion is also affected by the questionnaire and the relationship between the interviewer and the respondent. A survey is only as good as its questions: how they are worded and what order they are in. If they suggest a particular answer, then they force opinion rather than reflect it.

The focus of the questions is normally dictated by the objectives of the study. Public polls, such as those conducted by independent research organizations like Gallup and Harris and syndicated to newspapers and magazines, usually focus on who is ahead and on how different groups of people feel about the candidate. "If the election were held today, for whom would you vote?" is the key question.

In addition to random selection and sample size, the likelihood of those interviewed actually voting must also be considered. Pollsters regularly ask respondents a series of questions to differentiate potential voters from nonvoters. Those whose answers suggest that they probably will not vote are eliminated or separated from the others when analyzing the results.

Finally, pollsters and candidates alike are interested in the currency of their polls. A survey of public opinion measures that opinion only during the time in which interviews were conducted. To monitor changes as rapidly as possible, a technique known as tracking polls is used. Instead of simply interviewing the entire sample in one or two days and then analyzing the results, interviews are conducted continuously. As new responses are added, old ones are dropped. This produces a rolling sample. Continuous analyses of this sample can identify emerging issues, monitor a candidate's strength among various constituencies, and evaluate the impact of the candidate's media advertising.

cincts. These may be randomly or purposely selected. In either case, they should be roughly proportional to the number of urban, suburban, and rural precincts within the state. If they are purposely chosen, they should have a history of mirroring the state vote or should be reflective of the vote of a particular ethnic, racial, or religious group within the state. Finally, they must report early.[8]

The object of the analysis is to discern trends. As the votes are received, they are compared with the results from the same precincts in previous years. Computers are used to calculate the various combinations of voting patterns within a state. On the basis of these calculations, analysts project what the results of the election will be. Normally, the vote is not projected until a number of different checks, usually made by different people, confirm the same outcome. Occasionally, however, the race to beat the other networks is so compelling that analysts will go out on a limb, sometimes with embarrassing consequences.

The classic faux pas in election projections happened in 1960, when CBS News forecast a Nixon victory at 7:15 P.M. eastern standard time. The CBS error occurred because its computer had been programmed to evaluate the vote in the order in which it had been received in the last election and not on the basis of geographic areas. Thus, when midwestern votes were received more quickly than they had been four years earlier, the computer predicted Nixon would win. Once the returns from the East Coast began to be recorded, the computer revised its prediction.

The CBS error in 1960, combined with some hasty projections by the other networks, has led to greater caution in election-eve forecasts. In 1976, all three networks waited until the early hours of the morning before projecting a Carter victory. In 1984, however, they did not. At 8:01 P.M., CBS News projected that Reagan had won the election. By 8:30, ABC and NBC had declared Reagan the winner.

How were such quick projections made? Obviously, the results could not have been predicted on the basis of precinct votes, since they could not have been counted and reported so quickly. What CBS did in 1984 was to project the results on the basis of exit polls, which survey voters after they have cast their ballots.[9]

Exit polls work in the following manner: A large number of precincts across the country are randomly selected. Representatives of the networks, often college students, interview voters as they leave the polls. In the course of the interview, each voter is asked to complete a printed ballot and deposit it into a sealed box. Throughout the day, these ballots are collected and tabulated. Results are telephoned to a central computer bank. After the election in a state has been completed, the findings of the poll are broadcast.

The survey is usually very accurate. Because it is conducted over the course of the day, there is no time bias that would under- or overrepresent certain types of voters. Moreover, the large number of voters sampled, anywhere from 12,000 to 15,000, reduces the error to much less than that of the national surveys conducted by Gallup, Harris, and the Center for Political Studies of the University of Michigan. As a consequence, the attitudes, opinions, and choices of the electorate can be discerned in a fairly precise manner.

All three networks have depended on exit polls in recent years to analyze the vote. It was not until the 1980s, however, that the media also began to rely on them to forecast the winner of a presidential election. Current technology and survey techniques enable more rapid projections than ever before.

These projections have generated considerable criticism, primarily on the grounds that they discourage turnout and affect voting in states in which the polls are still open. This controversy was heightened in 1980. When the early returns and private polls all indicated a Reagan landslide, President Carter appeared before his supporters at 8:30 P.M. eastern standard time, while polls were still open in most parts of the country, and acknowledged defeat. His concession speech was carried live on each of the major networks. Almost immediately Carter's early announcement incurred angry protests, particularly from defeated West Coast Democrats, who alleged that the President's remarks discouraged many Democrats from voting. It is difficult to substantiate their claim, however.

In general, turnout declined more in the East and Midwest than it did in the Far West in 1980. Even if there was a decline after Carter's concession, there is little evidence to suggest that Democrats behaved any differently from Republicans and independents. Hawaii, the last state to close its polls, voted for Carter.

A number of researchers have studied the impact of television projections on voting at all levels, but their results are inconclusive. In a 1964 survey of approximately 1,700 registered voters in California, Harold Mendelsohn uncovered little evidence of vote switching as a consequence of television's projection of Johnson's victory before the polls closed in that state. Relatively few people watched the broadcasts and then voted. Most voted first.[10] However, in the 1972 election, political scientists Raymond Wolfinger and Peter Linquiti concluded that there was a small decline in the West Coast vote after the Nixon victory had been predicted on the basis of the East Coast vote.[11] Similarly, studies of other recent elections have found decreased turnout in the West associated with election night predictions by television networks.[12] One such study indicated that 7 percent of registered nonvoters felt less interested in voting after hearing projections of Reagan's victory in 1984. These discouraged voters, however, resembled the electorate at large in their candidate preferences.[13] Their participation would not have affected the outcome at the presidential level.

Responding to the criticisms of early projections, the legislature of Washington State passed a law prohibiting persons from conducting exit polls within 300 feet of a voting place. As a result, no exit polls were taken in that state during the 1984 election. After the election, however, the law was declared invalid by the courts. Other laws restricting exit polling are likely to be considered in western states, as the debate over the effects of early projections continues.

In summary, it is difficult to prove or disprove the impact of election-night broadcasts on the vote. In all likelihood they affect turnout or the rationale for not turning out more than they affect the actual decision how to vote.

INTERPRETING THE ELECTION

In addition to predicting the results, the television networks also provide an instant analysis of them on election night. This analysis, based primarily on exit polls, relates voting decisions to the issue positions, ideological perspectives, and partisan preferences of the electorate. Patterns between demographic characteristics, issue stances, and electoral choices are noted and used to explain why people voted for particular candidates.

Exit polls present a detailed picture of the electorate on election day. They do not, however, provide a longitudinal perspective. To understand changes in public attitudes and opinions, it is necessary to survey people over the course of the campaign, asking the same questions and, if possible, interviewing the same people. The nationwide polls conducted by Gallup and Harris often repeat questions, but they do not repeat respondents. Surveys conducted by the University of Michigan repeat the respondents and some of the questions. Utilizing the interview-reinterview technique, these surveys have provided social scientists with a wealth of data on the behavior of the American voter.

The Normal Vote

According to the Michigan studies (discussed in Chapter 3), the identification people make with political parties is the most stable and resilient factor affecting the voting decision. It is considered to be the single most important long-term influence on voting. Party identification has both direct and indirect effects. Partisan attitudes provide voting cues to party identifiers. They also influence their perceptions of the candidates and the issues, and this, in turn, affects their vote. Orientations toward the candidate and issues are short-term factors which change from election to election. If strong enough, they can, of course, cause people to vote against their partisan inclinations. Usually, however, they do not. In most cases, they serve as an inducement and a rationalization for supporting the party and its candidates.

The stability of party identification explains why much of the electorate votes as it does in election after election.[14] To be influenced by partisanship is normal for people who identify with a party, and even for many who theoretically consider themselves independent. Since a large majority of the electorate does identify with a political party or leans in a partisan direction, the candidate of the major party should win—*all other things being equal.*

That partisan attitudes are held by much of the electorate permits analysts to calculate the vote in any given election. By examining the rate of turnout among strong and weak partisan identifiers, researchers can project an expected or normal vote.[15] Actual votes can then be compared with the expected vote and the difference explained on the basis of short-term factors.

Some deviation from the expected partisan division of the electorate occurs in every election. Since 1952, the deviation seems to have been increasing at the presidential level. The weakening of partisan ties, the growth of media campaigning, and the increasing ideological/issue awareness on the part of some of the electorate have contributed to the influence of short-term factors on the outcome of the election. What are these factors, and which have been the most important?

In its evaluation of presidential elections since 1952, the Center for Political Studies of the University of Michigan has attempted to identify the major components of the electorate's decisions. Focusing on the interplay of candidate evaluation, issue awareness, and ideological attitudes, the center's analysts have sought to provide an explanation of the elections, an interpretation of the votes. What follows is a summary of their conclusions.

1952–1960: The Impact of Personality

In 1952, the short-term effect of the issues and the candidates contributed to the Republican victory. "Communism, corruption, and Korea" were the three principal issues.[16] The Republicans were seen as the party better able to deal with the problems of fighting Communism, promoting efficiency and better government, and ending the war in Korea. General Eisenhower was also perceived in a more favorable light than his opponent, Adlai Stevenson. While the public still regarded Democrats as more capable of handling domestic problems, the appeal of

Eisenhower, combined with the more favorable attitude toward the Republican party in the areas of foreign affairs and government management, resulted in an election that deviated from what would have been expected if only partisanship had affected the vote.

The presidential election of 1956 also deviated from partisan voting patterns. However, Eisenhower's reelection was far more a personal triumph for the President than it was a political victory for the Republicans. The Republican party did not win control of Congress, as it had in 1952.

One major factor seems to explain the presidential voting in 1956—the very positive evaluation of Eisenhower and the slightly negative evaluation of Stevenson in contrast to 1952, when Stevenson had been favorably perceived by most of the electorate. At other levels of government, however, the Democrats continued to benefit from their partisan majority. Their reputation in the domestic sphere more than compensated for the Republicans' image as the party best able to make and conduct foreign policy.[17] In electoral politics, it is the impact at home that counts the most.

Because he was the candidate of the majority party in 1960, Kennedy's victory was not surprising. What was surprising was the closeness of the election. Despite the Democrats' large partisan advantage, Kennedy received only 115,000 more votes than Nixon, 0.3 percent more of the total vote. Why was the presidential contest so close?

Most analysts agree that Kennedy's Catholicism cost him votes. The Michigan researchers estimate that he lost about 2.2 percent of the popular vote, or approximately 1.5 million votes, because of the religious issue.[18] The decline in Democratic voting was particularly evident in the heavily Protestant South, where 16.5 percent of the expected Democratic vote went to Nixon. Analysis of the Protestant defection reveals that it varied directly with church attendance. The more regular the attendance, the less likely the individual would vote for Kennedy.[19]

Outside the South, however, Kennedy registered a small net gain over the expected Democratic vote. The main reason for this gain was the heavy vote he received from Catholics. In 1960, it was almost 80 percent, 17 percent more than the Democrats normally achieved. The concentration of Catholics in the large industrial states may, in fact, have contributed to the size of his Electoral College majority.[20]

Religion, in short, was the main issue, even though the candidates focused on other concerns and generally downplayed the religious question.[21] Kennedy's religion dominated the attention of the voters and affected their assessments of the candidates. Nixon had a better image than Kennedy. His Vice Presidency during the popular Eisenhower years contributed to the public perception that he was the more experienced candidate, the more capable in foreign affairs, and—surprisingly, considering the events of his own Presidency—the more personable of the two candidates. In contrast, Kennedy was viewed as young, less mature, and lacking in experience. His performance during the debates, however, helped to counter Nixon's image advantage, especially among Democratic partisans.

The Michigan analysis of the election suggests that the vote turned on partisanship as modified by religion.[22] The Democratic candidate won, but barely. Kennedy's vote fell 4 percent below the expected Democratic vote.

1964–1972: The Importance of Issues

Lyndon Johnson's victory in 1964 can also be attributed to his being the candidate of the majority party. The size of his victory, however, exceeded the Democrats' partisan advantage. Moreover, there were significant deviations from the voting patterns of the past. The South, which had traditionally been Democratic, voted for Goldwater, while the Republican Northeast went Democratic.

Short-term factors explain the magnitude of the Johnson victory.[23] Goldwater was perceived as a minority candidate within a minority party, ideologically to the right of most Republicans. Moreover, he did not enjoy a favorable public image. In the Michigan survey, negative comments about Goldwater outnumbered positive comments two to one.[24] For Johnson, the pattern was reversed. He received twice as many complimentary remarks as uncomplimentary ones. Policy attitudes also favored the Democrats, even in foreign affairs. Goldwater's militant anticommunism scared many voters. They saw Johnson as the peace candidate.

Some analysts have concluded that voters in 1964 were more aware of and influenced by issues than in previous elections.[25] Goldwater's strong ideological convictions, coupled with his attempt to differentiate his positions from Johnson's, undoubtedly contributed to a greater issue awareness. Although most of the policy-conscious electorate had their views on the issues reinforced by their partisan attitudes, two groups did not. Southern Democrats, fearful of the party's civil-rights initiatives, cast a majority of their votes for Goldwater, while northern Republicans, who disagreed with their candidate's policy positions, voted for Johnson.[26]

The impact of issues on voting grew in 1968. With the Vietnam

War, urban riots, campus unrest, and civil rights dividing the nation and splitting the Democratic party, partisan desertions increased. The Democratic share of the vote declined 19 percent, while the Republican proportion increased 4 percent. The third-party candidacy of George Wallace accounted for much of the difference.

Wallace's support was much more issue based than Humphrey's or Nixon's.[27] The Alabama governor did not have as much personal appeal for those who voted for him as did his positions.[28] Unhappy with the Democratic party's handling of a wide range of social issues, white Democratic partisans, particularly in the South, and to a limited degree in the urban North, turned from their party's presidential candidate, Hubert Humphrey, to vote for Wallace, who received 13.5 percent of the vote.[29] Had Wallace not run, the Republican presidential vote undoubtedly would have been larger, since Nixon was the second choice of most Wallace voters.[30]

The results of the 1968 presidential election thus deviated from the partisan alignment of the electorate primarily because a significant number of Democrats had grievances against their party and against Lyndon Johnson's conduct of the Presidency and expressed them by voting for Wallace and, to a much lesser extent, for Nixon. A decline in the intensity of partisanship and a growth in the number of independents contributed to the issue voting that occurred in 1968. Had it not been for the Democrats' large partisan advantage and the almost unanimous black vote that Humphrey received,[31] the presidential election would not have been nearly so close.

The trend away from partisan presidential voting for the Democratic candidate continued in 1972. With a nominee who was ideologically and personally unpopular, the Democrats suffered their worst presidential defeat since 1920. What factors contributed to Nixon's win?

According to the Michigan researchers, the withdrawal of Senator Thomas Eagleton, McGovern's choice as vice presidential candidate, after Eagleton's history of mental depression became known, was not a factor, nor was McGovern's identification with the New Left.[32] These issues affected the electorate's perception of McGovern, but they were not directly associated with the vote he received.

Nixon enjoyed a better image. He was seen as the stronger presidential candidate. The electorate reacted to him positively, although less so than in 1960.[33] McGovern, on the other hand, was viewed negatively by non-Democrats and neutrally by Democrats. These perceptions contributed to Nixon's victory, as did his stands on most of the issues. Most of the electorate saw the Republican standard-bearer as closer to their own positions than the Democrat. McGovern was perceived as liberal on all issues and ideologically to the left of his own party. Thus, Democrats defected in considerable numbers but Republicans did not.

The large defection of Democrats in 1972 and 1968 and of Republicans in 1964 led election analysts to reevaluate the impact of partisanship, candidate orientation, and issue stands on voting. Some studies of electoral behavior during this period indicated that more people than before were holding consistent issue positions and were being influenced by them when voting.[34] How much more important issues and ideology had become, however, remained the subject of considerable controversy.

1976–1984: The Evaluation of Performance

Issue differences narrowed in 1976. Neither Ford nor Carter emphasized the social and cultural concerns that played a large role in the McGovern-Nixon contest. Rather, they both focused their attention on trust in government and on domestic economic matters. In the wake of Watergate and a recession that occurred during the Ford Presidency, it is not surprising that these issues worked to the Democrats' advantage.

Carter was also helped by a slightly more favorable personal assessment than that given to Ford.[35] Normally, an incumbent would enjoy an advantage in such a comparison. However, Ford's association with the Nixon administration, highlighted in the public mind by his pardon of the former President, his difficult struggle to win his own party's nomination, and his seeming inability to find a solution to the country's economic problems adversely affected his image as President.

Nonetheless, Ford was probably helped more than hurt by being the incumbent. He gained in recognition, reputation, and stature. He benefited from having a podium with a presidential seal on it. His style and manner in the office contrasted sharply with his predecessor's—much to Ford's advantage. As the campaign progressed, his presidential image improved.[36] It just didn't improve quickly enough to allow him to hold onto the office.

With sociocultural issues muted and the Vietnam War over, economic matters divided the electorate along partisan lines. This put the candidate of the dominant party into the driver's seat. Democrats had more faith in their party's ability to improve the economy. Carter won primarily because he was a Democrat, and secondarily because his personal evaluation was more favorable than Ford's.

Carter was also helped by being a southerner. He received the electoral votes of every southern state except Virginia. In an otherwise divided Electoral College, this proved to be decisive.

In 1980, being a Democrat, an incumbent, and a southerner was not enough. Poor performance ratings overcame the advantage partisanship and incumbency normally bring to a President of the dominant party. In 1976, Carter was judged on the basis of his potential *for* office. In 1980 he was judged on the basis of his performance *in* office. As the results of the election indicate, that judgment was very harsh. Carter's vote fell behind his 1976 percentages in every single state, and in approximately half the states it dropped at least 10 percent. Why did he lose so badly? What happened to his electoral support over the four years?

Whereas long-term factors still seemed to benefit the candidate of the dominant party,[37] short-term considerations in 1980 did not. Personal evaluations of Carter and assessments of his policies were not nearly so favorable as they had been four years earlier. Starting the campaign with the lowest approval rating of any President since the ratings were first begun in 1952, Carter saw his performance in office approved by only 21 percent of the adult population in July 1980. Personal assessments of Reagan were also low—although, in contrast to Carter's ratings, they became more favorable as the campaign unfolded.

These evaluations of the candidates colored the electorate's perceptions of Carter's and Reagan's ideological and policy positions. At the outset Carter was viewed as a centrist candidate and Reagan as the more extreme. By the conclusion of the campaign, this perception was reversed. Carter was seen as liberal, somewhat to the left of the electorate, and Reagan as more centrist.[38] Similarly, the policy-related assessments of the candidates also changed. Over the course of the campaign the public identified with Reagan's stands on a variety of issues more than with Carter's.[39]

The issues also seemed to benefit Reagan. Concerns about the economy, persistently high inflation, large-scale unemployment, and the decreasing competitiveness and productivity of American industry all worked to the out-party's advantage. For the first time in many years, the Republicans were seen as the party better able to invigorate the economy, return prosperity, and lower inflation. The Democrats, and particularly Carter, were blamed for the problems.

Dissatisfaction with the conduct of foreign affairs, culminating in frustration over the Soviet invasion of Afghanistan and over the United

States' failure to obtain the release of American hostages in Iran con-tributed to Carter's negative evaluation and to changing public attitudes toward defense spending and foreign affairs. In 1980 most Americans supported increased military expenditures, a position with which Reagan was closely identified, combined with a less conciliatory approach and a stronger posture in dealing with problems abroad.

These issues, combined with the negative assessment of Carter as President explain why he lost even though he was the dominant party's candidate. Twenty-seven percent of the Democrats who had supported Carter in 1976 deserted him in 1980. Approximately 80 percent of these deserters voted for Reagan. They represented all ideological groups, not just conservatives. And Carter's share of the independent vote declined substantially.

Independent John Anderson benefited from the disaffected voters. He was a protest candidate who drew equally from Democrats and Repub-licans. Anderson was unable, however, to attract a solid core of supporters. His candidacy did not appeal to particular ethnic, racial, or religious groups who were unhappy with the nominees of the major parties. Nor was Anderson able to differentiate his policy positions sufficiently from Carter's and Reagan's to generate an issue-oriented vote. In the end, his winning of no electoral votes and only 6.5 percent of the popular vote demonstrates the resiliency of the major parties and the legitimacy that their labels provide candidates for office.

In summary, Carter was repudiated by the voters because of his performance in office. In 1980 it was Reagan who offered greater poten-tial. He won primarily because he was the option that had become accept-able. He did not win because of his ideology or his specific policy positions. While there was a desire for change, there was little direct ideological or issue voting.[40] Nor did Reagan's personal appeal contribute significantly to his victory. According to Miller and Wattenberg, "Reagan was the least positively evaluated candidate elected to the presidency in the history of the national election studies, which date back to 1952."[41]

Four years later the voters rewarded President Reagan for what they considered to be a job well done. Reagan's 1984 victory was even more impressive than his previous win. He increased his share of the popular vote to 59 percent, more than eight percentage points higher than his 1980 level. Democratic candidate Walter Mondale matched the 41 per-cent gained by Carter four years earlier. Reagan carried 31 states by a margin of 20 percent or more, and with 525 electoral votes obtained the second-greatest share of electoral votes for any contested presidential election. A shift of fewer than 2,000 votes in Mondale's home state of Minnesota would have given the President a fifty-state sweep.

What factors contributed to Reagan's impressive victory? Was his landslide primarily a product of his ideology, of his issue stands, or of his performance in office?

Ideology did not work to Reagan's advantage in 1984 any more than it did in 1980. According to a Michigan study, the average voter considered himself or herself to be a moderate, holding issue positions slightly closer to the liberal Mondale than to the conservative Reagan.[42] This moderate perspective, however, did not easily translate into presidential voting. As a consequence, it did not adversely affect Reagan; nor did it help Mondale.

There was a potential for issue voting in 1984. The electorate did perceive a choice between the two candidates on a range of domestic matters. It was conditions more than positions, however, that seemed to influence the electorate's judgment. A resurgent economy, strengthened military, and renewed feelings of national pride brought the President broad support. While the voters agreed more with Mondale than Reagan on many of the problems confronting the nation for the future, they viewed Reagan as the leader better able to deal with these problems now.

Leadership was a dominant concern. Voters evaluated Reagan much more highly than Mondale in this regard. He was seen as the stronger and more independent of the two candidates, less beholden to special and parochial interests. When leadership was combined with the ability to deal with the most pressing problems, Reagan won hands down. In the words of political scientists Paul C. Light and Celinda Lake, "Mondale's image as a weak leader acted as a screen against the issues. Even when he made inroads against Reagan on specific policies, the voters doubted Mondale's ability to do any better."[43]

Reagan also used his position to blunt Mondale's attacks and to make appeals to potentially hostile groups. When Mondale chided him for failing to meet with Soviet leaders to pursue an arms-control agreement, Reagan responded by inviting the Soviet foreign minister to Washington. Criticism from small farmers, suffering from falling prices and large debt obligations, was countered by Reagan with the offer of a new loan program. Moreover, the President suffered little of the blame his predecessor had encountered from those who had been adversely affected by his administration. In short, he reaped the traditional advantages of incumbency.

Reagan won a retrospective vote. The electorate supported him primarily for his performance in office. In other words, they voted *for* him in 1984 just as they had voted *against* Carter four years earlier.

If this analysis is correct, then the 1984 election was a referendum on the present. It was not a mandate for the future. Good times and strong leadership won it for Reagan, not his specific issue positions. In fact, exit polls taken on election day reveal that of those who voted for the President, 20 percent had significant policy disagreements with him, while another 20 percent had no strong feelings one way or the other on most of his issue stands.[44]

As a consequence, Reagan cannot be said to have received a policy mandate by virtue of his huge electoral victory. What he did receive was a vote of confidence to continue his ways and maintain prosperity. How he would do this was for him to determine.

Figure 8–1   THE PRESIDENT'S MANDATE

Source: Copyright 1982 by Herblock in *Washington Post.*

CONVERTING ELECTORAL CHOICE INTO PUBLIC POLICY

The President's Imprecise Mandate

It is not unusual for the meaning of the election to be ambiguous. The reasons that people vote for a President vary. Some do so because of his party, some because of his issue stands, some because of their assessment of his potential or his performance. For most, a combination of factors contributes to their voting decision. This combination makes it difficult to discern exactly what the electorate means, desires, or envisions by its electoral choice.

The President is rarely given a clear mandate for governing. He has to construct one, to fashion his own policy agenda. The campaign and the election provide guidance, but they do not dictate priorities or long-term policy decisions, nor do they provide a ready-made coalition of supporters for the duration of a President's term. He must create and maintain this coalition as well.

Assuming that party is the principal influence on voting behavior, what cues can a President cull from his political connection? Party platforms contain a laundry list of positions and proposals, but there are problems in using them as a precise guide for new administrations. First and foremost, the presidential candidate may not have exercised a major influence on the platform's formulation. Or, second, he may have had to accept certain compromises in the interests of party unity. It is not unusual for a nominee to disagree with one or several of the platform's positions or priorities. Carter personally opposed his party's abortion stand in 1980, and had major reservations about reducing unemployment through a $12 billion jobs program.

In addition to containing items the President-elect may oppose, the platform may omit some that he favors, particularly if they are controversial. There was no mention of granting amnesty to Vietnam draft dodgers and war resisters in the 1976 Democratic platform, although Carter had publicly stated his intention to do so if he was elected.

Another limitation to using a platform as a guide to the partisan attitudes and opinions of the public is that many people, including party rank and file, are unfamiliar with most of its contents.[45] The platform per se is not the reason people vote for their party's candidates on election day.

On the other hand, presidential nominees usually do exercise some influence over the contents of the platform, and incumbents, in particular, exercise a lot. In 1964, 1972, and 1984 party platforms were crafted by White House aides and approved by the President himself. Thus, it is not surprising that a considerable number of party positions and campaign promises find their way into public policy.

Political scientist Jeff Fishel found that from 1960 to 1984 Presidents "submitted legislation or signed executive orders that are broadly consistent with about two-thirds of their campaign pledges."[46] Of these, a substantial percentage were enacted into law, ranging from a high of 89 percent of those proposed during the Johnson administration to a low of 61 percent during the Nixon years.[47] Although these figures do not reveal the importance of the promise, its scope, or its impact, they do suggest that, in general, campaign platforms and candidate pledges are important. They provide a foundation from which an administration's early policy initiatives emanate.

One reason campaign promises are important is that they are part of the public record; candidates and parties can be held accountable for them. Another is that they represent the interests of a significant portion of the population. To gain public approval, a President must respond to these interests. Third, organized groups, to whom promises have been made, have clout in Congress and in the bureaucracy. The President can either mobilize them to help him achieve his campaign promises, or be thwarted by them if he fails to do so.

Expectations and Performance

When campaigning, candidates also try to create an aura of leadership, conveying such attributes as assertiveness, decisiveness, compassion, and integrity. Kennedy promised to get the country moving, Johnson to continue the New Frontier-Great Society program, Nixon to bring us together. These promises created expectations of performance regardless of policy stands. In the 1976 election, Jimmy Carter heightened expectations by his constant reference to the strong, decisive leadership he intended to exercise as President. His decline in popularity stemmed in large part from his failure to meet these expectations. In contrast, Reagan in 1980 indicated his determination to steer a new and steadier course than his predecessor. His high approval ratings before, during, and after his reelection indicate that most of the public believed that he met, even exceeded, these goals.

All new administrations, and to some extent reelected ones, face diverse and often contradictory desires. By their ambiguity, candidates encourage voters to see what they want to see and to believe what they want to believe. Disillusionment naturally sets in once a new President begins to make decisions. Some supporters feel deceived while others may be satisfied.

One political scientist, John E. Mueller, has referred to the disappointment groups may experience with an administration as "the coalitions of minorities variable."[48] In explaining declines in popularity, Mueller notes that the President's decisions inevitably alienate parts of the coalition that elected him. This alienation, greatest among independents and supporters who identify with the other party, produces a drop in popularity over time.[49]

The campaign's emphasis on personal and institutional leadership also inflates expectations. By creating the aura of assertiveness, decisiveness, and potency, candidates help shape public expectations of their performance in office. Jimmy Carter contributed to the decline in his own popularity by promising more than he could deliver. Carter's problem was not unique to his Presidency. It is one that other successful candidates have faced and will continue to face. How can the promise of leadership be conveyed during the campaign without creating unrealistic and unattainable expectations of the candidate's performance as President?

The Electoral Coalition and Governing

Not only does the selection process inflate performance expectations and create a set of diverse policy goals, it also *lessens* the President's power to achieve them. His political muscle has been weakened by the decline in the power of party leaders, and the growth of autonomous state and congressional electoral systems.

In the past, presidential candidates were dependent on the heads of the state parties for delegate support. Today, they are not. In the past, the state party organizations were the principal means for conducting the general election campaign. Today, they are not. In the past, partisan ties united legislative and executive officials more than they currently do.

Today, presidential candidates are more on their own. They essentially designate themselves to run. They create their own organizations, mount their own campaigns, win their own delegates, and set their own convention plans. However, they pay a price for this independence. By winning the party's nomination a candidate gains a label, but not an organization. In the general election, he must expand his prenomination coalition, working largely on his own. Planning a strategy, developing tactics, writing speeches, formulating an appeal, organizing interest groups, and, perhaps with the help of the party, conducting a grass roots registration and a get-out-the-vote effort are all part of seeking the Presidency.

The personalization of the presidential electoral process has serious implications for governing. To put it simply, it makes coalition building more difficult. The electoral process provides the President with fewer political allies in the states and in Congress. It makes his partisan appeal less effective. It fractionalizes the bases of his support.

The establishment of candidate campaign organizations and the use of out-of-state coordinators have weakened the state parties. This has created competition, not cooperation. The competition cannot help but deplete the natural reservoir of partisan support a President needs to tap when he alienates parts of his electoral coalition.

Moreover, the democratization of the selection process has also resulted in the separation of state, congressional, and presidential elections. In the aftermath of Watergate, Jimmy Carter made much of the fact that he did not owe his nomination to the power brokers within his party, nor his election to them or members of Congress. The same could be said for members of Congress and, for that matter, governors and state legislators. Carter was not dependent on them, nor were they dependent on him for their nomination and election. The increasing independence of Congress from the Presidency decreases legislators' political incentives to follow the President's lead.

The magnitude of the President's problem is compounded by public expectations for his legislative leadership. Yet that leadership is difficult to achieve, because of the constitutional and political separation of institutions. Thus, the weakening of party ties during the electoral process carries over to the governing process, with adverse consequences for the President.

Finally, personality politics has produced factions within the parties. It has created a fertile environment for the growth of interest-group pressures. Without strong party leaders to act as brokers and referees, groups vie for the nominee's attention and favor during the campaign and for the President's after the election is over. This group struggle provides a natural source of opposition and support for almost any presidential action or proposal. It enlarges the arena of policy-making and contributes to the multiplicity of forces that converge on most presidential decisions.

Personality Politics and Presidential Leadership

What is a President to do? How can he meet public expectations, in light of the weakening of partisanship and the increased sharing of policy-making powers? How can a President lead, achieve his goals, and satisfy pluralistic interests at the same time?

Obviously, there is no set formula for success. Forces beyond the President's control may affect the course of events. Nonetheless, there are certain maxims that Presidents would be wise to follow in their struggle to convert promises into performance and to perhaps also get reelected.

1. A President must define and limit his own priorities, rather than have them defined and expanded for him.
2. A President must build his own coalitions, rather than depend solely or even mostly on existing partisan or ideological divisions.
3. A President must take an assertive posture, rather than let words and actions speak for themselves. He must actively shape public opinion. He must lead while also appearing to follow.

Priority-setting is a necessary presidential task. Without it, an administration appears to lack direction and leadership. People question what the President is doing and have difficulty remembering what he has done. This happened to Carter, and it contributed to the decline of his performance ratings in the public-opinion polls and his defeat in 1980. The Reagan administration understood this lesson and limited the issues, controlled the agenda, and, most important, focused the media on the President's policy objectives during his first term in office.

Presidential campaigns are not likely to provide a limited agenda. In fact, they usually do just the opposite. The promises made during the preconvention contest, the pledges contained in the party's platform, and the positions taken during the general campaign constitute a wide range of policy objectives that may or may not be consistent with one another. They provide the President with more discretion than direction. If he is skillful, he can actually manufacture a mandate, as Reagan did in 1980. Claiming that he was elected to implement his economic program, Reagan appealed for public support and then used that support to win congressional backing for his budget and revenue proposals.

While the absence of a clear electoral mandate can actually help the President, allowing him flexibility in designing his program, it can also hurt him. Setting priorities often takes time, time especially valuable at the beginning of an administration when presidential influence tends to be greatest. A failure to act at the start may make action later, when unity fades and partisan divisions reemerge, more difficult. A President may prolong his honeymoon, but he cannot do so indefinitely.

Extending the campaign debate over goals and policies into the presidential term is also likely to reduce support. Those whose positions are not accepted are not likely to keep their arguments and protests private for long, particularly if they represent vocal constituencies. One way a President can counter this debate is to preempt it by taking a position at the beginning of his administration. Another is to appoint loyalists who are on his ideological and partisan wavelengths.

Beyond establishing priorities and positions, the President has to get them adopted. His electoral coalition does not remain a cohesive entity within the governing system. This forces him to build his own alliances around his policy objectives. Constructing these alliances requires organizing skills different from those used in winning an election. Partisanship can no longer be so effectively appealed to, nor is it so cohesive an instrument. Recruiting public officials who have their own constituencies demands a variety of inducements and tactics; it also requires time, energy, and help. The President cannot do it alone.

As campaign organizations are necessary to win elections, so governing organizations are necessary to gain backing for presidential policies. Several offices within the White House have been established to provide liaison and to mobilize support for the President on Capitol Hill, in the bureaucracy, and with outside interest groups. By building and mending bridges, a President can improve his chances for success. He can commit, convince, cajole, and otherwise gain cooperation despite the constitutional and political separation of institutions and powers.

Unlike winning the general election, making and implementing public policy is not an all-or-nothing proposition. Assessments of performance are based on expectations, somewhat as they were in the primaries. Part of the President's image problem results from the contrast between an idealized concept of what his powers are or ought to be and his actual ability to get things done. This is why a President needs a public-relations staff, and why some grandstanding is inevitable.

If a President cannot achieve what he wants, he can at least shift the blame for failure. He can at least look good trying, and can perhaps even claim partial success. And finally, he can always change his public priorities to improve his batting average. Public appeals may or may not generate support within the governing coalition, but they can boost support outside it, and within the electoral coalition the next time around.

SUMMARY

Americans are fascinated by presidential elections. They want to know who will win, why the successful candidate has won, and what the election augurs for the next four years. Their fascination stems from four interrelated factors: elections are dramatic; they are decisive; they are participatory; and they affect future policy and leadership.

These factors suggest why so much attention has been devoted to predicting and analyzing presidential elections. Public-opinion polls constantly monitor the attitudes and views of the electorate. Gallup, Harris, and other pollsters reflect and, to some extent, contribute to, public interest through the hypothetical elections they continuously conduct. Private surveys also record shifts in popular sentiment, helping clients to know what to say, to whom to say it, and, in some cases, when and even how to say it.

Polls have become fairly accurate measures of opinion at the time they are taken. Practitioners use them as a guide; journalists present them as news. National opinion polls serve an additional purpose. They provide data that can be employed to help explain the meaning of the election: the issues that were most salient; the positions that were most popular; the hopes and expectations that are initially directed toward the elected leaders of government.

The most thorough analyses of presidential elections have been conducted by the Center for Political Studies of the University of Michigan. Using party identification as a base, Michigan analysts have evaluated the meaning of elections in terms of their deviation from the expected partisan vote. Deviations have been caused primarily by evaluations of the candidates and their ideological and issue stances. The declining intensity of partisan attitudes and the increasing number of independent voters have contributed to the impact of these short-range factors on voting behavior.

In 1960, it was Kennedy's religion that seemed to account for the closeness of the popular vote. In 1964, it was Goldwater's uncompromising ideological and issue positions that helped provide Johnson with an overwhelming victory in all areas but the Deep South. In 1968, it was the accumulation of grievances against the Democrats that spurred the Wallace candidacy and that resulted in Nixon's triumph. In 1972, ideology, issues, and the perception of McGovern as incompetent split the Democratic party, and culminated in Nixon's landslide. In 1976, however, partisanship was reinforced by issue, ideological, and personal evaluations to the benefit of the dominant party's nominee. In 1980 and 1984 it was not. Dissatisfaction with Carter's performance in office and satisfaction with Reagan's overcame the Democrats' numerical advantage, causing voters to cast their ballots for Reagan as the person they thought best qualified to lead.

When combined, the long- and short-term influences on voting behavior create a diverse and inflated set of expectations of the successful candidate, expectations upon which his Presidency is likely to be judged. That these expectations may be conflicting, unrealistic, or in other ways unattainable matters little. A President is expected to lead, to achieve, and to satisfy the interests of a heterogeneous coalition. His failure or success will depend in large part on his ability to fulfill these expectations.

Every newly elected President has a problem. The election provides him with an open-ended mandate that means different things to different people, including to himself, but that does not give him the political clout to get things done.

Parties seem to exercise less influence over public officials than they did in the past. Electoral systems have become more autonomous. Candidates now have to create their own organizations to win the election, and Presidents have to build their own alliances to govern. In the past, the electoral and governing coalitions were more closely connected by partisan ties than they are today.

This situation has presented serious governing problems for the President. To overcome them he must establish his own priorities, construct his own policy alliances, articulate his appeal clearly and convey it forcefully to those outside the government.

NOTES

1. Michael Wheeler, *Lies, Damn Lies, and Statistics* (New York: Dell, 1976), p. 84.

2. Moreover, the 2 million people who returned the questionnaire were not necessarily even typical of those who received it. By virtue of responding, they displayed more interest and concern than the others.

3. Archibald Crossley predicted that Roosevelt would receive 53.8 percent of the vote, George Gallup estimated that he would receive 55.7 percent, and Elmo Roper forecast 61.7 percent. Roosevelt actually received 62.5 percent.

4. "Gallup Report," No. 231 (December, 1984), p. 32.

5. The differences between the public and private polls in 1980 are listed below:

	Public Polls		Private Polls		Actual Results
	CBS/NY Times (Oct. 30–Nov. 1)	NBC/AP (Oct. 22–24)	Caddell (Carter) Nov. 3	Wirthlin (Reagan) Nov. 3	(Nov. 4)
Reagan	41	42	46	45	50.7
Carter	40	36	36	34	41.0
Anderson	7	9	9.5	9	6.6
Undecided/Other	11	10	8	12	1.7
N	2,264	1,574	1,200	2,000	

Weekend polls picked up the movement toward Reagan. By the day before the election, it was clear that he had pulled significantly ahead.

6. According to a Gallup Survey, only 16 percent of the voters intended at any time during the campaign to cast their ballots for a candidate other than one they finally selected. Four years earlier, 27 percent of the electorate had indicated that they had changed their minds during the campaign. See *The Gallup Poll: Public Opinion 1984* (Wilmington, Del.: Scholarly Resources, Inc., 1985), p. 263.

7. Paul Wilson, "Election Night 1980 and the Controversy over Early Projections," in William C. Adams (ed.), *Television Coverage of the 1980 Presidential Campaign* (Norwood, N.J.: Ablex, 1983); Joan Bieder, "Television Reporting," in Gerald Benjamin (ed.), *The Communications Revolution in Politics* (New York: Academy of Political Science, 1982), pp. 37–41.

8. The need for quick reporting eliminates those precincts that use paper ballots, which must be counted by hand, or punched ballots, which normally are tabulated by machine at the county board of elections. Thus, the media depend on those precincts that use automatic voting machines, which tend to be concentrated in metropolitan areas.

9. The other networks do this as well, although NBC also requires that some of the actual returns from its sample precincts be analyzed before projections can be broadcast and the races called.

10. Harold Mendelsohn and Irving Crespi, *Polls, Television, and the New Politics* (Scranton, Pa.: Chandler, 1970), pp. 234–236.

11. Raymond Wolfinger and Peter Linquiti, "Tuning In and Turning Out," *Public Opinion*, 4 (Feb/Mar. 1981), 57–59.

12. Michael X. Delli Carpini, "Scooping the Voters? The Consequences of the Networks' Early Call of the 1980 Presidential Race," *Journal of Politics*, 46 (1984), 866–885; Philip L. Dubois, "Election Night Projections and Voter Turnout in the West," *American Politics Quarterly*, 2 (1983), 349–364; John E. Jackson, "Election Night Reporting and Voter Turnout," *American Journal of Political Science*, 27 (1983), 615–635.

13. William C. Adams, "Early Projections in 1984: How the West Deplored But Ignored Them" (paper presented at the annual meeting of the American Association of Public Opinion Research, New Jersey, 1985).

14. While party identification has remained stable, the evaluation of parties by the electorate has not. Favorable evaluation has declined. According to Martin Wattenberg,

parties do not mean as much to the voters as they did two years ago. Martin Wattenberg, *The Decline of American Political Parties* (Cambridge, Mass.: Harvard University Press, 1984), p. 35. See also Charles H. Franklin and John E. Jackson, "The Dynamics of Party Identification" (paper presented at the annual meeting of the American Political Science Association, New York, September 3–6, 1981).

15. For a discussion of the concept of the normal vote and its application to electoral analysis, see Philip E. Converse, "The Concept of a Normal Vote," in Angus Campbell, Philip E. Converse, Warren E. Miller, and Donald E. Stokes (eds.), *Elections and the Political Order* (New York: Wiley, 1966), pp. 9–39; Warren E. Miller and Teresa E. Levitin, *Leadership and Change* (Cambridge, Mass.: Winthrop, 1976), pp. 37–40.

16. For an analysis of the components of the 1952 presidential election, see Angus Campbell, Philip E. Converse, Warren E. Miller, and Donald E. Stokes, *The American Voter* (New York: Wiley, 1960), pp. 524–527.

17. Ibid.; Donald E. Stokes, Angus Campbell, and Warren E. Miller, "Components of Electoral Decision," *American Political Science Review*, 52 (1958), 382.

18. Philip E. Converse, Angus Campbell, Warren E. Miller, and Donald E. Stokes, "Stability and Change in 1960: A Reinstating Election," in Campbell et al., *Elections and the Political Order*, p. 92.

19. Ibid., pp. 88–89.

20. Kennedy's Catholicism may have enlarged his Electoral College total by 22 votes. See Ithiel de Sola Pool, Robert P. Abelson, and Samuel Popkin, *Candidates, Issues, and Strategies* (Cambridge, Mass.: MIT Press, 1965), pp. 115–118.

21. Kennedy addressed a group of Protestant ministers in Houston, Texas. In his opening remarks, he advocated a complete separation of church and state. He then replied to question about how his Catholicism would affect his behavior as President. His responses, which received considerable media coverage, appeared to satisfy the apprehensions of a significant portion of the Protestant community.

22. Converse et al., "Stability and Change in 1960," p. 87.

23. For a discussion of the 1964 presidential election, see Philip E. Converse, Aage R. Clausen, and Warren E. Miller, "Electoral Myth and Reality: The 1964 Election," *American Political Science Review*, 59 (1965), 321–336.

24. Ibid., pp. 330–331.

25. Norman H. Nie, Sidney Verba, and John R. Petrocik, *The Changing American Voter* (Cambridge, Mass.: Harvard University Press, 1976); Miller and Levitin, *Leadership and Change;* Gerald Pomper, "From Confusion to Clarity: Issues and the American Voter, 1956–1968," *American Political Science Review*, 66 (1972), 415–428.

26. Nie, Verba, and Petrocik have concluded that 1964 was a critical transitional year for presidential elections:

> 1964 . . . is the year when the public becomes more issue oriented and when its issue positions develop a coherence they did not previously have. . . . It is the year when partisan commitment begins to erode. Pure party voting—that is, a vote for the candidate of the party with whom one identifies even if that vote is not in accord with one's issue inclination—declines.

Nie, Verba, and Petrocik, *The Changing American Voter*, p. 307.

27. Philip E. Converse, Warren E. Miller, Jerrold G. Rusk, and Arthur C. Wolfe,

"Continuity and Change in American Politics: Parties and Issues in the 1968 Election," *American Political Science Review*, 63 (1969), 1097.

28. Wallace claimed that there was not a dime's worth of difference between the Republican and Democratic candidates. He took great care in making his own positions distinctive. The clarity with which he presented his views undoubtedly contributed to the issue orientation of his vote. People know where Wallace stood.

29. In the South, the breakdown of the Wallace vote was 68 percent Democratic and 20 percent Republican. Outside the South, it was 46 percent Democratic and 34 percent Republican. Converse et al., "Continuity and Change," p. 1091.

30. Daniel A. Mazmanian, *Third Parties in Presidential Elections* (Washington, D.C.: Brookings Institution, 1974), p. 71.

31. Converse et al., "Continuity and Change," p. 1085.

32. Arthur H. Miller, Warren E. Miller, Alden S. Raine, and Thad A. Brown, "A Majority Party in Disarray: Policy Polarization in the 1972 Election," *American Political Science Review*, 70 (1976), 753–778.

33. Miller and Levitin, *Leadership and Change*, p. 164.

34. Gerald Pomper, "From Confusion to Clarity: Issues and American Voters, 1956–1968"; David E. RePass, "Issue Salience and Party Choice," *American Political Science Review*, 65 (1971), 389–400.

35. Arthur H. Miller and Warren E. Miller, "Partisanship and Performance: 'Rational' Choice in the 1976 Presidential Elections" (paper presented at the annual meeting of the American Political Science Association, Washington, D.C., September 1–4, 1977).

36. Ibid., p. 99.

37. The partisan predisposition of the electorate did not change appreciably. Between 1976 and 1980 the Republican party did not gain adherents at the expense of the Democrats. Public opinion did move slightly toward conservative policy positions, but the proportion of conservatives to liberals within the electorate remained approximately the same as it had since 1972.

38. Mainstream candidates tend to do better than those with more extreme political and ideological views. In 1964 and 1972, voters perceived conservative Republican Barry Goldwater and liberal Democrat George McGovern as less competent than their more centrist opponents. In 1980 this trend was reversed. It was Carter who was seen as the less competent candidate. John R. Petrocik and Sidney Verba with Christine Schultz, "Choosing the Choice and Not the Echo: A Funny Thing Happened to *The Changing American Voter* on the Way to the 1980 Election" (paper delivered at the annual meeting of the American Political Science Association, New York, September 3–6, 1981), p. 25.

39. Analysts at the University of Michigan have concluded that these perceptual shifts, which occurred among liberals, moderates, and conservatives, resulted from voters' allowing their impressions of the candidates to affect their judgments of the candidates' positions. As they became more disillusioned with Carter, they became more supportive of Reagan and more likely to vote for him. To rationalize that vote it was necessary to perceive his opinions and attitudes, and not Carter's, as closer to their own. Arthur H. Miller and Martin P. Wattenberg, "Policy and Performance Voting in the 1980 Election" (paper delivered at the annual meeting of the American Political Science Association, New York, September 3–6, 1981), p. 15.

40. Ibid., p. 7; Warren E. Miller, "Policy Directions and Presidential Leadership:

Alternative Interpretations of the 1980 Presidential Election" (paper delivered at the annual meeting of the American Political Science Association, New York, September 3–6, 1981).

41. Miller and Wattenberg, "Policy and Performance Voting in the 1980 Election," p. 6.

42. Paul R. Abramson, John H. Aldrich, and David W. Rohda, *Change and Continuity in the 1984 Elections* (Washington, D.C.: The Congressional Quarterly, 1986), pp. 171–180.

43. Paul C. Light and Celinda Lake, "The Election: Candidates, Strategies, and Decisions," in Michael Nelson (ed.), *The Elections of 1984* (Washington, D.C.: Congressional Quarterly, 1985), p. 92.

44. Adam Clymer, "Poll Finds Reagan Failed to Obtain a Policy Mandate," *New York Times*, November 11, 1984, p. A1.

45. In fact, it may even be difficult to obtain a complete copy of it. The number of platform summaries that are printed and circulated greatly exceeds the number of copies of the platforms that are available across the country during the campaign.

46. Jeff Fishel, *Presidents and Promises* (Washington, D.C.: Congressional Quarterly, 1985), p. 38.

47. Ibid, pp. 42–43.

48. John E. Mueller, *War, Presidents, and Public Opinion* (New York: Wiley, 1973), pp. 205–208 and 247–249.

49. Ibid.

Selected Readings

Abramson, Paul R., John H. Aldrich, and David W. Rohde. *Change and Continuity in the 1984 Elections.* Washington, D.C.: Congressional Quarterly Press, 1986.

Converse, Philip E., Angus Campbell, William E. Miller, and Donald E. Stokes. "Stability and Change in 1960: A Reinstating Election," *American Political Science Review,* 55 (1961), 269–280.

Converse, Philip E., Aage R. Clausen, and Warren E. Miller. "Electoral Myth and Reality: The 1964 Election," *American Political Science Review,* 59 (1965), 321–336.

Converse, Philip E., Warren E. Miller, Jerrold G. Rusk, and Arthur C. Wolfe. "Continuity and Change in American Politics: Parties and Issues in the 1968 Election," *American Political Science Review,* 53 (1969), 1083–1105.

Fishel, Jeff. *Presidents and Promises.* Washington, D.C.: Congressional Quarterly, 1985.

Kelley, Stanley. *Interpreting Elections.* Princeton, N.J.: Princeton University Press, 1983.

Miller, Arthur H. "The Majority Party Reunited? A Comparison of the 1972 and 1976 Elections," in Jeff Fishel (ed.), *Parties and Elections in an Anti-Party Age.* Bloomington: Indiana University Press, 1978, pp. 127–140.

Miller, Arthur H., Warren E. Miller, Alden S. Raine, and Thad A. Brown. "A Majority Party in Disarray: Policy Polarization in the 1972 Election," *American Political Science Review*, 70 (1976).

Miller, Arthur H., and Martin P. Wattenberg. "Throwing the Rascals Out: Policy and Performance Evaluations of Presidential Candidates, 1952–1980," *American Political Science Review*, 79 (1985), 359–372.

Miller, Warren E., and Teresa E. Levitin. *Leadership and Change*. Cambridge, Mass.: Winthrop, 1976.

Nelson, Michael (ed.). *The Elections of 1984*. Washington, D.C.: Congressional Quarterly, 1985.

Pomper, Gerald M., et al. *The Election of 1984*. Chatham, N.J.: Chatham House, 1985.

Ranney, Austin, (ed.). *The American Elections of 1984*. Durham, N.C.: Duke University Press, 1985.

Chapter 9

REFORMING THE ELECTORAL SYSTEM

Introduction

The American political system has evolved significantly in recent years. Party rules, finance laws, and media coverage are very different than they were twenty years ago. The composition of the electorate has changed as well with the expansion of suffrage and the reduction of legal obstacles to voting. And the Electoral College certainly does not function in the manner in which it was originally designed to do so.

Have these changes been beneficial? Has the system been improved? Are further structural or operational changes desirable? These questions have elicited a continuing, and sometimes spirited, debate.

Critics have alleged that the electoral process is too long, too costly, and too burdensome, that it wears down candidates and numbs voters, resulting in too much style and too little substance, too much rhetoric and too little debate. They have said that many qualified people are discouraged from running for office and much of the electorate is discouraged from participating in the election. Other criticisms are that the system benefits the rich, encourages factionalism, weakens parties, and focuses on the candidates and not the issues. It has also been contended that voters do not receive the information they need to make an intelligent, rational decision on election day.

In contrast, proponents argue that the political system is more democratic than ever. More, not fewer, people are involved, particularly at the nomination stage. Candidates, even lesser-known ones, have ample opportunity to demonstrate their competence, endurance, motivation, and leadership capabilities. Parties remain important as vehicles through which the system operates and by which governing is accomplished. Those who defend the process believe voters do receive as much information as they desire and that most people can make intelligent, informed, rational judgments.

The old adage "where you stand influences what you see" is applicable to the debate about electoral reform. No political process is completely neutral. There are always winners and losers. To a large extent the advantages that some enjoy are made possible only by the disadvantages that others encounter. Rationalizations aside, much of the debate about the system, about equity, representation, and responsiveness, revolves around a very practical, political question: Who gains and who loses?

Proposals to change the system need to be assessed in the light of this question. They also should be judged on the basis of how such changes would affect the operation of the political system. This section will discuss some of these proposals and the impact they could have on the road to the White House. The chapter is organized into two parts, one dealing with the more recent developments in party rules, campaign finance, and media coverage, and the other dealing with the long-term, democratic issues of participation and voting.

MODIFYING RECENT CHANGES

Party Rules

Of all the changes that have recently occurred in the nomination process, none has caused more persistent controversy than the reforms governing the selection of delegates. Designed to encourage grass roots participation and broaden the base of representation, these reforms have also lengthened the nominating period, made it more expensive, generated candidate-based organizations, weakened state party leaders, converted conventions into coronations, and loosened the ties between the parties and their nominees. As a consequence, governing has been made more difficult.

Since 1968, when the Democrats began to rewrite their rules for delegate selection, the parties have suffered from these unintended repercussions. Each succeeding presidential election has seen a new Democratic commission recommend new changes to the party rules, changes that have attempted to reconcile expanded participation and representation with the traditional need to unify the party for a national campaign. While less reform conscious than the Democrats, the Republicans have also tried to steer a middle course between greater rank-and-file involvement and more equitable representation on the one hand and the maintenance of successful electoral and governing coalitions on the other.

How to balance these oft-competing goals has been a critical concern. Those who desire greater public participation have lauded the trend toward having more primaries and a larger percentage of delegates selected in them. Believing that the reforms have opened up the process and made it more democratic, they favor the continued selection of pledged delegates based on the proportion of the popular vote a candidate receives. In contrast, those who believe that greater control by state and national party leaders is desirable argue that the reforms have gone too far. They would prefer fewer primaries, a smaller percentage of delegates selected in them, and more unpledged delegates, elected officials, and party leaders attending the nominating conventions. They would also favor a larger involvement by the national party in the presidential campaign. Giving federal funds to the party, and not to the candidate, has been proposed as one way to achieve this latter objective.

While the strong-party advocates appear to be in the ascendant, having dominated the latest series of Democratic party reforms, widespread public support continues for simplifying and shortening the nomination and making the selection of a candidate more reflective of the wishes of a majority in each party. Several proposals have been made and even introduced as legislation in Congress. One would limit the period during which primaries or caucuses could be held; a second would cluster primaries and caucuses geographically, forcing states in designated regions to have their elections on the same day; a third would create a national primary.

Having an official period during the spring of the election year for primaries and caucuses has been suggested as a way to reduce the impact the early contests have had on the nomination. A second but equally important objective has been to reduce the media's influence on public opinion during these initial stages of the process.

The Democratic party attempted to do this in 1984 and again in 1988 by imposing its own window period. Opposition, however, from several states, including Iowa and New Hampshire, forced the party to grant exceptions to the rule. The exceptions, in turn, continue to produce the problem that generated the proposal in the first place.

Theoretically, if the parties do not or will not impose a primary period, Congress can. Legislation has been proposed that would require all states to schedule their contests between the second Tuesday in March and the second Tuesday in June.

One problem with Congress establishing such a period is that it would involve the national government in an area traditionally reserved for the states. Another difficulty is that it might produce an effect precisely the opposite to the one intended. Instead of shortening the campaign and decreasing the media's influence, the imposition of a window, combined with the front-loading of the caucuses and primaries at the beginning of the period, might actually increase the time needed by candidates to develop their organization, raise money, and mount large-scale media efforts. No longer would they have the luxury of waiting until after the early caucuses and primaries had boosted their national recognition to provide the basis for a simultaneous multistate campaign.

In order to allow states to retain some discretion, yet encourage them to hold primaries and concentrate them at specific points in the nominating process, a system of regional or interregional primaries has been suggested. While these proposals have not received a ground swell of public support, they have been viewed more favorably than unfavorably by the electorate.[1]

A variety of plans have been introduced in Congress. Although they differ in specifics, they agree in essentials:

1. Divide the country into contiguous regions;
2. require states within those regions to hold primaries (if they have one) on the same day;
3. randomly choose the dates for the regional election;
4. schedule the regional votes two to four weeks apart.

A regional primary system would undoubtedly compress the process and better focus public attention in the area where the vote occurred. This might encourage turnout, which would also be spurred by the likelihood of a regional media blitz. The allocation of delegates in regional primaries would probably reflect the popularity of the candidates within the area. Under such a system, conventions would still be necessary to choose among the leading candidates or to ratify the selection of the winner, as well as to perform their other traditional functions—writing a platform, rallying the faithful, making a public appeal.

On the negative side, regional primaries might exacerbate sectional rivalries, encourage sectional candidates, and produce more organizations to rival those of the state and national parties. Moreover, they might impede the emergence of a consensus candidate, thereby extending the process through the convention and increasing, not decreasing, costs, time, and media attention. Finally, a system of regional primaries would deny states the option of setting their own date. For this reason alone, some state officials and their congressional representatives—especially those from Iowa and New Hampshire—have consistently opposed the idea.

Other state leaders, on the other hand, believe a regional primary system would enhance their state's influence and give them a greater voice in the selection of the nominee and the issues the candidates address. Southern Democrats, in particular, unhappy over their party's standard-bearers in 1972 and 1984, over their party's national image, and over its recent platforms, have regarded regional primaries as an opportunity to stamp the ticket with a southern imprint. These leaders have convinced their state legislatures—all incidentally controlled by the Democrats—to hold primaries on the same day in 1988 (the second Tuesday in March) and caucuses the following weekend. Thus, the first regional elections have been established, without congressional legislation or mandated changes in party rules.

Whether regional primaries will accomplish their political objectives is difficult to forecast. One possible consequence, however, of the southern states holding their 1988 nomination contests together at that beginning of the period could be to maintain or enhance the importance of Iowa and New Hampshire in initially shaping public opinion. Another might be to increase the pressure on other regions to hold their primaries on the same day and/or to encourage states within those regions to move their contests to a point earlier in the process.

Candidates for the nomination will be affected as well. They will need more extensive field organizations, and more funds, to take advantage of any boost that Iowa and New Hampshire might provide. Aspirants who were nationally recognized before Iowa and New Hampshire would be in a better position initially to mobilize and utilize these resources.

A third option, and the one that would represent the most sweeping change, would be to institute a national primary. While party leaders, including members of the reform commissions, have opposed such a proposal, and Congress has been cool to the idea, the general public seems to be more favorably disposed. Gallup polls taken over the last twenty years indicate that about two-thirds of the electorate would prefer such an election to the present system.[2]

Most proposals for a national primary call for a one-day election to be held during the summer. Candidates who wished to enter their party's primary would be required to obtain a certain number of signatures, equal to approximately 1 percent of the vote in the last presidential election. Any aspirant who won a majority would automatically receive the nomination. In some plans a plurality would be sufficient, provided it was at least 40 percent. In the event that no one received 40 percent, a runoff election would be held several weeks later between the top two finishers. Nominating conventions would continue to select the vice presidential candidates and to decide on the platforms, although they might have to convene after the national primary was completed.

A national primary would be consistent with the one person–one vote principle. All participants would have an equal voice in the selection. No longer would those in the early, small primary and caucus states exercise disproportionate influence.

It is likely that a national primary would stimulate turnout. The attention given to such an election would provide greater incentive for voting than currently exists, particularly in those states that hold their nomination contests after the apparent winner has emerged. A national primary would probably result in nomination by a more representative electorate than is currently the case. Moreover, if the vote were held on one day in the summer, a shorter campaign might result.

A single primary for each party would accelerate a nationalizing trend. Issues that affect the entire country would be the primary focus of attention. Thus, candidates for the nation's highest office would be forced to discuss the problems they would most likely address during the general election campaign and would most likely confront as President.

Moreover, the results of the election would be clear-cut. The media could no longer interpret primaries and caucus returns as they saw fit. An incumbent's ability to garner support through the timely release of grants, contracts, and other spoils of government might be more limited in a national contest. On the other hand, such an election would undoubtedly discourage challengers who lacked national reputations. No longer would an early victory catapult a relatively unknown aspirant into the position of serious contender and jeopardize a President's chances for renomination. In fact, lesser-known candidates such as George McGovern and Jimmy Carter would find it extremely difficult to raise money, build an organization, and mount a national campaign within the relatively short period in which such a contest would be waged. This would improve the chances that competent, experienced political leaders would be selected as their party's standard-bearers—or, depending on one's perspective, that older, tired, Washington-based politicians would be chosen.

From the standpoint of the party, a national primary would further weaken the ability of its leaders to influence the selection of the nominee. A successful candidate would probably not owe his victory to party officials. Moreover, a postprimary convention could not be expected to tie the nominee to the party, although it might tie the party to the nominee at least through the election. The trend toward personalizing politics would probably continue. At the very least, the successful candidate would have to wage a media campaign, further emphasizing image at the expense of substantive policy questions.

Whether the primary winner would be the party's strongest candidate is also open to question. With a large field of contenders, those with the most devoted supporters might do best. On the other hand, candidates who do not arouse the passions of the diehards, but who are more acceptable to the party's mainstream, might not do as well. Everybody's second choice might not even finish second, unless a system of approval voting were used. But approval voting, which allows the electorate to list their top two or three choices in order, would complicate the election, confusing the result and adding to the costs of conducting it.[3]

In addition to weakening the party, a national primary could lessen the ability of states to determine when and how their citizens would participate in the presidential nomination process. The ability of state party leaders and elected officials to affect the process and influence the outcome would suffer. These likely consequences have made it difficult to mobilize wide support for such a plan.

Finance Laws

Closely related to the period and process of delegate selection are the new finance laws. Enacted in the 1970s in reaction to secret and sometimes illegal bequests, to the disparity in contributions and spending among the candidates, and to the spiraling costs of modern campaigns, particularly the costs of television advertising, these laws were designed to improve accountability, subsidize nominations, and fund the general election. Some of these objectives have been achieved, but in the process other problems have been created.

The laws have taken campaign finance out of the back rooms and put it into the public spotlight. They have, however, also created a nightmare of compliance procedures and reporting requirements. Detailed records of practically all contributions and expenditures must now be kept by campaign organizations and must be periodically submitted to the Federal Election Commission. A good accountant and attorney are now as necessary as a pollster, image maker, and grass roots organizer.

The amount wealthy individuals can donate to presidential nominating campaigns, but not the amount they can spend independently, is limited by law. This has created incentives for broad-based public support but has not lessened the need for frequent appeals for funds. It has eliminated the burden of raising money during the general election, but has created severe budget constraints on the candidates.

Nor has government support equalized the financial status of the major party candidates. Republicans still enjoy an advantage by virtue of their party's superior organizational and financial base at the national, state, and local levels. Incumbents are also benefited by their capacity to make news, affect events, and use the perquisites of office.

Although the legislation has hurt third parties, it has not correspondingly strengthened the two major parties at the national level. On the contrary, federal subsidies and support have contributed to party factionalism and have encouraged the formation of separate candidate organizations. They have also made the parties more dependent on outside groups for contributions and organized support.

Several changes have been proposed to alleviate these problems. Compliance procedures could be eased. For example, the size of the contribution that must be reported could be increased, and the number of reports might be reduced. This would relieve campaign organizations of some of the burdens of record keeping but would also mean that less detailed information would be available less promptly to the public.

Independent spending cannot be prevented, but the limits on direct contributions to candidates could be increased, particularly for individual donors. This would provide candidates with more money and reduce their dependence on outside groups. Party organizations could benefit from a decline in PAC activity and would have more incentive to create and maintain a structure that could mobilize the vote for their nominees. The problem with increasing the amount individuals could give is that the wealthy would gain greater influence, and grass roots solicitation might suffer.

Similarly, the national party's contribution might be increased. This could strengthen its role in the presidential campaign, but could also divert funds from other candidates and accentuate the financial advantage the Republicans presently enjoy.

Finally, more money could be given by the federal government, if more money were available. With only 25 percent of the population contributing to the campaign fund, however, a large increase would require funding from the general treasury, placing election funds in competition with other programs. An alternative would be to permit private donations in the general election; but this raises the perennial problem of the increased influence that those in the upper-income groups would have as a consequence of their greater ability to give.

Although many lawmakers see problems with the finance laws, they cannot agree on solutions. The difficulty with amending the law lies in ensuring that no one party benefits or suffers at the expense of the other. Maintaining this objective, however, decreases the partisan motive for passing the legislation.

In addition to the question of political equity, there is an even more fundamental issue for a democratic society. Competing needs have created contradictory goals. Freedom of speech implies the right to give and to spend. Equality of opportunity requires that the wealthy not be advantaged. Yet campaign appeals to the entire electorate are very expensive. There are no easy answers. In all likelihood, unless and until there is a major problem that attracts public attention and demands resolution, finance issues are more likely to be debated than legislated.

Media Coverage

A third significant change in the electoral process is in the way in which information about the campaign is communicated to the voters. Beginning in the 1950s, television became the principal medium through which candidates made their appeals and by which those appeals were assessed. Since then, television's emphasis on the contest, the drama, and the style of campaigning has affected public perceptions of the candidates and influenced the images they sought to create.

Changes in party rules and finance laws have also contributed to the media's impact. The increasing number and complexity of preconvention contests has provided the media with greater inducements to cover these events and interpret their results. The desire of the party to obtain maximum exposure for its nominating convention has further extended such coverage and interpretation. The limited funds for presidential campaigns have also increased the importance of news about the election, and may have contributed to its impact on the voters. Today, candidates do not leave their coverage to chance. They attempt to influence it by carefully releasing favorable information, by staging events, and by paying for many commercial messages.

Is the coverage adequate? Do voters receive sufficient information from the media to make an intelligent decision? Many believe they do not. Academics, especially, have urged that greater attention be paid to policy issues and less to the horse race. One proposal would have the networks and wire services assign special correspondents to cover the issues of the campaign, much as they assign people to report on its color, drama, and personal aspects.

In addition to criticizing the media's treatment of the issues, academics and others have frequently called into question the amount and accuracy of election reporting. The law states that if the networks provide free time to some candidates, they must provide equal time to all running for the same position, including those of fringe parties. This "equal time" provision has in fact resulted in no or little free time, although coverage of presidential debates as news events has circumvented the rule to some extent. Networks are also required to be impartial in their coverage. Station licenses can be challenged and even revoked if biases are consistently evident in the presentation of the news.

Other than requiring fairness, preventing obscenity, and ensuring that public-service commitments are met, there is little the government can do without impinging on the freedom of the press. The media are free to choose which elections and candidates to emphasize, what kind of coverage to provide, how to interpret the results of primaries and caucuses, and even to predict who will win before the election is concluded.

Projecting the returns on election night has caused particular controversy. Since 1964, when a Johnson landslide was predicted before the polls on the West Coast had closed, proposals have been advanced to limit or prohibit these glimpses into the immediate future. One proposal, sponsored by the League of Women Voters, would request the networks and wire services to voluntarily desist from making any forecasts until voting across the country has been completed. In 1984 the networks consented to a variation of this proposal, agreeing not to predict the outcome in any one state until its polls had closed. Even with this voluntary restriction, however, all the networks had projected President Reagan the winner by 8:30 P.M. eastern standard time—several hours before the polls closed in the West.

A second proposal, introduced in the form of legislation, would establish a uniform hour at which all polls in the continental United States would close. In order to provide as long a voting day as possible in the West, the plan would extend daylight saving time in Pacific states until the Sunday following each presidential election. The polls would then remain open until 7 P.M. Pacific time and 9 P.M. eastern time.

A third proposal, the most far-reaching, would eliminate the polls altogether and have all votes cast by mail. Ballots would be distributed by the state to all eligible voters within that state. They would have to be returned (postmarked) by a specific date.

Each of these proposals has encountered criticism. Could the networks be expected to wait until voting ended across the nation, given the competitive character of news reporting? Could uniform hours for the entire country be agreed upon? What about the logistical problems this would cause on the West Coast? Besides, there still would be no guarantee that early forecasts could be eliminated. They could still be made on the basis of exit polling, even if exit polling were made more difficult by restricting network interviewers to a certain distance from the polls. Voting by mail would be expensive, time-consuming, and potentially subject to the most fraud.

In addition to the obvious First Amendment problems that such proposals would engender, the restrictions on the media might meet other objections. Americans seem to want their election returns reported rapidly. After a lengthy campaign, workers and sympathizers are eager to know the results and to celebrate or commiserate. Second, the presidential transition is short enough without having to wait another few days for every state to conclude its official count. Even exit polls have value. Knowledge about the beliefs, attitudes, and motivations of the voters is useful information, particularly for those who are elected. In a democracy, it is essential to get as clear a reading of the pulse of the electorate as possible. At the very least this prevents mythical mandates from being claimed and implemented.

ENHANCING ELECTORAL CHOICE

Turnout

While suffrage has expanded, voter turnout has declined (not in whole numbers but as a proportion of the total electorate). It has declined in part because the number of eligible voters has increased and in part because partisan attitudes have weakened. A number of other factors, including legal obstacles, continue to confound and confuse would-be voters. As a result only a little over 50 percent of the electorate exercises its franchise and votes during presidential elections.

This relatively low turnout in a free and open society has been a source of embarrassment to the United States and of concern to its elected officials. How can a President legitimately claim a public mandate with the electoral support of only about one-quarter of those eligible to vote? How can the government claim to be representative if half the electorate chooses not to participate in its selection?

Concern over low turnout has generated a number of proposals for remedying it. One proposal would make election day in presidential years a holiday. Presumably this would, for the bulk of the population, prevent work-related activities from interfering with voting.[4] Many countries follow this practice, or hold their elections on Sunday. The problem here is that another national holiday would cost employers millions of dollars in lost productivity, with no guarantee that turnout would be increased. For workers in certain service areas the holiday might be a workday anyway.

Another proposal would be to ease registration by making it automatic or extending it, perhaps even to election day itself. That way people could automatically vote or simply register and vote at the same time. Since approximately 85 percent of those who register vote, either proposal should increase the percent of voters. In fact, two political scientists, Raymond E. Wolfinger and Steven J. Rosenstone, have estimated that abolishing the requirement practiced in many states, that registration be completed thirty days prior to the election, would increase turnout 3 to 9 percent for the nation as a whole.[5]

There are a number of problems with automatic registration or simultaneous registration and voting. The potential for voting fraud might be increased; the ability of states to monitor federal elections could be impaired; and citizens' responsibilities might be lessened. Should it be the duty of the national government or the states to conduct elections? The Constitution specifies that the states hold elections for national officials, although amendments extending suffrage have limited a state's authority to determine who is eligible to vote. Similarly, where should the line be drawn between responsibility of the government to oversee the electoral process and the obligation of the citizenry to participate in it?

The most radical proposal would be to simply compel people to vote: to force them to go to the polls and cast a ballot. Penalties would be imposed on those who refused to do so.

If everybody who was eligible had to vote, parties and candidates would have to broaden their appeal. They would have to address the needs and desires of all the people and not concentrate on those who were most likely to vote. Those who have not participated as frequently in the current voluntary system of voting—the poorer, less educated, less fortunate—would receive more attention not only from candidates for office but from elected officials in office. More equitable policies might result. The ideal of a government of, by, and for the people might be a step closer to reality.

One obvious problem with compelling people to vote is the compulsion itself. Some may be physically or mentally incapable of voting. Others may not care, have little interest, and have very limited information. They might not even know the names of the candidates. Would the selection of the best qualified person be enhanced by the participation of these uninformed, uninterested, uncaring voters? Might demagogy be encouraged, or even slicker and more simplistic advertising develop? Would government be more responsive and more popular, or would it be more prone to what British philosopher John Stuart Mill referred to as "the tyranny of the majority?" Finally, is it democratic to force people to vote? Should voting be a responsibility of government or of the citizenry? If the right to vote is an essential component of a democratic society, then what about the right not to vote? Shouldn't it be protected as well?

The Electoral College

In addition to the problem of who votes, another source of contention is how the votes should be aggregated. Theoretically, the Electoral College allows electors chosen by the states to vote as they please. In practice, all votes are cast for the popular-vote winner in the state. The reason for this is simple. The vote for President and Vice President is actually a vote for competing slates of electors. The slate that wins is the slate proposed by the winning candidate's party. Naturally they are expected to vote for their party's nominees.

This de facto system has been criticized as undemocratic, as unrepresentative of minority views within states, and as potentially unreflective of the nation's popular choice. Over the years, there have been numerous proposals to alter it. The first was introduced in Congress in 1797. Since then, there have been over five hundred others. The first actual modification occurred in 1804 with ratification of the Twelfth Amendment. While other constitutional amendments have tangentially affected presidential elections, none has changed the basic structure of the college.

In urging changes, critics have pointed to the college's archaic design, its electoral biases, and the undemocratic results it can produce.[6] In recent years, four major plans—automatic, proportional, district, and direct election—have been proposed to alleviate some or all of these problems. This section will examine these proposals and the impact they could have on the way in which the President is selected.

The Automatic Plan. The actual electors in the Electoral College have been an anachronism since the development of the party system. Their role as partisan agents is not and has not been consistent with their exercising an independent judgment in choosing a President. In fact, sixteen states plus the District of Columbia prohibit such a judgment, by requiring electors to cast their ballots for the winner of the state's popular vote. Although probably unenforceable because they seem to clash with the Constitution, these laws strongly indicate how electors should vote.

The so-called automatic plan would do away with the danger that electors may exercise their personal preferences. First proposed in 1826, it has received substantial support since that time, including the backing of Presidents John Kennedy and Lyndon Johnson. The plan simply keeps the Electoral College intact but eliminates the electors. Electoral votes are automatically credited to the candidate who has received the most popular votes within the state.

Other than removing the potential problem of faithless or unpledged electors, the plan would do little to change the system. It has not been enacted because Congress has not felt the problem to be of sufficient magnitude to justify a constitutional amendment. There have in fact been only eight faithless electors, who failed to vote for their party's nominees—six since 1948.[7]

The Proportional Plan. Electing the entire slate of presidential electors has also been the focus of considerable attention. If the winner takes all the electoral votes, the impact of the majority party is increased within the state and the larger, more competitive states are benefited.

From the perspective of the minority party or parties within the state, the selection of an entire ticket is not desirable. In effect, it disenfranchises people who do not vote for the winning candidate. And it does more than that: It discourages a strong campaign effort by a party that has little chance of winning the presidential election in that state. Naturally this affects the success of other candidates of that party as well. All this works to reduce voter turnout.

One way to rectify this problem would be to have proportional voting. Such a plan has been introduced on a number of occasions. Under a proportional system, the electors would be abolished, the winner-take-all principle would be eliminated, and a state's electoral vote would be divided in proportion to its popular vote. A majority of electoral votes would still be required for election. If no candidate received a majority, most proportional plans call for a joint session of Congress to choose the President from among the top two or three candidates.

The proportional proposal would have a number of major consequences, It would decrease the influence of the most competitive states, where voters are more evenly divided, and increase the importance of the least competitive ones, where they are likely to be more homogeneous. Under such a system, it would be the size of the victory that counts. To take a dramatic example, if the electoral votes of Vermont and New York in 1960 had been calculated on the basis of the proportional vote for the major candidates within the states, Nixon would have received a larger margin from Vermont's 3 votes (1.759 to 1.240) than Kennedy would have gotten from New York's 45 (22.7 to 22.3). Similarly, George Wallace's margin over Nixon and Humphrey in Mississippi in 1968 (3.8) would have been larger than Humphrey's over Nixon in New York (2.3).

While the proportional system rewards large victories in relatively homogeneous states, it also seems to encourage competition within those states. Having the electoral vote proportional to the popular vote provides an incentive to the minority party to mount a more vigorous campaign and establish a more effective organization. However, it might also cause third parties to do the same, thereby weakening the two-party system.

The proportional plan contains a pattern of biases far different from the one found in the Electoral College. As noted in Chapter 1, the Electoral College benefits the very smallest and, to a greater extent, the very largest states. Within the larger and more competitive states, the system favors geographically concentrated groups with cohesive voting patterns. A proportional system, however, would advantage smaller states, disadvantage larger states, and would not benefit geographically concentrated groups nearly so much as the current system does.[8]

Finally, operating under a proportional plan would in all likelihood make the Electoral College vote much closer, thereby decreasing the President's mandate for governing. Carter would have defeated Ford by only 11.7 electoral votes in 1976 and Nixon would have won by only 6.1 in 1968. (See Table 9–1.) In at least one recent instance, it might also have changed the election results. Had this plan been in effect in 1960, Richard Nixon would probably have defeated John Kennedy by 266.1 to

Table 9–1 VOTING FOR PRESIDENT, 1952–1984: FOUR METHODS FOR AGGREGATING THE VOTES

Year	Electoral College	Proportional Plan	District Plan	Direct Election (percentage of total vote)
1952				
Eisenhower	442	288.5	375	55.1 %
Stevenson	89	239.8	156	44.4
Others	0	2.7	0	.5
1956				
Eisenhower	457	296.7	411	57.4
Stevenson	73	227.2	120	42.0
Others	0	7.1	0	.6
1960				
Nixon	219	266.1	278	49.5
Kennedy	303	265.6	245	49.8
Others	0	5.3	0	.7
1964				
Goldwater	52	213.6	72	38.5
Johnson	486	320.0	466	61.0
Others	0	3.9	0	.5
1968				
Nixon	301	231.5	289	43.2
Humphrey	191	225.4	192	42.7
Wallace	46	78.8	57	13.5
Others	0	2.3	0	.6
1972				
Nixon	520	330.3	474	60.7
McGovern	17	197.5	64	37.5
Others	1	10.0	0	1.8
1976				
Ford	240	258.0	269	48.0
Carter	297	269.7	269	50.1
Others	1	10.2	0	1.9
1980				
Reagan	489	272.9	396	50.7
Carter	49	220.9	142	41.0
Anderson	0	35.3	0	6.6
Others	0	8.9	0	1.7
1984				
Reagan	525	317.6	468	58.8
Mondale	13	216.6	70	40.6
Others	0	3.8	0	.7

Source: Figures on Proportional and District Vote for 1952–1980 were supplied to the author by Joseph B. Gorman of the Congressional Research Service, Library of Congress. Calculations for 1984 were completed by Mark Drozdowski on the basis of data reported in the *Almanac of American Politics* (Washington, D.C.: National Journal, 1985) and *Congress and the Nation* (Washington, D.C.: Congressional Quarterly, 1985), vol. 6, p. 1093.

265.6. However, it is difficult to calculate the 1960 vote precisely because the names of the Democratic presidential and vice presidential candidates were not on the ballot in Alabama and because an unpledged slate of electors was chosen in Mississippi.

The District Plan. The district electoral system is another proposal aimed at reducing the effect of winner-take-all voting. While this plan has had several variations, its basic thrust would be to keep the Electoral College but to change the manner in which the electoral votes within the state are determined. Instead of selecting the entire slate on the basis of the statewide vote for President, only two electoral votes would be decided in this manner. The remaining votes would be allocated on the basis of the popular vote within individual districts (probably congressional districts). A majority of the electoral votes would still be necessary for election. If the Electoral College were not decisive, then most district plans call for a joint session of Congress to make the final selection.

For the very smallest states, those with three electoral votes, all three electors would have to be chosen by the state as a whole. For others, however, the combination of district and at-large selection would probably result in a split electoral vote. On a national level, this would make the Electoral College more reflective of the partisan division of the newly elected Congress rather than of the popular division of the national electorate.

The losers under such an arrangement would be the large, competitive states and, most particularly, the organized, geographically concentrated groups within those states. The winners would include small states. Third and minority parties might also be aided to the extent that they were capable of winning specific legislative districts. It is difficult to project whether Republicans or Democrats would benefit more from such an arrangement, since much would depend on how the legislative districts within the states were apportioned. If the 1960 presidential vote were aggregated on the basis of one electoral vote to the popular-vote winner of each congressional district and two to the popular-vote winner of each state, Nixon would have defeated Kennedy 278 to 245 with 14 unpledged electors. In 1976 the district system would have produced a tie, with Carter and Ford each receiving 269 votes. (See Table 9–1.) The state of Maine is the only state that presently chooses its electors in this manner.

The Direct Election Plan. Of all the plans to alter or replace the Electoral College, the direct popular vote has received the most attention and support. Designed to eliminate the College entirely and count the votes on a nationwide basis, it would elect the popular-vote winner provided the winning candidate received a certain percentage of the total vote. In most plans, 40 percent of the total vote would be necessary. In some, 50 percent would be required.[9] In the event that no one got the required percentage, a runoff between the top two candidates would be held to determine the winner.[10]

A direct popular vote would, of course, remedy a major problem of the present system—the possibility of electing a nonplurality President. It would better equalize voting power both among and within the states. The large, competitive states would lose some of their electoral clout by the elimination of winner-take-all voting. Party competition within the states and perhaps even nationwide would be increased. Turnout should also improve. Every vote would count in a direct election.

However, a direct election might also encourage minor parties, which would weaken the two-party system. The possibility of denying a major party candidate 40 percent of the popular vote might be sufficient to entice a proliferation of candidates and produce a series of bargains and deals in which support was traded for favors with a new administration. Moreover, if the federal character of the system were changed, it is possible that the plurality winner might not be geographically representative of the entire country. A very large sectional vote might elect a candidate who trailed in other areas of the country. This would upset the representational balance that has been achieved between the President's electoral constituency and Congress's.

The organized groups that are geographically concentrated in the large industrial states would have their votes diluted by a direct election. Take Jewish voters, for example. Highly supportive of the Democratic party since World War II, Jews constitute approximately 3 percent of the total population but 14 percent in New York, the second largest state with 39 electoral votes. Thus, the impact of the New York Jewish vote is magnified under the present Electoral College arrangement.[11]

The Republican party has also been reluctant to lend its support to direct election. Republicans perceive that they benefit from the current arrangement. Moreover, as the smaller of the two major parties in terms of partisan identifiers, the Republicans would not necessarily have their chances for winning improved by a direct, popular vote. While Republican Benjamin Harrison was the last nonplurality President to be elected, Gerald Ford came remarkably close in 1976. On the other hand, Richard Nixon's Electoral College victory in 1968 could conceivably have been upset by a stronger Wallace campaign in the southern border states.

A very close popular vote could also cause problems with a direct election. The winner might not be evident for days, even months. Voter fraud could have national consequences. Under such circumstances, challenges by the losing candidate would be more likely.

The provision for the event that no one received the required percentage has its drawbacks as well. A runoff election would extend the length of the campaign and add to its cost. Considering that some aspirants begin their quest for the Presidency more than three years before the election, a further protraction of the process might unduly tax the patience of the voters and produce an even greater numbing effect than currently exists. Moreover, it would also cut an already short transition period for a newly elected President, and would further drain the time and energies of an incumbent seeking reelection.

There is still another difficulty with a contingency election. It could reverse the order in which the candidates originally finished. This might undermine the mandate of the eventual winner. It might also encourage spoiler candidacies. Third parties and independents seeking the Presidency could exercise considerable power in the event of a close contest between the major parties. Imagine Wallace's influence in 1968 in a runoff between Humphrey and Nixon.

Nonetheless, the direct election plan is supported by public opinion and has been ritualistically praised by recent Presidents. Recent Gallup Polls have consistently found the public favoring a direct election over the present electoral system by substantial margins.[12] Carter and Ford have both urged the abolition of the Electoral College and its replacement by a popular vote.

In 1969 the House of Representatives actually voted for a constitutional amendment to establish direct election for President and Vice President, but the Senate refused to go along. Despite this support, it seems unlikely that sufficient impetus for such a change will occur until the issue becomes salient to more people and until the opposition of certain liberal and conservative groups weakens. It may take the election of a nonplurality President or some other electoral crisis to produce the public outcry and political momentum needed to change the Electoral College system.[13]

SUMMARY

There have been changes and continuities in the way we select a President. In general the changes have made the system more democratic. The continuities link it to its republican past.

The nomination process has been affected more than the general election. Significant modifications have occurred in the rules for choosing delegates, in the laws regulating contributions and spending, and in the media through which appeals are made. The composition of the electorate has been altered as well. In contrast, the Electoral College has continued to function in much the same way for the last century and a half, although certainly not as the framers intended.

Have these changes been beneficial or harmful? Have they functioned to make the system more efficient, more responsive, and more likely to result in the choice of a well-qualified candidate? Political scientists disagree in their answers.

Much of the current controversy over campaign reform has focused on party rules. Designed to encourage greater rank-and-file participation in the selection of delegates, the new rules have helped democratize presidential nominations. In the process, however, they have also factionalized and personalized the parties and weakened the position of their leadership. These unintended consequences have stimulated a debate over the merits of the changes.

A consensus seems to be emerging that some of the reforms have gone too far and that stronger party control over the nomination process is needed. The Democrats have moved in this direction, modifying some of their reforms; the Republicans have not, but neither have they imposed national guidelines on their state parties, as the Democrats have done.

There have been proposals that the government get involved as well. Although Congress has not acted on these proposals, the southern states have cooperated in 1988 by scheduling their caucuses and primaries for the second week in March. In effect, this will create a system of regional elections.

Despite the inclinations of Democratic leaders to retrench and of some members of Congress to control the undesirable effects of the nomination process, a majority of the electorate would go even further— but in the opposite direction. They would have more participatory democracy, not less. They would abolish the present patchwork of state caucuses and primaries and replace it with a single, national primary.

New finance legislation has also been designed to improve accountability, equalize contributions, and control spending. This legislation has enhanced public information, but has done so only by increasing the burden on candidate organizations to keep detailed records and submit frequent reports. The law has succeeded in decreasing the influence of large donors but not the influence of professional fund-raisers. It has also contributed to the factionalizing of parties, encouraging multiple candidacies for the nomination. Moreover, it has weakened parties by giving aid directly to the candidates, encouraging the development of separate organizations, and providing incentives for political action committees. Whether the end result has been to lessen the advantage of wealth and effectively open the process to a much larger group of aspirants is difficult to say. No consensus on how to improve the law is apparent.

Media coverage has also been the subject of considerable controversy. Television has brought more people into contact with presidential candidates than in the past, but that contact has also tended to be indirect and passive. The reporting of information about personalities and events far exceeds that of substantive policy issues. Television, in particular, is often blamed for the average voter's low level of knowledge and for exercising undue influence on the electorate.

Whether or not this accusation is accurate, it is widespread and has generated persistent criticism. Few changes are likely, however, in the short run because the public is less concerned about media coverage than are the candidates, and any nonvoluntary attempt to affect coverage is apt to run up against the guarantees of the First Amendment.

Who votes and how the votes should be aggregated continues to prompt debate and elicit concern. The expansion of suffrage has made the election process more democratic in theory, but the decline in turnout and lower rates of participation have called this theoretical improvement into question. While the failure of almost one-half of the electorate to exercise its franchise has been a source of embarrassment and dismay, there is little agreement on how to deal with this problem in a federal system that values individual initiative and individual fulfillment of civic responsibility.

Finally, the equity of the Electoral College has also been challenged, but none of the proposals to alter or abolish it, except by the direct election of the President, has received much public support. With no outcry for change, Congress has been reluctant to alter the system and seems unlikely to do so until an electoral crisis or unpopular result forces its hand.

Does the electoral process work? Yes. Can it be improved? Of course. Will it be changed? Probably, but if the past is any indication, there is no guarantee that the changes will produce only, or even, the desired effect. If politics is the art of the possible, then success is achieved by those who can adjust most quickly to the change and turn it to their own advantage.

NOTES

1. A Gallup Poll taken in 1985 found a plurality of the population favoring regional primaries. Support was greater among Republicans than Democrats and outside the South than in the South. *Gallup Report,* No. 237 (June 1985), p. 13.

2. *Gallup Report,* No. 226 (July 1984), p. 23.

3. Steven J. Brams and Peter C. Fishburn, "Approval Voting," *American Political Science Review,* 72 (1978), 831–847.

4. Current law requires that employers give their employees time off to vote.

5. Raymond E. Wolfinger and Steven J. Rosenstone, *Who Votes?* (New Haven: Yale University Press, 1980), p. 130.

6. See the discussion of the Electoral College structure, biases, and consequences in Chapter 1, pp. 17–20.

7. There is some controversy whether three other electors in 1796 might also have gone against their party when voting for President. They supported Adams although they were selected in states controlled by the Democratic-Republicans. However, the fluidity of the party system in those days, combined with the weakness of party identification, makes their affiliation (if any) difficult to establish.

In 1960 eleven unpledged electors from two southern states, Alabama and Mississippi, were chosen. They did not support the national Democratic ticket, voting instead for Harry F. Byrd and Strom Thurmond.

8. Lawrence D. Longley and James D. Dana, Jr., "New Empirical Estimates of the Biases of the Electoral College for the 1980s," *Western Political Quarterly,* 33 (1984), 172–173.

9. Lincoln was the only plurality President who failed to attain the 40 percent figure. He received 39.82 percent, although he probably would have received more had his name been on the ballot in nine southern states.

10. Other direct-election proposals have recommended that a joint session of Congress decide the winner. The runoff provision was contained in the resolution that passed the House of Representatives in 1969. A direct election plan with a runoff provision failed to win a two-thirds Senate vote in 1979.

11. Kennedy carried New York by approximately 384,000 votes. He received a plurality of more than 800,000 from precincts that were primarily Jewish. Similarly, in Illinois, a state he carried by less than 9,000, Kennedy had a plurality of 55,000 from the so-called Jewish precincts. Mark R. Levy and Michael S. Kramer, *The Ethnic Factor* (New York: Simon & Schuster, 1972), p. 104.

12. A 1980 Gallup Poll found 67 percent favoring direct election over the present system, with only 19 percent opposed and the rest undecided. In Gallup surveys dating back to 1966, similar majorities have supported direct election and the elimination of the Electoral College:

	Favor	Oppose	No Opinion
1966	63%	20	17
1967 (Jan.)	58	22	20
1967 (Oct.)	65	22	13
1968	81	12	7
1977	73	15	12
1980	67	19	14

George Gallup, Jr., *The Gallup Poll* (Wilmington, Del.: Scholarly Resources, Inc.), pp. 258–260.

13. A proposal, known as the national bonus plan, has also been advanced by a task force on election reform sponsored by the Twentieth Century Fund. The plan would retain the electoral vote but weight it more heavily toward the popular vote winner. A pool of 102 electoral votes (2 for each state plus the District of Columbia) would automatically be awarded on a winner-take-all basis to the candidate who received the most popular votes. This bonus would be added to the candidate's regular electoral vote total. A majority of the electoral vote would still be required for election. If no one received the requisite votes (321 under the bonus plan), a runoff would be held between the two candidates who had the most popular votes.

The bonus plan practically assures that the popular-vote winner will also be the electoral-vote winner. Moreover, it reduces the chances for deadlock in the Electoral College. Had this system been in effect in 1976, Carter would have won a much larger Electoral College victory. In 1960, Kennedy also would have been a more decisive winner, assuming he had the most popular votes. However, the 1960 vote count problem in Alabama and possibly in Illinois suggests one of the difficulties with the bonus plan. In close elections, the Electoral College winner cannot be determined until the popular-vote count is completed and a winner certified. Fraud and election irregularities would present the same kinds of problems for the national bonus plan as they do for direct election. In general, many of the disadvantages of direct election would also apply to the bonus plan.

Selected Readings

Best, Judith. *The Case Against Direct Election of the President: A Defense of the Electoral College.* Ithaca, N.Y.: Cornell University Press, 1975.

Caeser, James W. *Reforming the Reforms: A Critical Analysis of the Presidential Selection Process.* Cambridge, Mass.: Ballinger, 1982.

Crotty, William. "The Philosophies of Party Reform," in Gerald M. Pomper (ed.), *Party Renewal in America.* New York: Praeger, 1980, pp. 31–50.

Hunter, Robert, ed. *Electing the President: A Program for Reform, Final Report of the Commission on National Elections.* Washington, D.C.: The Center for Strategic and International Studies, April 1986.

Keech, William R., ed. *Winners Take All: Report of the Twentieth Century Task Force on Reform of the Presidential Election Process.* New York: Holmes & Meier, 1978.

Longley, Lawrence D., and Alan G. Braun. *The Politics of Electoral College Reform.* New Haven: Yale University Press, 1975.

Peirce, Neal R., and Lawrence D. Longley. *The People's President.* New Haven: Yale University Press, 1981.

Polsby, Nelson W. *Consequences of Party Reform.* New York: Oxford University Press, 1983.

Sundquist, James L. *Constitutional Reform.* Washington, D.C.: The Brookings Institution, 1986.

Walker, Jack. "Presidential Campaigns: Reforming the Reforms," *Wilson Quarterly,* 5 (1981), 88–101.

PART V

APPENDIXES

Appendix A
Results of Presidential Elections, 1860–1984

Year	Candidates Democrat	Candidates Republican	Electoral Vote Democrat	Electoral Vote Republican	Popular Vote Democrat	Popular Vote Republican
1860(a)	Stephen A. Douglas Herschel V. Johnson	Abraham Lincoln Hannibal Hamlin	12 4%	180 59%	1,380,202 29.5%	1,865,908 39.8%
1864(b)	George B. McClellan George H. Pendleton	Abraham Lincoln Andrew Johnson	21 9%	212 91%	1,812,807 45.0%	2,218,388 55.0%
1868(c)	Horatio Seymour Francis P. Blair Jr.	Ulysses S. Grant Schuyler Colfax	80 27%	214 73%	2,708,744 47.3%	3,013,650 52.7%
1872(d)	Horace Greeley Benjamin Gratz Brown	Ulysses S. Grant Henry Wilson		286 78%	2,834,761 43.8%	3,598,235 55.6%
1876	Samuel J. Tilden Thomas A. Hendricks	Rutherford B. Hayes William A. Wheeler	184 50%	185 50%	4,288,546 51.0%	4,034,311 47.9%
1880	Winfield S. Hancock William H. English	James A. Garfield Chester A. Arthur	155 42%	214 58%	4,444,260 48.2%	4,446,158 48.3%
1884	Grover Cleveland Thomas A. Hendricks	James G. Blaine John A. Logan	219 55%	182 45%	4,874,621 48.5%	4,848,936 48.2%
1888	Grover Cleveland Allen G. Thurman	Benjamin Harrison Levi P. Morton	168 42%	233 58%	5,534,488 48.6%	5,443,892 47.8%
1892(e)	Grover Cleveland Adlai E. Stevenson	Benjamin Harrison Whitelaw Reid	277 62%	145 33%	5,551,883 46.1%	5,179,244 43.0%
1896	William J. Bryan Arthur Sewall	William McKinley Garret A. Hobart	176 39%	271 61%	6,511,495 46.7%	7,108,480 51.0%
1900	William J. Bryan Adlai E. Stevenson	William McKinley Theodore Roosevelt	155 35%	292 65%	6,358,345 45.5%	7,218,039 51.7%

Year	Candidates	Electoral Vote	%	Popular Vote	%
1904	Theodore Roosevelt / Charles W. Fairbanks	336	71%	7,626,593	56.4%
	Alton B. Parker / Henry G. Davis	140	29%	5,028,898	37.6%
1908	William H. Taft / James S. Sherman	321	66%	7,676,258	51.6%
	William J. Bryan / John W. Kern	162	34%	6,406,801	43.0%
1912(f)	Woodrow Wilson / Thomas R. Marshall	435	82%	6,293,152	41.8%
	William H. Taft / James S. Sherman	8	2%	3,486,333	23.2%
1916	Woodrow Wilson / Thomas R. Marshall	277	52%	9,126,300	49.2%
	Charles E. Hughes / Charles W. Fairbanks	254	48%	8,546,789	46.1%
1920	Warren G. Harding / Calvin Coolidge	404	76%	16,133,314	60.3%
	James M. Cox / Franklin D. Roosevelt	127	24%	9,140,884	34.2%
1924(g)	Calvin Coolidge / Charles G. Dawes	382	72%	15,717,553	54.1%
	John W. Davis / Charles W. Bryant	136	26%	8,386,169	28.8%
1928	Herbert C. Hoover / Charles Curtis	444	84%	21,411,991	58.2%
	Alfred E. Smith / Joseph T. Robinson	87	16%	15,000,185	40.8%
1932	Franklin D. Roosevelt / John N. Garner	472	89%	22,825,016	57.4%
	Herbert C. Hoover / Charles Curtis	59	11%	15,758,397	39.6%
1936	Franklin D. Roosevelt / John N. Garner	523	98%	27,747,636	60.8%
	Alfred M. Landon / Frank Knox	8	2%	16,679,543	36.5%
1940	Franklin D. Roosevelt / Henry A. Wallace	449	85%	27,263,448	54.7%
	Wendell L. Willkie / Charles L. McNary	82	15%	22,336,260	44.8%
1944	Franklin D. Roosevelt / Harry S. Truman	432	81%	25,611,936	53.4%
	Thomas E. Dewey / John W. Bricker	99	19%	22,013,372	45.9%
1948(h)	Harry S. Truman / Alben W. Barkley	303	57%	24,105,587	49.5%
	Thomas E. Dewey / Earl Warren	189	36%	21,970,017	45.1%
1952	Dwight D. Eisenhower / Richard M. Nixon	442	83%	33,936,137	55.1%
	Adlai E. Stevenson / John J. Sparkman	89	17%	27,314,649	44.4%

Appendix A

Results of Presidential Elections, 1860–1984 (Continued)

Year	Candidates Democrat	Candidates Republican	Electoral Vote Democrat	Electoral Vote Republican	Popular Vote Democrat	Popular Vote Republican
1956(i)	Adlai E. Stevenson / Estes Kefauver	Dwight D. Eisenhower / Richard M. Nixon	73 / 14%	457 / 86%	26,030,172 / 42.0%	35,585,245 / 57.4%
1960(j)	John F. Kennedy / Lyndon B. Johnson	Richard M. Nixon / Henry Cabot Lodge	303 / 56%	219 / 41%	34,221,344 / 49.8%	34,106,671 / 49.5%
1964	Lyndon B. Johnson / Hubert H. Humphrey	Barry Goldwater / William E. Miller	486 / 90%	52 / 10%	43,126,584 / 61.0%	27,177,838 / 38.5%
1968(k)	Hubert H. Humphrey / Edmund S. Muskie	Richard M. Nixon / Spiro T. Agnew	191 / 36%	301 / 56%	31,274,503 / 42.7%	31,785,148 / 43.2%
1972(l)	George McGovern / Sargent Shriver	Richard M. Nixon / Spiro T. Agnew	17 / 3%	520 / 97%	29,171,791 / 37.5%	47,170,179 / 60.7%
1976(m)	Jimmy Carter / Walter F. Mondale	Gerald R. Ford / Robert Dole	297 / 55%	240 / 45%	40,828,657 / 50.1%	39,145,520 / 48.0%
1980	Jimmy Carter / Walter F. Mondale	Ronald Reagan / George Bush	49 / 10%	489 / 90%	35,483,820 / 41.0%	43,901,812 / 50.7%
1984	Walter F. Mondale / Geraldine Ferraro	Ronald Reagan / George Bush	13 / 2%	525 / 98%	37,577,137 / 40.6%	54,455,074 / 58.8%

Source: *Congress and the Nation* (Washington, D.C.: The Congressional Quarterly, 1985), Vol. VI, pp. 1090–1091. Copyrighted material reprinted with permission of Congressional Quarterly Inc.

(a) 1860: John C. Breckenridge, Southern Democrat, polled 72 electoral votes; John Bell, Constitutional Union, polled 39 electoral votes.
(b) 1864: 81 electoral votes were not cast.
(c) 1868: 23 electoral votes were not cast.
(d) 1872: Horace Greeley died after election, 63 Democratic electoral votes were scattered. 17 were not voted.
(e) 1892: James B. Weaver, People's party, polled 22 electoral votes.
(f) 1912: Theodore Roosevelt, Progressive party, polled 88 electoral votes.

(g) 1924: Robert M. LaFollette, Progressive party, polled 13 electoral votes.
(h) 1948: J. Strom Thurmund, States' Rights party, polled 39 electoral votes.
(i) 1956: Walter B. Jones, Democrat, polled 1 electoral vote.
(j) 1960: Harry Flood Byrd, Democrat, polled 15 electoral votes.
(k) 1968: George C. Wallace, American Independent, polled 46 electoral votes.
(l) 1972: John Hospers, Libertarian party, polled 1 electoral vote.
(m) 1976: Ronald Reagan, Republican, polled 1 electoral vote.

Appendix B
1984 Presidential Election Results
Total Popular Vote: 92,652,793
Reagan's Plurality: 16,877,937

State	Ronald Reagan (Republican) Votes	%	Walter F. Mondale (Democrat) Votes	%	David Bergland (Libertarian) Votes	%	Lyndon H. LaRouche Jr. (Independent) Votes	%	Other Votes	%	Plurality
Alabama	872,849	60.5	551,899	38.3	9,504	0.7			7,461	0.5	320,950
Alaska	138,377	66.6	62,007	29.9	6,378	3.1			843	0.4	76,370
Arizona	681,416	66.4	333,854	32.5	10,585	1.0			42	—	347,562
Arkansas	534,774	60.5	338,646	38.3	2,221	0.2	1,890	0.2	6,875	0.8	196,128
California	5,467,009	57.5	3,922,519	41.3	49,951	0.5			65,954	0.7	1,544,490
Colorado	821,817	63.4	454,975	35.1	11,257	0.9	4,662	0.4	2,669	0.2	366,842
Connecticut	890,877	60.7	569,597	38.8	204				6,222	0.4	321,280
Delaware	152,190	59.8	101,656	39.9	268	0.1			458	0.2	50,534
D.C.	29,009	13.7	180,408	85.4	279	0.1	127	0.1	1,465	0.7	151,399
Florida	2,730,350	65.3	1,448,816	34.7	754				131	—	1,281,534
Georgia	1,068,722	60.2	706,628	39.8	152		34		584	—	362,094
Hawaii	185,050	55.1	147,154	43.8	2,167	0.6	654	0.2	821	0.2	37,896
Idaho	297,523	72.4	108,510	26.4	2,823	0.7			2,288	0.6	189,013
Illinois	2,707,103	56.2	2,086,499	43.3	10,086	0.2			15,400	0.3	620,604
Indiana	1,377,230	61.7	841,481	37.7	6,741	0.3			7,617	0.3	535,749
Iowa	703,088	53.3	605,620	45.9	1,844	0.1	6,248	0.5	3,005	0.2	97,468
Kansas	677,296	66.3	333,149	32.6	3,329	0.3			8,217	0.8	344,147
Kentucky	821,702	60.0	539,539	39.4			1,776	0.1	6,328	0.5	282,163
Louisiana	1,037,299	60.8	651,586	38.2	1,876	0.1	3,552	0.2	12,509	0.7	385,713
Maine	336,500	60.8	214,515	38.8					2,129	0.4	121,985
Maryland	879,918	52.5	787,935	47.0	5,721	0.3			2,299	0.1	91,983
Massachusetts	1,310,936	51.2	1,239,606	48.4					8,911	0.3	71,330
Michigan	2,251,571	59.2	1,529,638	40.2	10,055	0.3	3,862	0.1	6,532	0.2	721,933
Minnesota	1,032,603	49.5	1,036,364	49.7	2,996	0.1	3,865	0.2	8,621	0.4	3,761
Mississippi	582,377	61.9	352,192	37.4	2,336	0.2	1,001	0.1	3,198	0.3	230,185
Missouri	1,274,188	60.0	848,583	40.0					12	—	425,605
Montana	232,450	60.5	146,742	38.2	5,185	1.3					85,708

Appendix B
1984 Presidential Election Results (Continued)

State	Ronald Reagan (Republican) Votes	%	Walter F. Mondale (Democrat) Votes	%	David Bergland (Libertarian) Votes	%	Lyndon H. LaRouche Jr. (Independent) Votes	%	Other Votes	%	Plurality
Nebraska	460,054	70.6	187,866	28.8	2,079	0.3			2,091	0.3	272,188
Nevada	188,770	65.8	91,655	32.0	2,292	0.8			3,950	1.4	97,115
New Hampshire	267,050	68.6	120,347	30.9	735	0.2			418	0.1	146,703
New Jersey	1,933,630	60.1	1,261,323	39.2	6,416	0.2	467	0.1	16,493	0.5	672,307
New Mexico	307,101	59.7	201,769	39.2	4,459	0.8			1,041	0.2	508,870
New York	3,664,763	53.8	3,119,609	45.8	11,949	0.2			10,489	0.1	545,154
North Carolina	1,346,481	61.9	824,287	37.9	3,794	0.2			799	—	522,194
North Dakota	200,336	64.8	104,429	33.8	703	0.2	1,278	0.4	2,225	0.7	95,907
Ohio	2,678,560	58.9	1,825,440	40.1	5,886	0.1	10,693	0.2	27,040	0.6	853,120
Oklahoma	861,530	68.6	385,080	30.7	9,066	0.7					476,450
Oregon	685,700	55.9	536,479	43.7					4,348	0.3	149,221
Pennsylvania	2,584,323	53.3	2,228,131	46.0	6,982	0.1			25,467	0.5	356,192
Rhode Island	212,080	51.8	197,106	47.9	277	0.1			1,029	0.2	14,974
South Carolina	615,539	63.6	344,459	35.6	4,359	0.4			4,172	0.4	1,271,080
South Dakota	200,267	63.0	116,113	36.5					1,487	0.5	84,154
Tennessee	990,212	57.8	711,714	41.6	3,072	0.2	1,852	0.1	5,144	0.3	278,498
Texas	3,433,428	63.6	1,949,276	36.1			14,613	0.3	254	—	1,484,152
Utah	469,105	74.5	155,369	24.7	2,477	0.4			2,735	0.4	313,736
Vermont	135,865	57.9	95,730	40.8	1,002	0.4	423	0.2	1,541	0.6	40,135
Virginia	1,337,078	62.3	796,250	37.1			13,307	0.6			540,828
Washington	1,051,670	56.2	807,352	42.9	8,844	0.5	4,712	0.6	11,332	0.6	244,318
West Virginia	405,483	54.7	328,125	44.3					2,134	0.2	77,358
Wisconsin	1,198,584	54.3	995,740	45.1	4,883	0.2	3,791	2.0	8,691	0.4	202,844
Wyoming	133,241	69.1	53,370	27.7	2,357	1.2					79,871
Totals	54,455,074	58.77	37,577,137	40.56	228,314	.25	78,807	.08	241,261	.26	

Source: Congress and the Nation (Washington, D.C.: The Congressional Quarterly, 1985), Vol. VI, p. 1093. Copyrighted material reprinted with permission of Congressional Quarterly Inc.

Appendix C
Tentative Presidential Primary and Caucus Dates, 1988*
(in Chronological Order by Date)

Date	State	Method
JANUARY		
29–30 (Republicans)	Michigan	Convention
FEBRUARY		
8	Iowa	Caucus
16	New Hampshire	Primary
23	South Dakota	Primary
28	Maine	Caucus
MARCH		
1	Vermont	Preference primary
5 (Republicans)	South Carolina	Preference primary
(Democrats)	Wyoming	Caucus
8	Alabama	Primary
	Arkansas	Primary
	Florida	Primary
	Georgia	Primary
(Democrats)	Hawaii	Caucus
(Democrats)	Idaho	Caucus
	Kentucky	Primary
	Louisiana	Primary
	Maryland	Primary
	Massachusetts	Primary
	Mississippi	Primary
	Missouri	Primary
(Democrats)	Nevada	Caucus
	North Carolina	Primary
	Oklahoma	Primary
	Rhode Island	Primary
	Tennessee	Primary
	Texas	Primary
	Virginia	Preference primary
(Democrats)	Washington	Caucus
(Democrats)	American Samoa	Caucus
MARCH		
11 (Democrats)	Delaware	Caucus

Appendix C
Tentative Presidential Primary and Caucus Dates, 1988*
(in Chronological Order by Date) (Continued)*

Date	State	Method
MARCH		
12 (Democrats)	South Carolina	Caucus
	Virginia	Caucus
13 (Democrats)	Alaska	Caucus
14 (Democrats)	North Dakota	Caucus
15	Illinois	Primary
	Minnesota	Caucus
	Ohio	Primary
19 (Democrats)	Kansas	Caucus
(Republicans)	Wyoming	Caucus
20 (Democrats)	Puerto Rico	Primary
22 (Democrats)	Democrats Abroad	Primary
26 (Democrats)	Michigan	Primary
29	Connecticut	Primary
APRIL		
2 (Democrats)	Virgin Islands	Caucus
4 (Democrats)	Colorado	Caucus
5 (Republicans)	Nevada	Caucus
	New York	Primary
	Wisconsin	Primary
16 (Democrats)	Arizona	Caucus
18 (Democrats)	Utah	Caucus
19 (Democrats)	Vermont	Caucus
25 (Republicans)	Utah	Caucus
26	Pennsylvania	Primary
MAY		
3	District of Columbia	Primary
	Indiana	Primary
10	Nebraska	Primary
	West Virginia	Primary
17	Oregon	Primary

Appendix C
Tentative Presidential Primary and Caucus
Dates, 1988*
(in Chronological Order by Date) (Continued)*

Date	State	Method
MAY		
(Republicans)	Alaska	Caucus
24 (Republicans)	Idaho	Primary
JUNE		
7	California	Primary
	Montana	Primary
	New Jersey	Primary
	New Mexico	Primary
14 (Republicans)	North Dakota	Primary

Source: Kevin J. Coleman and Thomas H. Neale, Congressional Research Service of the Library of Congress. Updated by author on the basis of information available June 1, 1987.

*Several state parties had yet to decide on a date at the time this appendix was prepared.

INDEX